A lively hope

*The Suffering, Death, Resurrection,
and Exaltation of Jesus Christ*

RICHARD NEITZEL HOLZAPFEL

Bookcraft
Salt Lake City, Utah

Library of Congress Catalog Card Number 98-74767
ISBN 1-57008-562-5

First Printing, 1999

Printed in the United States of America

For my son,
Elder Nathanael Reid Holzapfel,
Chile Osorno Mission,
1997-1999

"God's fishers of men are
those whose nets do not
catch, but set free."

CONTENTS

$\mathcal{A}$CKNOWLEDGMENTS

I appreciate the efforts of Jeni Broberg Holzapfel for reading the final manuscript draft and offering suggestions and insights about the Greek New Testament text during the entire process of writing. Bobbie Z. Peterson, Paul H. Peterson, and Joseph B. Romney were kind enough to take time from their heavy responsibilities at the BYU Jerusalem Center for Near Eastern Studies to read early manuscript drafts of the first chapters. Their suggestions were insightful and helpful. Other administrators, faculty, staff, and students at the Jerusalem Center offered unique feelings about the subject while we journeyed through the Holy Land during the 1997–98 academic year. I would like to specifically mention Richard H. Berrett, David F. Boone, Terry W. Call, Jeffery R. Chadwick, Dana M. Pike, Craig J. Ostler, R. J. Snow, and Clark T. Thorstenson.

Upon my return to the United States, Paul Y. Hoskisson, Ray L. Huntington, Kent P. Jackson, Robert L. Millet, Joseph F. McConkie, Stephen E. Robinson, David R. Seely, D. Gene Taylor, and Keith J. Wilson kindly reviewed various chapters. Their sensitivity to tone and larger interpretive issues helped make some needed changes. My friendly and competent student assistants, Wendy Agle, McKay H. Bateman, and Matthew J. Grey did source checking and other important library work helping to get the manuscript ready for the publisher.

I am also indebted to Bookcraft, Inc., for their help in expanding my university classroom beyond the walls of campus to reach a larger audience. Cory H. Maxwell, Jana S. Erickson, and Janna L. DeVore's hard works in this effort deserve special mention.

Finally, the endnotes reveal the extent to which others' work allowed me to prepare this book. A poster on the BYU campus has the following statement printed on it: "Some of my best thoughts are thoughts belonging to others." My endnotes will clearly demonstrate this point. All those noted above made this a better book, catching many errors. Those that remain are mine.

Eugène Burnand's Les disciples Pierre et Jean courant au sépulcre.

$\mathscr{P}$REFACE:
THE FIRST DAY OF THE WEEK

Early in the morning on the first day of the week a group numbering as many as one hundred huddled together behind locked doors in an Upper Room in the Holy City. Saddened and confused, their world had collapsed suddenly and unexpectedly just days before. Dazed by the crushing events that had occurred on that fateful Friday, the assembled men and women discussed and perhaps even debated just what direction they should take, what future course they should follow.[1] Indeed, now that their leader had died a slow and painful death under the sagging weight of his bruised, stripped body on a Roman cross, a few probably wondered whether there even was a future course to be followed.

Whether Mary Magdalene was among the group, we do not know. The record does tell us that she slipped into the darkness of the early dawn and made her way through the city to one of its many gates. Carrying spices, she proceeded beyond the city wall to a garden where she expected to find a sealed stone and a standing guard. However, the guards were apparently gone and the tomb open. She peered inside. Once again, her world was irrevocably shaken: the sepulchre was empty.

As the sun rose over the Mount of Olives, enveloping Jerusalem in morning light, Mary hurried through the city. Excitedly, she told the disciples what she had *not* seen—the body of Jesus. While many of the group were skeptical, the leader among them, one called Simon Peter, was sufficiently curious that he immediately headed for the tomb. Another disciple joined Simon. It was John, and it would appear they were the only two who wanted (or perhaps dared) to go.

Running together, the more-fleet-of-foot John soon outdistanced his companion and arrived at the tomb first. As described by John himself: "Then cometh Simon Peter following him, and went into the sepulchre, and seeth the linen clothes lie, and the napkin, that was about his head, not lying with the linen clothes, but wrapped together in a place by itself. Then went in also that other disciple, which came first to the sepulchre, and he saw, and believed" (John 20:6–8). Now for the first time the beloved disciple began to understand in a fuller sense that fellowship with Jesus was stronger than death, as the Master had told him on the night of His betrayal (see John 16:16–17, 22).

A Lively Hope

Eugène Burnand's painting *Les disciples Pierre et Jean courant au sépulcre*, reproduced on page x and on the book jacket, effectively captures the countenances of these two disciples as they neared the tomb. The artist depicts John as younger; dressed in white, his hands tightly clasped together, his hair flowing, his countenance reflecting both concern and hopeful anticipation. Trying to keep pace with him, Peter's face is likewise etched with hopeful emotion as he moves forward, one hand holding his cloak against his chest, while the other hand, free flowing, depicts the pathos of the moment. In the background the rising sun breaks forth against the early morning sky, replacing darkness with light.

Within days of this epoch event, the disciples found new purpose and direction in life. The empty tomb, the appearances of the risen Lord—linked in a matter of days with the marvelous outpouring of the Spirit at Pentecost—such events quickened their souls and spirits, and they came to understand, if not fully, at least more completely than ever before, the significance and far-reaching effect of their Master's suffering and death. The emphasis was not on "Jesus died," but on that he "died for our sins"; even more, he "died for our sins *according to* the scriptures" (1 Corinthians 15:3; emphasis added); or further, he was "crucified and slain: whom God hath raised up, . . . being by the right hand of God exalted" (Acts 2:23–24, 33). For these first disciples, Jesus did not simply exist in their memory, he was a living reality.

Like Peter and John and the other disciples, most of us at some juncture in life find ourselves overwhelmed—our dreams, expectations, and longings seemingly dashed by forces beyond our control. We sometimes misunderstand our temporary loneliness for being "God forsaken." Like the disciples, however, we move forward by setting aside these temporary interruptions and setbacks, anticipating with hope the life that exists for all because of what occurred in the Roman province of Judea. It should be noted that the New Testament Greek word for *hope,* like that which pervades modern English usage, "had an overtone of uncertainty . . . ('I hope to see you next summer, but am by no means confident of doing so'). Whereas in Hebraic thought hope was expectation of good and (as in Rom. 4.18) closely allied to trust, hope as confidence in God."[2] Robert Millet, dean of Religious Education at BYU, captured the spirit of our usage best when he wrote: "A closely associated fruit of the Spirit—and a sure sign of rebirth—is hope. Our hope is in Christ. Our hope cannot rest solely on mortal men and women, no matter how good or noble they may be. . . . Gospel hope is more than wishing, more than yearning for some eventuality or some possession. It is a solid and sure conviction. It is expectation. Anticipation. Assurance."[3]

To the ancient Saints "scattered throughout Pontus, Galatia, Cappadocia, Asia, and Bithynia," Peter wrote: "Blessed be the God and Father of our Lord Jesus Christ, which according to his abundant mercy hath begotten us again unto *a lively hope* by the resurrection of Jesus Christ from the dead. . . . Wherein ye greatly rejoice, though now for a season, if need be, ye are in heaviness through manifold temptations: that the trial of your faith, being much more precious than of gold that perisheth, though it be tried with fire, might be found unto praise and honour and glory at the appearing of Jesus Christ: whom having not seen, ye love; in whom, though now ye see him not, yet believing, ye rejoice with joy unspeakable and full of glory: receiving the end of your faith, even the salvation of your souls" (1 Peter 1:1, 3–9; emphasis added).

A lively hope rises in our hearts as we understand the apostolic teaching announced on Pentecost about the risen Christ, which correctly interpreted Jesus' suffering and death and was taught by the early Saints. We are first inspired by and then inextricably bound in a common cause with the messages and testimonies of the early disciples who preserved for us the story of Jesus' atoning sacrifice, of how God through him extended the blessings of universal resurrection. Grounded and rooted in the same gospel soil, we face the world renewed and determined to follow Jesus, "receiving the end of [our] faith, even the salvation of [our] souls" (1 Peter 1:9).

This "Good News," as first proclaimed by Peter on the day of Pentecost, helps to place in proper focus those painful stories, the longest sections of the Gospels themselves, that deal with Jesus' agony and death, the scenes of which continue to stimulate the imaginations of painters, sculptors, filmmakers, and writers. His life still fascinates the media. For Easter 1996, for example, the three most popular news journals in North America, *Time, Newsweek,* and *U.S. News and World Report,* featured a depiction of Jesus on the covers of their magazines. The accompanying articles focusing on Jesus' life and current scholarly debate surrounding his identity caused one author to write an essay entitled, "Jesus: Darling of the Media" shortly thereafter.[4] And so it is after two thousand years: Jesus of Nazareth continues to capture our hearts, minds, and souls.

Methods, Objectives, and Limitations

The Restoration provides the Latter-day Saint community with additional insights about Jesus' suffering, death, resurrection, and exaltation, particularly a doctrinal reaffirmation of those truths declared and preserved by the original authors. Additionally, just as the New Testament provides a window through which the believer can interpret the Old Testament, Restoration scripture and the teachings of the living prophets and apostles provide a window through which we can interpret the New Testament. The doctrinal truths, therefore, are accessible to all who carefully read the New Testament, using the Restoration as an interpretive key to its stories and sayings.

The historical and cultural aspects of these stories may not always be addressed by the doctrinal Restoration. Thus, additional scholarly tools may be needed to help us gain a deeper appreciation for the New Testament's historical setting beyond the saving truths so plainly taught and affirmed through our glorious dispensation. Remember, however, that any conclusions gained through such tools are subject to revision and adjustment when revelation, instruction, and counsel are given by those who hold the authority to interpret scripture for the Church.

The scriptural narratives of Jesus' suffering, death, resurrection, and exaltation were written a long time ago and for completely different audiences. As BYU English professors Richard H. Cracroft and Neal E. Lambert explained so well, the Gospel authors "take for granted the laws, the traditions, and the social customs of their times, things that have greatly changed over nearly two millennia. They often leave unanswered those questions that interest us today but were of little concern to those who had either known Jesus personally or knew of him through others who had. Two thousand years later we look in vain to find a description of Jesus. . . . We must sift through accounts that speak of 'whited sepulchres,' of unusual social traditions, of Sabbath customs with which we are totally unfamiliar."[5]

The original reader, as Cracroft and Lambert observed, was expected to assume certain things. Bruce J. Malina and Richard L. Rohrbaugh explain in plain language this important aspect of any reading of the New Testament: "This 'unwritten' part includes the things an author presumes the audience knows about how the world works, which he or she can leave between the lines of a text, so to speak, yet which are crucial to its understanding. Such an implied understanding of the world is always shared by conversation partners. . . . A writer in contemporary America, for example, when referring to a 'Big Mac' for the first time in a story, has no need to explain that this item is a hamburger. Nor is an explanation required that this hamburger is made by a particular fast-food chain whose logo is the golden arches. An American reader can be counted on to understand and provide the necessary visual imagery. Such pictures are not only worth a thousand words, they can save that many and more if they can be supplied by the reader rather than the writer. . . . Because the reader must interact with the text and 'complete' it if it is to make sense, every text invites immediate participation on the part of a reader. Texts thus provide what is necessary, but cannot provide everything."[6]

In order to take into consideration this "unwritten" part of the story, we need to understand that for some, if not many, of the first-generation Christians their first encounter with the story of Jesus' suffering, death, resurrection, and exaltation did not come by reading or hearing one of the four Gospel accounts. Many had a background we do not have: they heard the story from the eyewitnesses themselves or at least from someone who had heard the story from an eyewitness. Additionally, as noted above, the original audience had a cultural and historical connection with the authors we do not share. They understood and responded to aspects of the story in ways we do not because of their situation—just as the authors intended. It is therefore helpful to ask questions about the original audience in order to appreciate more subtle aspects of the Gospel narratives. By so doing we can hope to arrive at some partial understanding of the concrete historical setting. Many issues may elude us during this process that involves weighing probabilities; as Carolyn Osiek observed, modern scholars are "vividly aware of one major reality: we cannot go back. There is no way that we as twentieth century Westerners can completely shed our assumptions and horizon of experience and take on the mindset of a person who has had no exposure to our culture."[7]

We need to acknowledge this limitation as we attempt to reconstruct the historical setting of the Gospel narratives. Additionally, we must also be aware of what D. A. Carson calls the fallacy of "uncontrolled historical reconstruction."[8] Carson aptly notes that we should not give "speculative reconstruction of first-century Jewish and Christian history [more] weight in the exegesis of the New Testament documents."[9]

The above limitation may lead us into the academic trap of dealing with issues that are not as important as sin, atonement, and forgiveness. I will attempt to avoid these minefields as I pursue my goals as stated below.

Kent P. Jackson, LDS biblical scholar, provides a concise and thoughtful list of ways to help us read and understand the Gospels better.[10] Utilizing scriptural teachings and counsel from Church leaders, he suggests: "Reading scripture is a life-changing exercise, and reading the Gospels will draw us nearer to Christ."[11]

An early review of the subject at hand was published in 1991.[12] This book expands on that discussion but remains a study intended for the general readership, rather than my professional colleagues at the university. As an introductory survey it is not intended to replace important scholarly works dealing with the issues raised. For those interested in a more technical discussion, the endnotes will lead to some important sources that are part of the current scholarly dialogue on the subject.

These efforts, therefore, are to introduce to a nonspecialist readership some of the insights from recent New Testament research that may benefit the believer and help him or her gain a deeper appreciation for the richness of the narratives left to us as a gift from the writers of the four Gospels.

In pursuit of this objective, I will suggest and illustrate a range of ways in which the stories of Jesus' suffering, death, resurrection, and exaltation may be read and interpreted in a first-century context. In the atttempt to reconstruct the historical and social setting of the events, I hope to approximate, where possible, the original author's intent and therefore allow the modern reader, in light of the data, to reflect on the story as the original readers or hearers may have done two thousand years ago. In this way I hope to reveal the meaning of the text in ways very different from what was at first supposed. In some cases it will challenge the images of Jesus created by some of us, the "Jesus-as-I-personally-like-to-imagine-him," as one biblical scholar expressed it.[13] This approach does not suggest that there is one single way in which these stories can be understood, let alone applied in one's life (see 1 Nephi 19:23).

The first difficulty we encounter in this particular effort is the general assumption that first-century people thought, acted, and felt the way we do today. While there are many ways in which we are alike, there are just as many ways in which we are different. In all likelihood, the authors and the audiences of these wonderful books would find certain aspects of our world quite unintelligible, just as we would expect to find the same in their world.

I will marshall many historical, cultural, and linguistic insights provided by recent developments in New Testament research to pursue this examination. And while the Lord expects us to increase our understanding by study, including the use of scholarly tools that may help reconstruct the original historical setting, he also wants us to approach the scriptures with faith (see D&C 88:118).[14]

The tools of modern scholarship can enhance our scripture study, but they can never replace sincere prayer, fasting, meditation, and obedience to the word of the Lord as revealed in inspired scriptural records and through the teachings of modern appointed prophets, seers, and revelators. These fundamental aspects of serious scripture study are presupposed in this book. In fact, our study of Jesus' last hours among his disciples "will remain spiritually empty, emotionally hollow and doctrinally unsound" unless we include a spiritual dimension to our personal reflection and search.[15]

Like Malcolm Muggeridge, I feel that "future historians . . . are likely to conclude that the more we knew about Jesus [and his world] the less we knew him, and the more precisely his words were translated the less we understood or heeded them."[16]

I desperately hope that the historical, cultural, linguistic, and social backgrounds provided in this examination will in nowise impoverish the original accounts of Matthew, Mark, Luke, and John. In the end, each believer can apply the principles found in the scriptures without any help beyond the words of the original writers, the teachings of the living prophets and apostles, and finally, the guidance of the Holy Spirit. Everything else, including this book, is commentary and of secondary importance.

To raise new questions, suggest possible contexts, and provide historical, linguistic, and cultural background may help us move beyond assumptions derived from our own culture in order to recreate, as best we can, the same lenses through which the first readers understood the text themselves.

With such a lofty goal in mind, it is admitted that John was right when he made his final statement to his Gospel witness: "And there are also many other things which Jesus did, the which, if they should be written every one, I suppose that even the world itself could not contain the books that should be written" (John 21:25). In his conclusion John reminds us that it is impossible to fully reconstruct Jesus' activity (especially the suffering and death narratives) in the pages of any book, even a book such as the fourth Gospel, let alone this book.

This attempt to discuss these important stories, like other efforts by thoughtful commentators and faithful scholars, is really an effort to help us come to life in Christ Jesus more fully. As John wrote: "These are written, that ye might believe that Jesus is the Christ, the Son of God; and that believing ye might have life through his name" (John 20:31).

NOTES

1. There are variant opinions about which day of the week Jesus was executed. However, this study assumes Friday as the generally accepted day.

2. James D. G. Dunn, *The Theology of Paul the Apostle* (Grand Rapids, Michigan: Wm. B. Eerdmans, 1998), 387, no. 217.

3. Robert L. Millet, *Alive in Christ: The Miracle of Spiritual Rebirth* (Salt Lake City: Deseret Book Company, 1997), 168.

4. Herschel Shanks, "Jesus: Darling of the Media," *Bible Review* 12 (August 1996): 4.

5. Richard H. Cracroft and Neal E. Lambert, " 'After the Manner of Their Language': The Persuasive Voices of the Scriptures," *New Era* (December 1972): 32–33.

6. Bruce J. Malina and Richard L. Rohrbaugh, *Social Science Commentary on the Synoptic Gospels* (Minneapolis: Fortress Press, 1992), 9.

7. Carolyn Osiek, *What Are They Saying About the Social Setting of the New Testament?* (New York: Paulist Press, 1984), 25.

8. D. A. Carson, *Exegetical Fallacies* (Grand Rapids, Michigan: Baker Book House, 1984), 131.

9. Ibid.

10. Kent P. Jackson, "Jesus and the Gospels," in *Studies in Scripture:*

Volume 5, The Gospels, Kent P. Jackson and Robert L. Millet, eds. (Salt Lake City: Deseret Book Company, 1986), 8–9.

11. Ibid., 8.

12. Richard Neitzel Holzapfel, "The Passion of Jesus Christ: An Intimate Look at the Gospel Narratives," in *The Lord of the Gospels*, Bruce A. Van Orden and Brent L. Top, eds. (Salt Lake City: Deseret Book, 1991), 69–82.

13. James D. G. Dunn's description is found in promotional notices of Luke Timothy Johnson's *The Real Jesus: The Misguided Quest for the Historical Jesus and the Truth of the Traditional Gospels* (San Francisco: HarperSanFrancisco, 1997) by the publisher.

14. For a more complete discussion of this issue see Richard Neitzel Holzapfel, "Questions, But No Doubts?" in *Expressions of Faith: Testimonies of Latter-day Saint Scholars* (Provo and Salt Lake City: Foundation for Ancient Research and Mormon Studies and Deseret Book Company, 1996), 182–92.

15. Gerald O'Collins, *What Are They Saying About Jesus?* (New York: Paulist Press, 1977), 24.

16. Malcolm Muggeridge, *Jesus: The Man Who Lives* (New York: Harper & Row, 1975), 8.

$\mathcal{G}$OSPEL MOSAICS:
SEPARATE WITNESSES

To any reader who approaches the Gospels of Matthew, Mark, Luke, and John with more than a cursory glance, two realizations quickly come to mind: First, there are some striking similarities among the four accounts, most especially so with Matthew, Mark, and Luke, which are known as the synoptic Gospels because they share similar material (the Greek word *synoptikos* means "seeing the whole together, taking a comprehensive view").[1]

Second, there are some differences among the various accounts.[2] These differences and even variances are to be expected. After all, the Gospels were written by four different people, at different times, in different locales, and for different audiences. Elder Bruce R. McConkie observed: "It is apparent, however, that each inspired author had special and intimate knowledge of certain circumstances not so well known to others, and that each felt impressed to emphasize different matters because of the particular people to whom he was addressing his personal gospel testimony."[3]

Early Efforts to Make One Gospel

Early on, some endeavored to remove the kinks by elimination. That is, they retained only their favorite or preferred gospel and eliminated the others. Perhaps the best-known eliminator was Marcion (second century), who accepted only the Gospel of Luke, ostensibly because Luke was thought to be Paul's traveling companion.[4]

Then there was Tatian (also second century), who composed a gospel harmony called *Diatessaron*.[5] A gospel harmony, sometimes called a synopsis (from the Greek *synoptos*), endeavors to weave all the details of the Gospel tradition into a single chronological strand, one composite order, or sequence.[6] A Gospel harmony should be distinguished from another important study tool, a Gospel parallel, which places all the Gospel narratives in parallel columns for comparison (we will discuss this format in greater detail later in this chapter).

Traceable to at least Tatian is the effort to combine the various Gospel narratives into one account. However, his attempt hardly shared a common goal with other such efforts made to achieve "a better understanding of the life, ministry, and teachings of the Saviour and his Apostles," as some have postulated.[7] Rather, Tatian's effort to produce one Gospel was partly an attempt to eliminate any passages that Jewish or pagan critics might use to hinder Christianity in its claims concerning Jesus. Another purpose was to eliminate passages that Christians themselves found problematic.

For these reasons, Tatian's solution to the differences found in the four Gospels, the creation of a harmony, was surprisingly successful for a long time among certain groups of Christians.

In its modern counterpart, the harmony author selects unique characteristics or aspects of various events and arranges them in what seems to be a rational, cohesive order, ostensibly in an attempt to make things easier for the reader. One of the disadvantages to such an arrangement or compilation is that it eliminates the individuality of the Gospel writers. For example, it is difficult under such an arrangement to understand or get a feel for how Matthew understood the events of Resurrection day as compared with Luke.

The Acceptance of Four Gospels

Among the most monumental decisions made within early Christianity was the acceptance of a fourfold Gospel canon.[8] Although most of us today do not consider questioning why we have four approaches to telling the story of Jesus, the significance of the choice to preserve and finally accept four gospels "becomes clear once we recognize that alternative solutions nearly won the day in the first and second centuries."[9]

For most people these one-gospel approaches are not very appealing, yet the strong pull to accept and use only one in the early scripture canon cannot be underestimated. It was a frequent possibility for several centuries.[10] There were in fact strong tides moving in the various Christian communities towards acceptance of only one Gospel. We probably need to thank Irenaeus (second century Bishop of Lyons in Gaul) for mounting "what seems to have been the first full theological defence of the fourfold Gospel."[11] While some contend that Irenaeus's defense was intended to eliminate from consideration the use of apocryphal texts, the historical setting suggests the main objective was to reject all attempts to select either one single Gospel or a harmony of known gospels.

While most Christians finally accepted the fourfold Gospels, it was not an easy struggle. If lost it would have had tremendous consequences on the amount of primary source material which we have to study Jesus' life and teachings.

Gospel Harmonies and Gospel Parallels

As noted above, Gospel harmonies and Gospel parallels are not the same. A Gospel harmony creates a single Gospel using material from all four Gospels. The second and more common study tool presents Gospel events in parallel columns on the same page in such a way that the reader can, with some study, isolate or extricate both the similarities and differences.[12] Thomas M. Mumford, a respected LDS scholar, argues that Gospel "harmonies [and parallels] are based upon the Gestalt principle that the whole of anything is greater than the sum of its parts. Since each gospel represents a part, the greater message of the life of Jesus can only be seen when all four are arranged together."[13]

Mumford is correct when he states that a study of Jesus' life should examine all relevant texts (in particular the four Gospels). As Latter-day Saints we also have additional voices giving us expanded and profound views of the suffering, death, resurrection, and exaltation of Jesus Christ. Many have undertaken to discuss these events using this broader range of sources. However, this is not the scope nor goal of this book. The intent here is to examine in context what Matthew, Mark, Luke, and John individually had to say about these transcendent events and how each audience originally read or heard the Gospel narratives.

When a person harmonizes the Gospel narratives, there is a tendency to distort the historical setting of each story and as a result miss certain themes and insights originally intended by each author. Undoubtedly each writer preserved a separate and distinct account of Jesus' ministry—including the suffering, death, resurrection, and exaltation—for a good reason. This does not deny the usefulness of a Gospel parallel, as noted by Mumford above. It suggests only that a study of the individual Gospels provides a nuanced portrayal of the events of Jesus' life which will enhance the understanding we gain from studying the scriptures in other ways.

The approach, however, is admittedly not without its own deficiencies. Some readers may be concerned that they will learn *too much* about Matthew, Mark, Luke, and John and not enough about Jesus. Frankly, this problem is inherent in any approach. The only real difference is that we may be more acutely aware of the author's presence when we study each individually and ask specific questions about his themes, audience, and purposes.

We would like to know what Jesus himself did, said, and thought. However, for some unknown reason Jesus did not leave us an account of his life. In fact, we do not have any record of Jesus writing anything, except on one occasion when he wrote something "on the ground" (see John 8:6–8). We are, therefore, left with what others said, recalled, and recorded about him. Not one of them provided the details we might be interested in today because their audience is separated from us by time and, for the most part, by place. Yet among them were those who knew him best—his disciples. They not only told us who he was, how they gradually discovered who he really is, but also how coming to know him changed their lives.

The Proclamation of the Gospel

Jesus proclaimed the gospel—the Good News. The English word *gospel* derives from the Anglo-Saxon *godspell*, which essentially means "a story about god."[14] When it is used to translate the Greek word *euangelion*, *gospel* acquires the popular meaning of "good news" or "glad tidings."[15]

Jesus declared, "The time is fulfilled, and the kingdom of God is at hand: repent ye, and believe the gospel" (Mark 1:15). In substance, the Good News was that the kingdom of God was present because his Son was among them. Later, after his suffering, death, and resurrection, the New Testament writers presented the Good News about Jesus. Their Gospel accounts are "as much the gospel of Jesus" as they are "about Jesus".[16] That is, they are "the glad tidings . . . that he came into the world, even Jesus" (D&C 76:40–41). Eventually, the term *Good News* became associated with the narratives written by Matthew, Mark, Luke, and John.

The titles given to the four Gospels from the second century onward are significant: "the Gospel according to Matthew," "the Gospel according to Mark," and so on. In the Joseph Smith Translation, two of the titles are changed to read "The Testimony of St. Matthew" and "The Testimony of St. John."[17]

Although Jesus proclaimed a single gospel, the Gospel authors presented Jesus' words and deeds in accordance with what they understood and experienced and with what they felt was important for their original audience. Each writer thus gave his particular testimony; as a result we now have four Gospels.[18] In the thirteenth century the word *gospel* "took on the figurative meaning, 'an authoritative account.' "[19]

Separate and Distinct Views

In the Gospels we have four accounts of Jesus' suffering, betrayal, trial, crucifixion, resurrection, and exaltation. The differences between them are not always related to the events described but to the significance of the events each author chose to highlight. As noted at the beginning, each narrative was written at a different time for a different audience by a different author, and each author chose those aspects of the story which they felt would most help them communicate the message of hope and salvation to his audience. Because of the particular needs of his audience, the author sometimes wrote of aspects of the events in ways others did not and thus gave that audience a different framework for receiving the story.

To maintain the integrity of these stories as a whole, we need to examine each narrative independent of the others. Keeping the accounts separated offers us a rich way to understand the demands of discipleship in our own lives. Doing the reverse may lead us away from certain messages and insights that each Gospel writer intended to preserve through his witness of Jesus.

Additionally, by artificially combining the four individual stories into one, we sometimes create false images not necessarily found or intended in the original gospel stories. This is analogous to many university students who are exposed to Hollywood movies on Bible subjects or who grew up watching cartoon versions of the scriptures, either at home or in various church settings. They tend to visualize scenes and reproduce dialogue in their minds that do not exist in the text itself. The reality is that for the most part we tend to remember the Hollywood remake, with its color and background music, better than we do the silent black-and-white original.

Although we have a tendency to want one picture of Jesus' life—a single Gospel, as it were—the Gospel narratives do not make a single picture of Jesus, but four beautiful mosaics. LDS New Testament scholar Roger R. Keller uses the analogy of a diamond instead: "In reality each gospel is like a facet of a diamond. It brightens and highlights the picture of Jesus that we receive, and just as a diamond would be terribly uninteresting without its facets, so also would the picture of Jesus be flat and one-dimensional without the composite picture of him that is presented when the four Gospels are brought together."[20]

Whether we compare the four Gospels to the facets of a diamond or to mosaics, they contain Jesus' words and actions as interpreted by authentic witnesses, authors who faithfully recorded what they personally knew or who recorded Jesus' words received through eyewitnesses.

One of the greatest evidences for the truthfulness of the four Gospels is the frank portrayal of the disciples' fundamental misunderstanding of Jesus' words and deeds during his mortal ministry, including those closest to him. Of note, in the cases of Matthew and John at least, their Gospels portray themselves at times in less than a positive light. Their candid admissions of struggles remind me of Joseph Smith's testimony published in the Pearl of Great Price (see

Joseph Smith—History) and the revelations he received from the Lord which challenged him to live up to his calling (see, for example, D&C 3; 93:47). This is one indication that we can trust these records as being a faithful account of what they experienced and witnessed.

And while the Gospels sometimes reveal the disciples' lack of understanding of Jesus' mission prior to his resurrection, these testimonies come from individuals who found forgiveness, grace, and mercy from God through Jesus Christ. We should not be blind to Jesus' own positive prophecies about their future labors. Additionally, the positive characterizations of the disciples are numerous (for example, see Mark 1:18, 20; 2:14; 3:14; 4:11, 33; 6:1, 7), all in all giving us a balanced view.

We do not need to always cut and paste them together to form a single picture. New Testament scholar Heinrich Greeven argues, "['The first harmonies'] declared purpose was to fuse parallel texts into one single text"; to do so, the compilers had to harmonize and diminish the differences or supposed contradictions between the stories.[21]

Four Mosaics

If we had four ancient mosaics giving different representations of the same scene, it would not occur to us to say, "These mosaics are so beautiful that I do not want to lose any of them; I shall demolish them and use the enormous pile of stones to make a single mosaic that combines all four of them."[22] Trying to combine the pieces of the mosaics in order to produce a single one would be an affront, not only destroying the mosaics themselves but also negating the individuality of the artist who created them in the first place. Because the four Gospels differ from each other, we should from time to time study each one for itself, without demolishing it and using the debris to reconstruct a life of Jesus by making the four Gospels into one Gospel.

Proper Use of a Gospel Parallel

Following a careful reading of each Gospel narrative on its own terms, we then need to study each episode in all four Gospels simultaneously. This is where a Gospel parallel serves us well. Built upon the earlier foundation of individual attention to each Gospel, a parallel will bring to light another set of important insights by comparing and contrasting all four Gospels. This is particularly helpful when reading John, because he probably assumed his audience already knew the general outlines of the synoptic Gospel narratives, and in many cases were very familiar with specific details from them.

Focusing on each Gospel narrative individually provides a fresh approach from the one generally taken in group gospel study sessions and in our personal study of Matthew, Mark, Luke, and John. I personally believe that examining the four Gospels individually will enrich fourfold a person's study of the subject of Jesus' suffering and death. And as I have learned, variety in approaches generally has its benefits.

NOTES

1. H. G. Liddell and Scott, *An Intermediate Greek-English Lexicon* (Oxford, Clarendon Press, 1975), 779.

2. Some of these differences relate to the size of the text: Mark has roughly 11,000 words; John, 15,000; Matthew, 18,000, and Luke, 19,000. These differences are particularly important when one uses word count studies to demonstrate some theological nuance in a particular text since a greater numerical use of a word by one author against another may in fact turn out to be merely less of a percentage of usage by a particular author when compared to the total length of his Gospel narrative.

3. Bruce R. McConkie, *Doctrinal New Testament Commentary: Volume 1, The Gospels* (Salt Lake City: Bookcraft, 1987), 69.

4. See John J. Clabeaux, "Marcion," in *The Anchor Bible Dictionary*, 6 vols. (New York: Doubleday, 1992), 4:514–16.

5. O. C. Edwards Jr., "Tatian," in *The Anchor Bible Dictionary*, 6 vols. (New York: Doubleday, 1992), 6:335; for a more detailed discussion see William Petersen, *Tatian's Diatessaron: Its Creation, Dissemination, Significance, and History in Scholarship* (Leiden, Netherlands: E. J. Brill, 1994).

6. Greek *synoptos*, "that can be seen at a glance, in full view." H. G. Liddell and Scott, *An Intermediate Greek-English Lexicon* (Oxford: Clarendon Press, 1975), 779.

7. Steven J. Hite and Julie M. Hite, *The New Testament with the Joseph Smith Translation* (Orem, Utah: The Veritas Group, 1994), vii.

8. Graham N. Stanton, "The Fourfold Gospel," *New Testament Studies* 43 (July 1997):318.

9. Ibid., 341.

10. Tatian's *Diatessaron* eventually fell into disfavor and all accessible copies were destroyed by either Theodoret (c. 393–c. 466), Bishop of Cyrrhus in Syria, or Rabbula (died c. 435), Bishop of Edessa in Syria.

11. Stanton, "The Fourfold Gospel," 317–46; especially 341.

12. An excellent and accessible Gospel parallel is found in the LDS Bible Dictionary under the subheading, "Gospel," published in the LDS version of the King James Version of the Bible (Salt Lake City: The Church of Jesus Christ of Latter-day Saints, 1979), 684–96. Two Gospel parallels with scholarly apparatus, noncanonical material, and variant manuscript readings are Burton H. Throckmorton Jr., *Gospel Parallels: A Synopsis of the First Three Gospels* (Nashville, Tenn.: Thomas Nelson Publishers, 1979) and Robert W. Funk, *New Gospel Parallels*, 2 vols. (Philadelphia: Fortress Press, 1985). A Gospel parallel utilizing the Joseph Smith Translation is Steven J. and Julie M. Hite, *The New Testament with the Joseph Smith Translation* (Orem, Utah: The Veritas Group, 1994). For a Latter-day Saint audience, the best Gospel parallel is Monte Nyman, *New Testament Restoration Harmony* (no publisher: 1996).

13. Thomas M. Mumford, *Horizontal Harmony of the Four Gospels in Parallel Columns* (Salt Lake City, Utah: Deseret Book Co., 1976).

14. Walter W. Skeat, *A Concise Etymological Dictionary of the English Language* (Oxford: Clarendon Press, 1967), 218.

15. The Greek *euangelion* (good news) was known to secular authors and was used to announce a victory or great events in the life of the emperor. For a fuller discussion of its usage, see William F. Arndt and Wilbur F. Gingrich, *A Greek-English Lexicon of the New Testament and Other Early Christian Literature* (Chicago: University of Chicago Press, 1957), 318.

16. Edward Schillebeeckx, *Jesus: An Experiment in Christology* (New York: The Crossroad Publishing Company. 1981), 110. Though Schillebeeckx described only Mark's Gospel in this way, the concept seems applicable to all four.

17. See Robert J. Matthews, *Joseph Smith's Translation of the Bible: A History and Commentary* (Provo, Utah: Brigham Young University Press, 1985), 242–43.

18. For a recent discussion on the relationship of the Gospels to each other, see Kloppenborg, *Q Parallels*, xxi-xxxiv.

19. Michael Macrone, *Brush Up Your Bible!* (New York: Harper Collins, 1993), 163.

20. Roger R. Keller, "Mark and Luke: Two Facets of a Diamond," in *The Lord of the Gospels: The 1990 Sperry Symposium on the New Testament*, Bruce A. Van Orden and Brent L. Top, eds. (Salt Lake City: Deseret Book Company, 1991), 83.

21. Heinrich Greeven in Albert Huck, *Synopse der drei ersten Evangelien/Synopsis of the First Three Gospels with the Addition of the Johannine Parallels* (Tubingen, W. Germany: J. C. B. Mohr [Paul Siebeck], 1981), xxxvi.

22. See Etienne Charpentier, *How to Read the New Testament* (New York: Crossroad Publishing Company, 1984), 18.

The Suffering and Death of Jesus

Part One

$\mathscr{I}$NTRODUCTION

W ell-known German biblical scholar Martin Hengel persuasively argues: "No human death has influenced and shaped the world of late antiquity, and indeed the history of mankind as a whole down to the present day, more than that of the Galilean craftsman and itinerant preacher who was crucified before the gates of Jerusalem in AD 30."[1] Hengel indicates that countless thousands of Jews were executed by the imperial legions of Rome who imposed *pax Romana* (Roman peace) on the inhabitants of Judea from the death of King Herod in 4 B.C. through the end of the First Jewish Revolt in A.D. 70.[2] For the most part, those so cruelly executed are completely forgotten, their names lost forever. That Jesus was not forgotten and that his name is remembered today is among the most remarkable historical facts of our time.

No longer do scholars seriously doubt that Jesus lived and was executed. Even one of the well-known members of the "Jesus Seminar," a group whose majority believe that the Gospels in general and the words attributed to Jesus in particular are a complex blend of fact and fiction, categorically declared: "Jesus' death by execution under Pontius Pilate is as sure as anything historical can ever be."[3]

The Significance of Jesus' Death and Resurrection

Even some well-meaning Christians argue that God offered salvation through the death of his Son even though Jesus himself was caught off guard in Jerusalem. One scholar perceptively wrote, "One would have to declare Jesus something of a simpleton if it were

maintained that he went up from Galilee to Jerusalem in all innocence, without any idea of the deadly opposition he was to encounter
there."4 This is an important point which we will review again and
again as we read the narratives of his suffering and death. The authors of the Gospels clearly noted on several occasions that Jesus was
fully aware of how his last journey to the Holy City would end.

Another important point of study is how Jesus' suffering and
death in Jerusalem was interpreted by himself and his disciples. He
and his closest followers understood it as an atoning sacrifice on behalf of humanity (see Matthew 20:28; Romans 4:25; 5:8; 8:32; 1
Corinthians 15:3–5; Galatians 1:4; Ephesians 5:2; 1 Timothy 2:6; 1
Peter 2:21–24). Additionally, while Jewish beliefs in the resurrection
are presupposed by every author of the New Testament, an important factor that transformed these earlier beliefs is the early disciples'
absolute assurance that the Father had begun the resurrection of the
dead by raising the crucified Jesus. The raising of Jesus had indeed
demonstrated the Father's eternal overruling of the human court's
inhumane and unthinkable decision, which brought about the trial
and crucifixion of Jesus.

With the great outpouring of the Holy Spirit, beginning on the
day of Pentecost, Jesus' resurrection gave the early Saints a new lens
through which to interpret Jesus' mortal ministry. The Resurrection
made sense of Jesus' suffering and death, facilitated Jesus' exaltation
as Lord, and finally promised resurrection to all humanity and eternal
life to those who believe.5 In the end, this was virtually the whole
essence of the Gospel for the early disciples, especially for Paul.6

A Personal Approach

As a trained historian, my interest in the historical aspect of the
Gospel events is self-evident in both my study and my writing. From
a scholarly point of view, a historian is pleased to have four separate
sources available to help reconstruct Jesus' words and actions on that
fateful last day of life. However, the authors of the Gospels did not
have my professional bias. They were not solely interested in recording the historical details of Jesus' suffering and death but rather
recorded their individual witness for a much different and more im-

portant purpose—the proclamation of the gospel of peace and reconciliation to a fallen world.

Therefore, on a personal level I prefer to emphasize dimensions of
Gethsemane, those that caused him, "the greatest of all, to tremble because of pain, and to bleed at every pore, and to suffer both body and
spirit—and would that I might not drink the bitter cup, and shrink—
Nevertheless, glory be to the Father, and I partook and finished my
preparations unto the children of men" (D&C 19:18–19). The unspeakable suffering in Gethsemane, which far surpasses any physical
torment inflicted by those involved in his arrest, trial, and crucifixion, is not the fault of any one person, ethnic group, or even nation.
Too often our discussions focus on who was responsible, which sometimes leads to anti-Jewish statements. Of the estimated four to five
million Jews living in the Greco-Roman world at the time, few had
contact with Jesus or his disciples. Only a small minority of the estimated 150,000 to 180,000 Passover visitors to Jerusalem during Jesus'
last week could have participated in the events described in the
Gospels. As we will discover, the Jewish leadership, with the support
of some of the common people, rejected Jesus and handed him over to
the Romans to be executed. This does not negate the fact that Jesus'
disciples were Jewish and that many other Jews, including priests and
Pharisees, converted in large numbers shortly after his resurrection
(see Acts 2:41; 4:4; 5:15). In a real and fundamental sense I am as
much at fault as anyone. If like Paul we can declare: "This is a faithful
saying, and worthy of all acceptation, that Christ Jesus came into the
world to save sinners; of whom I am chief, . . . [and] gave himself a
ransom for all" (1 Timothy 1:15; 2:6), then we come to realize that
any preoccupation with who was responsible for the physical abuse
Jesus experienced can, in fact, divert our attention from the real
drama and the essential issues raised by each Gospel's author.

The same can be said of the strictly scholarly tools (historical
and exegetical methodology) used to enhance a study of Jesus' suffering and death. Any tool of study that prevents us from asking
such eternally important questions as "Whom seekest thou?" and
"Lovest thou me?" (John 20:15; 21:15–17) is antithetical to the very
mission of the Gospels themselves and the early Christians who read
or heard these personal and authentic testimonies.

After realizing how easily I could be enticed and led away from the most important issues raised in the Gospels, I chose, no matter how painful, to imagine myself playing the parts of the individual characters in the story.[7] Some of the questions I ask in order to place myself within the story include: Have I sometimes acted like Pilate, washing my hands of personal responsibilities because society allows me to do so? Am I like the unnamed disciple who ran away naked from Gethsemane, willing to flee a commitment in the face of personal cost? Like Peter, do I pretend not to understand the questions, thus avoiding the hard decisions of life? Do the Roman soldiers' actions remind me of times when I joined in with others without questioning my actions, because everyone else was doing the same?

I am persuaded that the terrible story of Jesus' last mortal hours are meant to be read personally, and the issues involved are intended to challenge us to ask hard questions about ourselves instead of focusing on others. At first we may feel personal anguish, contrition, and profound sadness for our own sins. In the end, the resurrection of Jesus replaces these natural feelings with divine love, hope, peace, and reconciliation. With this view in mind, let us turn our attention to a discussion of the suffering and death of Jesus as portrayed by the authors of the Gospel narratives.

The Passion Narratives

Like the infancy narratives (Matthew 1:1–2:23; Luke 2:1–39) and the Resurrection narratives (Matthew 28:1–20; Mark 16:1–20; Luke 24:1–53; and John 20:1–21:25), the *Passion narratives* are a subset of the larger Gospel story.[8] The Passion (from *pathos*, meaning "something that befalls someone; suffering") includes "the sections of the canonical gospels that recount the suffering and death of Jesus of Nazareth" and includes most of the material found in Matthew 26–27; Mark 14–15; Luke 22–23; and John 12–19.[9] Note that the Passion narratives represent "the longest consecutive action recounted of Jesus" in the Gospels, which seems to indicate that the Gospel writers considered the Passion as most important.[10] That emphasis reflects Jesus' own words before Pilate: "To this end was I born, and for this cause came I into the world" (John 18:37).

Elder Jeffery R. Holland, picking up the message behind Jesus' announcement to Pilate, insightfully wrote about an earlier episode in Jesus' life, recorded in Luke 2:25, 29–35: "There is a profound . . . message in the one [Simeon] gave to sweet and pure Mary in that first Christmas season. He was joyously happy. . . . But his joy was not of the superficial kind. . . . His joy had something to do . . . with this child's life—or at least his death—which would be like a sword piercing through his beloved mother's soul. . . . Surely such [an ominous warning] was untimely, even unseemly, at *that* moment—when the son of God was so young and tender and safe, and his mother so thrilled with his birth. . . . [But] it was appropriate *and* important. . . . It is in the life at the *other* end of the manger scene that gives this moment of nativity in Bethlehem its ultimate meaning. . . . Wise old Simeon understood all of this—that the birth was ultimately for the death."[11]

Earlier Telling of the Story

In all likelihood, the story of Jesus' suffering and death was already committed to writing before any of the Gospels were written; one such source may have been used by both Mark and Luke.[12] As one scholar notes: "Certainly, the telling of the stories of Jesus' death was a central Christian concern long before" any Gospel was written.[13]

More likely, Paul was also acquainted with the "story of the cross" (*ho logos gar ho tou staurou*) as described in Corinthians and that he was summarizing a well-known and oft-repeated story of Jesus' suffering and death to the early Saints living in the Roman port city on the Peloponnesian coast of Greece (see 1 Corinthians 1:18).

Note the following aspects (which include the story of the Resurrection as a natural conclusion to the Passion narratives) found in Paul's writings, usually ascribed to have been written before any of the Gospel narratives: "For I have received of the Lord that which also I delivered unto you, That the Lord Jesus *the same night in which he was betrayed took bread:* And when he had given thanks, he brake it, and said, Take, eat: this is my body, which is broken for you: this do in remembrance of me. After the same manner also he took the cup, when he had supped, saying, This cup is the new testament in my blood: this do ye, as oft as ye drink it, in remembrance of me. For as often as ye eat this bread, and drink this cup, ye do *shew the Lord's death* till he come" (1 Corinthians 11:23–26; emphasis added). And finally: "I delivered unto you first of all that which I also received, how that *Christ died for our sins* according to the scriptures; *and that he was buried, and that he rose again the third day* according to the scriptures: *and that he was seen of Cephas, then of the twelve*" (1 Corinthians 15:3–5; emphasis added).[14]

Additionally, while Paul does not focus on Jesus' mortal ministry, he makes numerous allusions and references to the events described in the Passion narratives of the four Gospels (all written after his probable execution in Rome): his sufferings (Philippians 3:10); the cross (Philippians 2:8); the crucifixion (Galatians 2:20; 3:1; 1 Corinthians 1:23; 2 Corinthians 13:4); being "hung on a tree" (Galatians 3:13); his death (1 Thessalonians 5:10; 1 Corinthians 11:26; 15:3; Romans 4:25; 5:8–10; 6:3); his burial (1 Corinthians 15:3; Romans 6:4); the significant truth that "the Jews. . . . killed the Lord Jesus" (1 Thessalonians 2:14–15); and his being nailed to the cross (Colossians 2:14).

The many citations and allusions to the book of Psalms in the Passion narrative and in Peter's discourses as recorded in the early chapters of the book of Acts show how firmly Jesus' disciples believed that his suffering, death, resurrection, and exaltation were truly "according to the scriptures" and thus part of the Father's plan to save the world (see John 3:16).

The difficulty of properly telling the story of Jesus can be seen in that the disciples had to make sense of Jesus' suffering and death themselves, as well as for those to whom they preached soon after the Resurrection. Paul captured the problematic nature of the message the first missionaries presented to a skeptical world when he wrote: "But we preach Christ crucified, unto the Jews a stumbling-block, and unto the Greeks foolishness" (1 Corinthians 1:23).

The earliest mention of Christianity by a Roman writer dates from the beginning of the second century. Pliny, a governor in the province of Bithynia, now modern Turkey, wrote letters to the Roman Emperor Trajan seeking advice about how he should handle

Christians living in this region. Later, many other Roman authors wrote much more about the dominant societies' attitudes and re-sponses to the message of the cross.[15]

And while these written sources are important, a dramatic dis-covery in 1856 of a graffito dating from the Roman period may graphically illustrate Paul's contention. It was found on a wall in the servants' quarters of the Imperial Palace on the Palatine Hill in Rome. The graffito includes a drawing of a man gesturing with his right hand towards a cross with a man crucified on it. The man on the cross is depicted with a donkey's head. The statement scrawled below is often translated: "Alexamenos, worship god."[16] While some date the graffito to the first century, no one is certain. However, "one can easily assume such a derogatory cartoon did indeed mock the Christian [proclamation of the Good News about Jesus Christ]."[17]

In light of the above it does not seem hard to believe that some-one may have asked early Christians: "If Jesus was the Messiah, then why did God allow him to be crucified as a criminal?" To this ques-tion, and others like it, Peter gave the first response on Pentecost: "Therefore let all the house of Israel know assuredly, that God hath made that same Jesus, whom ye have crucified, both Lord and Christ" (Acts 2:36). That is, God vindicated Jesus, who had been tried and convicted in a human court, through raising him from the dead and exalting him (making him Lord). Therefore, the story of the events leading up to and including the crucifixion were of real significance and an important part of the message now proclaimed by the disciples.

Different Views—One Climax

As one examines the four Passion narratives one thing becomes quite clear: while we see similarities in presentation, we also see con-siderable differences in content. Each one tells the story from his par-ticular viewpoint, highlighting some points, excluding other aspects of the story, or simply reordering incidents. In fact, it seems certain that no one Gospel author has told the whole story. Nevertheless, each of the synoptic Gospels inevitably finds its climax in the proclamation: "He is risen; he is not here"! (Mark 16:6; cf. Luke

24:6; Matthew 28:6). Thus, while the story of Jesus' passion is recounted, the purpose is not to focus on some setback to his ministry but to demonstrate his complete and total victory against the forces of darkness. The implicit crux of the Passion narrative is no more and no less than the accomplishment of God's plan of salvation.

NOTES

1. Martin Hengel, *The Atonement: The Origins of the Doctrine in the New Testament* (Philadelphia: Fortress Press, 1981), 1.

2. Overview based on Hengel, *The Atonement*, 1–2.

3. John Dominic Crossan, *Who Killed Jesus?: Exposing the Roots of Anti-Semitism in the Gospel Story of the Death of Jesus* (San Francisco: HarperCollins Publishers, 1996), 5; for a devastating but fair critique of the Jesus Seminar's method and approach, see Luke Timothy Johnson, *The Real Jesus: The Misguided Quest for the Historical Jesus and the Truth of the Traditional Gospels* (San Francisco: HarperCollins Publishers, 1997).

4. Edward Schillebeeckx, *Jesus: An Experiment in Christology* (New York: The Crossroad Publishing Company, 1981), 299.

5. See George W. E. Nickelsburg, "Resurrection," *The Anchor Bible Dictionary*, 6 vols. (New York: Doubleday, 1992), 5:688.

6. The term *Gospel* has different meanings, depending on context, in the writings of the early apostles and prophets. Today, we generally use the term in a more expansive way to include all of the revealed truths and practices of the modern-day kingdom.

7. See Raymond E. Brown, *A Crucified Christ in Holy Week: Essays on the Four Gospel Passion Narratives* (Collegeville, Minnesota: The Liturgical Press, 1986), 10–11.

8. This summary is based on Joseph A. Fitzmyer, *The Anchor Bible: The Gospel According to Luke* (2 vols.) (New York: Doubleday, 1985), 2:1360–69.

9. George W. E. Nickelsburg, "Passion Narratives," in *The Anchor Bible Dictionary*, 6 vols. (New York: Doubleday, 1992), 5:172–73; see also a standard dictionary under the entry "passion" for its common definition. For example, *The New Merriam-Webster Dictionary* (Springfield, Massachusetts: Merriam-Webster Inc., Publishers, 1989), 533.

10. Raymond E. Brown, *The Death of the Messiah: From Gethsemane to the Grave*, 2 vols. (New York: Doubleday, 1994), 1:11.

11. Jeffery R. Holland, *Christmas Comfort* [pamphlet] (Salt Lake City: Bookcraft, 1996), 3–4.

12. While many scholars hold this view, Raymond Brown notes, "Mark's passion account, however, need not depend directly on an earlier written Passion narrative"; see R. E. Brown, *A Crucified Christ in Holy Week*, 9.

13. David L. Barr, *New Testament Story: An Introduction*, 2nd edition (New York: Wadsworth Publishing Company, 1995), 230. While accepting the existence of an earlier Passion story I do not, however, believe the so-called "Cross Gospel" theory presently discussed in such popular publications as *Newsweek, Time,* and *U.S. News & World Report* by scholars like John Dominic Crossan, co-director of the Jesus Seminar. One scholar notes: "In this bullish market, the most remarkable entrepreneurship has been demonstrated by the Jesus Seminar, a ten-year exercise in academic self-promotion that has succeeded in drawing an extraordinary amount of attention to itself. Indeed, it has come to symbolize, for better or worse, the controversy over 'the Historical Jesus.'" See Luke Timothy Johnson, *The Real Jesus: The Misguided Quest for the Historical Jesus and the Truth of the Traditional Gospels* (San Francisco: Harper SanFrancisco, 1997), 1.

14. Many modern translations and New Testament scholars no longer print the term *twelve* with a lowercase *t* but rather with an uppercase *T*, because it seems that this term, *the Twelve*, is a proper name representing the quorum, not just the numeric composition of the group. In this sense, then, we may distinguish between three important terms found in the New Testament: disciples, Apostles, and the Twelve. Disciples are followers of Jesus, Apostles are those "sent" by Jesus (this is what the term means in Greek), and the Twelve are ordained members of the inner circle. Therefore, the Twelve are by definition Apostles and disciples, but disciples may not necessarily be Apostles or members of the Twelve. Later, the term *Apostles* took on specific meaning in the Restoration as "special witnesses of the name of Christ" and refers to those specifically ordained to the office; see the index to the triple combination under the term *Apostle*.

15. See Robert L. Wilken, *The Christians as the Romans Saw Them* (New Haven: Yale University Press, 1984).

16. Graydon F. Snyder, *Ante Pacem: Archaeological Evidence of Church Life Before Constantine* (n.p.: Mercer University Press, 1985), 27–28.

17. Ibid., 26.

$\mathcal{M}$ARK'S PASSION NARRATIVE

I n the judgment of most New Testament students, the oldest Gospel book is Mark.[1] It was apparently written by John Mark (see Acts 12:12) with the help of Peter, or, more likely, based on Peter's teachings. Quoting Papias, the second-century bishop of Hierapolis (in modern Turkey), a third-century bishop of Caesarea named Eusebius wrote: "Mark, having become the interpreter of Peter, wrote down accurately, though not indeed in order, whatsoever he remembered of the teachings said or done by Christ."[2]

For this reason it is sometimes called "Peter's Memoirs," making Mark more of a faithful recorder than an author.[3] There appears to be a correlation between Peter's discourse at Caesarea in the home of Cornelius and Mark's outline. Just as Mark begins his Gospel with the baptism of John (see Mark 1:1–11), so Peter begins with the baptism of John as he presents the gospel to Cornelius (see Acts 10:37). Both conclude with Jesus' resurrection (Mark 16; Acts 10:39–41).

In all likelihood, Mark composed his Gospel in Rome during the Neronian persecution beginning in A.D. 64 or during the "last stages of the civil turmoil that gripped the empire in A.D. 68–69 and before the fall of the temple in Jerusalem in August 70."[4] Whether during Nero's persecution or following his death (A.D. 68), the early Saints in Rome experienced unprecedented social and political disruptions—and officially and unofficially sanctioned persecution.

This period of turmoil began when Nero made "the Christians the scapegoats for the disastrous fire" in July 64, a fire which lasted more than a week and left only four of nineteen districts in Rome untouched. Though short-lived, according to Christian tradition this persecution caused the death of nearly one thousand Christians, including Paul and Peter.[5]

Writing nearly fifty years later, Roman historian Tacitus described the madness of the emperor Nero's campaign to kill Christians in Rome: "But neither human help, nor imperial munificence, nor all the modes of placating Heaven, could stifle scandal or dispel the belief that the fire had taken place by order. Therefore, to scotch the rumour, Nero substituted as culprits, and punished with the utmost refinements of cruelty, a class of men, loathed for their vices, whom the crowd styled Christians. . . . First, then, the confessed members of the sect were arrested; next, on their disclosures, vast numbers were convicted, not so much on the count of arson as for hatred of the human race. And derision accompanied their end: they were covered with wild beasts' skins and torn to death by dogs; or they were fastened on crosses, and when daylight failed were burned to serve as lamps by night. Nero had offered his Gardens for the spectacle, and gave an exhibition in his Circus, mixing with the crowd in the habit of a charioteer, or mounted on his car. Hence, in spite of a guilt which had earned the most exemplary punishment, there arose a sentiment of pity, due to the impression that they were being sacrificed not for the welfare of the state but to the ferocity of a single man."[6]

As a result of this setting, Mark seems to emphasize things that would be of particular help to his Roman audience, then experiencing intense pressure from the dominant society, the loss of Paul and Peter, and the overwhelming social, political, and economic effects caused by civil turmoil rippling through the Roman Empire at the time. Remember that the Gospel authors did not simply report the events of Jesus' life for purely historical recollection: they chose, organized, and customized sources, including their own memory, to stress important themes and doctrinal teachings.

Mark seems more interested in what Jesus did than what he taught, though he clearly identifies Jesus as a teacher. Mark is very familiar with details of the stories he presents, some of which are sometimes unnecessary. Mark's Gospel is the shortest of the four canonical accounts, some 661 verses. As one Jewish scholar noted,

"Mark is short enough to read at one sitting."[7] Yet, his Passion narrative is longer than one might expect and is the most word-for-word and hour-by-hour sequence in his entire narrative. Perhaps because it is so detailed, sequential, and logical, it was used by the other Gospel writers as an important source for their own telling of the story.

The material that Mark presents in the chapters before he formally begins his Passion narrative was once thought to be a long introduction to it. Mark depicts Jesus' ministry as a "way to the cross" from the beginning.[8] Although scholars no longer hold strongly to that notion, Mark does present a journey towards suffering, towards death on the cross. His message is grounded in the fact that Jesus suffered, died, and rose from the dead. For Mark the passion is intrinsically bound up with Jesus himself, both words and deeds.

We will discuss ways in which Peter's memoirs (recorded in Mark's Passion narrative) may have influenced the other Gospel authors later. It is true that longer or shorter versions of the stories do not necessarily prove which was the earlier source because an author can always move in either direction with a source, yet there are some interesting examples about Matthew's text that seem to be explained only by Mark's narrative being written first. (More about that later.)

Mark's particular difference from the other accounts is the flight of the naked young disciple (see Mark 14:51–52), traditionally identified as Mark himself. If so, Mark's description of events may include insights from himself, an eyewitness.

Jesus Announces His Suffering and Death
(Mark 8:29–33; 9:31–32; 10:32–34)

At what point Jesus came to understand the particular details about how his mortal mission would end, we cannot be sure from the scriptural accounts. Nevertheless, Mark does inform the reader that at some point Jesus no longer remained silent on the subject, at least among his most intimate disciples. Indeed, Jesus makes three separate prophecies of his forthcoming suffering, death, and resurrection in Jerusalem. "They are," as one scholar notes, "climactically arranged from indirect speech and from general statement to very specific detail."9

The first prophecy follows immediately after Peter testifies that Jesus is the Christ as the disciples meet with their Master somewhere near Caesarea Philippi in Upper Galilee: "And he saith unto them, But whom say ye that I am? And Peter answereth and saith unto him, Thou art the *Christ*" (Mark 8:29; emphasis added). Christ is an anglicized form of the Greek word *christos*, meaning "anointed one." It is equivalent to the Hebrew word *mashiaḥ*, meaning "anointed one," from which we have the English word *Messiah*.

After Peter's confession, which in some respects is incomplete, Mark continues: "[Jesus] began to teach them, that the *Son of man* must suffer many things, and be rejected of the elders, and of the chief priests, and scribes, and be killed, and after three days rise again. And he spake that saying openly. And Peter took him, and began to rebuke him" (Mark 8:31–32; emphasis added). In turn, Jesus rebukes Peter in the sharpest of terms, placing him on the side of Satan: "But when he had turned about and looked on his disciples, he rebuked Peter, saying, Get thee behind me, Satan: for thou savourest not the things that be of God, but the things that be of men" (Mark 8:33). LDS New Testament scholar Roger Keller put it nicely when he wrote: "Clearly, Peter—and perhaps we as observers—missed something. What was wrong with Peter's desire that Jesus not suffer? Everything—for Jesus came precisely to suffer and die!"10 Apparently Peter, like the other disciples, was tempted by the satanic suggestion that Jesus could fulfill his mission without suffering and dying.

Capitalization of *Son of man* is a convention of the King James Version translators; there are no case distinctions in the original Greek texts. Only Jesus uses the phrase in the synoptic Gospels, and he uses it more often than any other title (such as Messiah or Son of God) to reveal who he is. In all likelihood, the context of Jesus' usage is a passage found in the book of Daniel in which the suffering righteous one was conjoined with martyrdom; that is, suffering, death, deliverance and exaltation came to be closely associated together (see Daniel 7–9).

The context of this particular pericope (Greek *perikopē*, meaning

the act of cutting around; a section or unit of material) may suggest
that this was the first time Jesus taught his disciples that he was the
"Righteous Sufferer" of Psalms, the "Son of man" of Daniel, and the
"Suffering Servant" of Isaiah, not the warrior-king Messiah so commonly expected by many at the time.[11]

Another important aspect of the prophecy is *rejection:* "the Son
of man must suffer many things, and be rejected of the elders, and of
the chief priests, and scribes." Yet, as Mark reveals even before the
"fateful Friday," Jesus is the "rejected one."[12] Those arrayed in opposition to him are Jewish religious leaders who question, accuse, and
reject him. Therefore, he came to Jerusalem after his message to "repent and believe" was rejected in Galilee. He arrived then as the
"one who with the rejection of the offer [of reconciliation] is himself
rejected."[13]

The second prophecy came on the heels of the Mount of Transfiguration experience and just shortly after the prophecy at Caesarea
Philippi: "For he taught his disciples, and said unto them, The Son
of Man is delivered into the hands of men, and they shall kill him;
and after that he is killed, he shall rise the third day. But they understood not that saying, and were afraid to ask him" (Mark
9:31–32).

A third prophecy recorded in Mark occurs as Jesus and his disciples begin their journey for the final Passover feast together in the
Holy City. In a most dramatic way Mark highlights Jesus' action as
he moves towards Jerusalem, where he faces certain death: "And
they were in the way going up to Jerusalem; *and Jesus went before
them:* and they were amazed; and as they followed, they were afraid"
(Mark 10:32; emphasis added). Mark continues: "And he took again
the twelve, and began to tell them what things should happen unto
him, saying, Behold, we go up to Jerusalem; and the Son of man
shall be delivered unto the chief priests, and unto the scribes; and
they shall condemn him to death, and shall deliver him to the Gentiles: and they shall mock him, and shall scourge him, and shall spit
upon him, and shall kill him: and the third day he shall rise again"
(Mark 10:32–34).

It is essential to realize that these three prophecies do not talk
about the possibility or even probability of execution, but in a real

sense they specify the ultimate outcome of a ministry that looked forward to an atoning sacrifice for humanity. Additionally, observe that Jesus does not simply rely upon former biblical prophecies to announce his passion and resurrection but also provides the disciples with his own prophecies about his mission, thus providing a double prophecy (old and new).

What later became clear to the disciples was that "the Son of man *must* suffer many things, and be rejected of the elders, and of the chief priests, and scribes, and be killed, and after three days rise again" (Mark 8:31; emphasis added). The "must suffer" and "rise again" are interconnected, as we will see later, and represent a profound doctrinal revelation. Jesus will, at the Last Supper, give his disciples a meaningful interpretation—indeed, his insight into the "must" on that night is the very heart of the Passion narrative.

All in all these three specific prophecies made by Jesus about his suffering, death, and resurrection surprised his disciples. Following the first prophecy Peter "began to rebuke" Jesus; following the second, the disciples "were afraid to ask" Jesus about what he meant; and finally, on the third occasion there is only deafening silence in the text about their reaction as they walked with Jesus towards Jerusalem.

The kind of death Jesus foresaw was most likely crucifixion, since he told the disciples that he would be delivered into the "hands of the Gentiles." While crucifixion (literally "fixed to the cross") originated in Mesopotamia, the Romans ("Gentiles" in Mark's Gospel narrative) used it as a political and military punishment to kill an enemy, primarily inflicted on the lower classes, slaves, violent criminals, and the unruly elements in rebellious provinces, not the least of which was Judea.[14]

All in all, Jesus' statements took on a cold and deadly reality, for the disciples understood that it was *legally* possible to be put to death in three ways at the time: first, the Romans had the power to execute those found guilty of serious criminal acts or rebellion; second, Herod Antipas had the royal prerogative (*ius gladii*) to behead someone living within his jurisdiction (for example, John the Baptist); and last, the Jewish leadership in Jerusalem was apparently empowered to stone someone (as in the case of Stephen).[15]

And while the real possibility of execution was present in Jesus' world from three separate and distinct forces, the prophecies take on added significance to the reader as Mark has carefully outlined the fierce opposition to Jesus' ministry by segments of the many groups within Judaism, including the Pharisees and the Herodians (possibly Essenes).[16]

The Pharisees (*pharisaioi* or "separatists") are pictured by scholars in various ways, ranging from a mere sect within Judaism to a powerful religious leadership body.[17] They are depicted very early in the Gospel narrative as opposing Jesus' activities (see Mark 2:16–17, 24). Later they joined with the Herodians to consider Jesus' death (see Mark 3:6). Finally, during Jesus' last week, the plotting of the Pharisees and the Herodians is noted again just days before Jesus' betrayal, trial, and death (see Mark 12:13).

However, rather surprisingly it is the chief priests, primarily composed of the Sadducean faction, who hand Jesus over to the Romans at Passover. While Mark does not make particular mention of it, it is not hard to imagine that "tension between Jesus and the Sadducees dated from an earlier period than the story of the Passion would suggest."[18] With information gleaned from John's Gospel, we learn that Jesus came to Jerusalem during the first year of his ministry and cleansed the temple (see John 2:13–22). Most likely, this event initiated an eventually deadly collision with the chief priests.

What Mark implies is that opposition to Jesus came from all segments of the religious continuum within Judaism, but mainly from the "Pharisees and, especially towards the end, the Sadducces."[19] We must not forget that many from these groups acted fairly towards the early Christians (see Acts 5:34–39), and others among them accepted Jesus' teachings and joined the Church following his death (see Acts 6:7; 15:5).

It was to celebrate this important religious feast, Passover, that Jesus and his male and female disciples made the long journey from Galilee to Jerusalem. As they did so, they left behind the Jewish kingdom ruled by Herod Antipas, son of King Herod, and arrived in a province of the Roman empire. The chief representative of Rome, the prefect (the title procurator came later), was Pontius Pilate. This was the setting of the Passion narrative found in Mark.

A Plot Against Jesus (Mark 14:1–2, 10–11)

Mark's Passion narrative (see Mark 14:1–15:47) begins on a malevolent note: "After two days was the feast of the passover, and of unleavened bread: and the chief priests and the scribes sought how *they might take him by craft*, and put him to death. But they said, Not on the feast day, lest there be an uproar of the people" (Mark 14:1–2; emphasis added). Passover and Unleavened Bread were originally two festivals (see Leviticus 23:5–6), but now were celebrated as one recalling Israel's liberation from bondage.

Mark alludes to several cultural traits that North Americans find difficult to understand. Apparently, it was not unexpected for elites in the first century to use craft (stealth) as a means of achieving their goals. They did so without bringing dishonor to themselves. Additionally, they used bribery (see Mark 14:11), false witnesses (see Mark 14:56), trumped-up charges (see Mark 15:3), crowd manipulation (see Mark 15:11), and public mocking (see Mark 15:31–32).[20]

Among these activities, all of which we find unacceptable today in North America, some are not only accepted as a normal course of business in certain cultures but are adopted by people without shame. Additionally, Mark informs us that the chief priests and scribes decided to wait until after Passover to take Jesus because they feared that those coming to Jerusalem for the feast might react negatively, even violently.

While the conspiracy to kill Jesus is announced here in ominous tones, Mark reassures us that nothing will happen *until after* the feast. This report is followed by the anointing of Jesus in Bethany (see Mark 14:3–9). Through the action of an unnamed woman we learn that Jesus understood the immediacy of his forthcoming death: "She hath done what she could: she is come aforehand to anoint my body to the burying" (Mark 14:8).[21] Jesus' statement implies that there will not be sufficient time for the traditional burial procedures following his death; thus are we informed that the plot to kill him will be successful.

Following this anointing in Bethany comes an astonishing and deadly turn of events. To the surprise of the chief priests an opportunity presents itself that requires them to unexpectedly change their plans: "And Judas Iscariot, one of the twelve, went unto the chief priests, to betray him unto them. And when they heard it, they were glad, and promised to give him money. And he sought how he might conveniently betray him" (Mark 14:10–11).

When reading the accounts of Jesus' appearances before the Jewish leaders following his arrest, the story line seems hurried and in many cases the meetings appear unorganized: they fail to obtain false witnesses who agree among themselves for example. Obviously Judas' unexpected offer to hand Jesus over to Jewish leaders *before* they planned to take him has thrown off their plans, causing them to improvise almost on the run. On the other hand, his offer gives them exactly what they need—someone from the inside who will act as an instrument for a discreet and precise arrest.

Mark provides no previous warning or reason for Judas' defection, but he agrees with the other synoptic writers on an important point: Judas was "one of the twelve" (see Matthew 26:14; Luke 22:3), highlighting the profound scandal of this act. The Joseph Smith Translation offers this insight about Judas' motive: "Nevertheless, Judas Iscariot, even one of the twelve, went unto the chief priests to betray Jesus unto them; *for he turned away from him, and was offended because of his words*. And when the chief priests heard of him they were glad, and promised to give him money; and he sought how he might conveniently betray Jesus" (JST, Mark 14:28; emphasis added). In all likelihood Judas rejected Jesus' interpretation of his own mission—one that embraced suffering and the cross. The Bread of Life sermon in John 6 suggests this for many disciples.

Judas betrayed not only Jesus but also the way of life he himself had once espoused. He thus qualified himself according to the classical definition as an apostate, for he was in a state of "rebellion [and] abandonment."[22] Additionally, while the actions of the chief priests in first-century society would not be shamed by their bribing Judas, "it would surely be shameful for Judas. As a core group member in the Jesus [movement], Judas surely had given his word of honor to be personally committed to Jesus and his [mission]. Further, since loyalty to one's family, group, or patron is among the highest virtues of an honor-shame society, betrayal is one of the lowest sins."[23]

And while Jesus states that his death is in accord with his Father's divine will, Judas is nevertheless severely condemned for his action (see Mark 14:21). This is one of the so-called paradoxes of our faith: even though God makes use of our actions, we are nevertheless still responsible for them (evil or good).

Mark's account next moves to the Last Supper, held in Jerusalem on the night before his death.

The Upper Room

Everything in Mark's Gospel leads to the Upper Room as a turning point in the narrative. Somewhere in the city, Jesus spent his last night with the disciples in "a large upper room" (Mark 14:15). The *Coenaculum,* the current name of the site, based on Jerome's Latin Vulgate translation of the Greek *hyperōon* and *anagaion* (upper room), is traditionally located in the southern part of the upper city, between Herod's palace and the Gate of the Essenes, on Mount Zion. This site was marked in Constantine's time by the Church of Holy Sion, which appears on the Madaba Map, the oldest map of the Holy Land.

Tourists today are shown an Upper Room in a building dating from the Crusaders period, except some large hewn stones (called "ashlars") dating from the Roman period (which might have originally been Herodian stones from the Temple Mount that the Romans reused after destroying the temple). One knowledgeable scholar argues that the early Christians arrived in the city shortly after the Roman destruction in A.D. 70 and rebuilt a Jewish-Christian Synagogue on the former site of the Upper Room, thus keeping its memory alive.[24]

While just outside of the Old City near Zion's Gate today, this location was well within the ancient city walls of the first century. Certain clues within the scriptural record give credence to the notion that this room was somewhat established as a meetingplace for Jesus and his followers. For Luke, the location of the Last Supper and the meetings discussed in Acts 1 and 2 are identical. Luke seems to have been well acquainted with Jerusalem; from the first-person account in Acts 21:15–18, he apparently visited the Holy City at

least once. The use of the article *the* before "upper room" in Acts
1:13 in the Greek text implies that Luke himself knew the location
of this room.[25]

    While there are many uncertainties, one learned speculation is
that this Upper Room was the same place mentioned later in Acts
after Peter's miraculous release from prison: "[Peter] came to the house
of Mary the mother of John, whose surname was Mark; where many
were gathered together praying" (Acts 12:12).[26] If this reconstruction
is accurate, then Mary may well have been a wealthy landowner with
a servant (see Mark 14:13) and a large room that could accommodate
one hundred and twenty people (see Acts 1:13–15).

    The author of Acts is clear on several points about Mary: (1) she
was a disciple; (2) her home served as a place of gathering for the
early Saints in Jerusalem; (3) her son was John Mark; and (4) she
was related to another wealthy disciple, Barnabas (see Acts 4:36–37;
12:12; Colossians 4:10).[27]

    While the exact location of the Upper Room seems of minimum
importance to Mark, the fact that a long tradition established the
site here demonstrates the early Church's interpretation of the importance of the Last Supper. The action continues when Jesus sends
"two of his disciples, and saith unto them, Go ye into the city, and
there shall meet you a man bearing a pitcher of water: follow him"
(Mark 14:13). The man's identity is debated by modern commentators. Perhaps he was a servant from the household performing an unusual assignment. If Essenes were present in this part of the city, a
man carrying water would not have drawn any unnecessary attention (because no women were allowed in their movement, thus requiring men to perform those duties usually assigned to women).
Jesus told them what they would find if they followed him. It would
be "a large upper room furnished and prepared" (literally "an upper
room large being spread ready") (Mark 14:15).

    The Greek *estromēnon* (KJV "furnished") usually refers to
"couches on which to recline while eating."[28] Some suggest it refers
to "a room *furnished* w[ith] carpets or couches for the guests to recline on as they ate."[29] A rare but nevertheless attested usage during
this period is "to prepare a room for a banquet."[30] Here in the large
Upper Room, furnished apparently for the Passover feast, Jesus met

with his disciples to celebrate the fulfillment of the Passover meal.[31] I will discuss the physical arrangements of the dinner in my review of John's account.

The Last Supper (Mark 14:12–25)

The question whether the Last Supper was a Passover Seder (dinner) has drawn the attention of New Testament scholars for years. The synoptic Gospels suggest that it was (Mark 14:12–20; Matthew 26:17–30; Luke 22:7–20), while John seems to indicate that Jesus died at the very moment when the Passover lambs were being ritually slaughtered in preparation for the Passover (John 18:28; 19:14).[32] Many attempts to solve this well-known chronological inconsistency have been published by competent scholars. One suggestion proposes that two different calendars were in use by different groups operating in Judea Palestine at the time—a solar calendar and a lunar calendar.

In the ancient Near East the traditional calendar was based on the monthly cycle of phases of the moon or twenty-nine and a half days. Such a calendar required the addition of an extra month every two or three years. While the ancient Israelites used this system, an Egyptian solar calendar of 364 days was apparently adopted by some Jews, resulting in a 52-week calendar, months of exactly 30 days, and seasons of 13 weeks. "The first day of the year and of each season always fell on the same day of the week, as did all the major festivals."[33]

While we cannot be sure about the specific location and calendar calculations, Mark portrays the Last Supper as a Passover; since the Passover, more than any other meal, was considered a family meal, we start to realize the implication of Jesus' earlier teaching: "There came then his brethren and his mother, and, standing without, sent unto him, calling him. And the multitude sat about him, and they said unto him, Behold, thy mother and thy brethren without seek for thee. And he answered them, saying, Who is my mother, or my brethren? And he looked round about on them which sat about him, and said, Behold my mother and my brethren! For whosoever shall do the will of God, the same is my brother, and my sister, and mother" (Mark 3:31–35).

Mark's story continues: "And in the evening he cometh with the twelve. And as they sat and did eat, Jesus said, Verily I say unto you, One of you which eateth with me shall betray me. And they began to be sorrowful, and to say unto him one by one, Is it I? and another said, Is it I? And he answered and said unto them, It is one of the twelve, *that dippeth with me in the dish*" (Mark 14:17–20; emphasis added).

Like the three separate prophecies about his death, Jesus now begins to provide the disciples with three additional prophecies, all fulfilled before the night was over. They deal specifically with his closest disciples: Judas, the Twelve, and Peter. The first noted here speaks of Judas' betrayal. Mark implicitly refers to a passage in Psalms: "Yea, mine own familiar friend, in whom I trusted, which did *eat of my bread* hath lifted up his heel against me" (Psalm 41:9; emphasis added). Here Jesus applies the Old Testament prophecy to an immediate event, just as he will regarding a prophecy about the disciples scattering later in the evening. This prophecy about Judas is a prelude to the institution of the sacrament.

Incidentally, another interpretive framework in which the disciples made sense of Jesus' passion was the book of Psalms, as alluded to above. In almost all cases when Psalms is either cited or alluded to, the author associates Jesus with the righteous one who suffers, who endures persecution but knows himself to be in God's power. Importantly, we should understand that individual suffering is not a sign of righteousness, but rather that the suffering one is being delivered from his present predicament by God. In the case of Jesus, vindication comes after death through the Resurrection and exaltation on the right hand of God.

Mark, who has identified the ritual context of the meal when he associated it with Passover, records Jesus' words and acts during the meal: "And as they did eat, Jesus took bread, and blessed, and brake it, and gave to them, and said, Take, eat: this is my body. And he took the cup, and when he had given thanks, he gave it to them: and they all drank of it. And he said unto them, This is my blood of the new testament, which is shed for many. Verily I say unto you, I will drink no more of the fruit of the vine, until that day that I drink it new in the kingdom of God" (Mark 14:22–25).

There are several important aspects of this particular passage. It is quite certain that this last statement, "I will drink *no more* of the fruit of the vine, until that day that I drink it new in the kingdom of God," is a forceful pronouncement that he is face-to-face with death; in other words, this is a farewell meal, the last one he will share with his disciples until he comes into his Father's kingdom.

Yet Jesus' death is not the end. To make this point he swears an oath to this effect ("Verily I say unto you"), that he has unshaken faith in the promises of his Father: "I will drink no more of the fruit of the vine, *until* that day that I drink it new in the kingdom of God."

At this point you might recall Jesus' earlier teaching: "And whosoever of you will be the chiefest, shall be servant of all. For even the Son of man came not to be ministered [served] unto, but to minister [serve], and to give his life a ransom for many" (Mark 10:44–45). *Diakonein,* a Greek word meaning "minister" (serve) had a distinct secular meaning denoting waiting at tables, but in Hellenistic Jewry this was weakened to cover various ways to provide a service. Eventually, within the first-century Church, the word took on added meaning as it was used specifically for religious activity.[34]

The shift in meaning from its original Greek usage to the ecclesiastical one by the early Saints can only be understood in light of the Last Supper. Here the teaching and the reality combine as Jesus "serves" his disciples the emblems that represent his "service" for humankind. Schillebeeckx reminds us that "Jesus' act of self-surrender, the shedding of his blood 'for (or in place of) you', is here interpreted as a service that benefits the rest of the company. The Last Supper is seen as a *diakonia* performed on behalf of the disciples."[35] The same theme, readiness to serve, is discernable in John's portrayal of the Last Supper when he discusses the washing of feet (see John 13:1–20). Both actions, foot washing and instituting the sacrament, represent Jesus' atoning sacrifice, and both are preserved for us in the context of the Last Supper narrative.

In the end Mark's narration of the institution of the sacrament dramatically contrasts Jesus' life-giving sacrificial offering with Judas' life-taking offering to the chief priests. The story of the Last Supper, which promises that the Passion will mediate a new covenant between the Father and his children, is preliminary to the climactic finale of a ministry in which *every* action announced, promised, and offered salvation. Even here Jesus continues to serve by offering salvation through the bread and wine in spite of his own impending death.

The chronological order is not precise at this point in the narrative, but the Joseph Smith Translation seems to place the next story before the disciples leave the Upper Room.

Jesus talks with his disciples and tells them again that it is the Father's will that Jesus die. His disciples, however, have not yet accepted this reality. Jesus states, "The sheep shall be scattered" (Mark 14:27). Mark thus explicitly refers to Zechariah's prophecy: "Awake, O sword, against my shepherd, and against the man that is my fellow, saith the Lord of hosts: smite the shepherd, and the sheep shall be scattered" (Zechariah 13:7).

Jesus, however, promises them: "But after I am risen, I will go before you into Galilee" and then the Joseph Smith Translation adds: "And he said unto Judas Iscariot, What thou does, do quickly; but beware of innocent blood" (JST, Mark 14:28). Does this reveal the chronological setting?

Peter characteristically denies that he will ever abandon Jesus (see Mark 14:29), only to be told by the Master that he would yet deny the Lord three times: "And Jesus saith unto him, Verily I say unto thee, That this day, even in *this night, before the cock crow twice*, thou shalt deny me thrice. But he spake the more vehemently, If I should die with thee, I will not deny thee in any wise. Likewise also said they all" (Mark 14:30–31; emphasis added). Jesus is very specific, *this very night*, and then becomes more specific, *"before the cock crow twice."* Peter responds with "the most powerful adverb available,"[36] rendered in English as "vehemently."

While both Judas' betrayal and the disciples' loss of will were foretold in scripture and interpreted by Jesus, there is no biblical prophecy alluded to in the case of Peter's denial either explicitly or implicitly.

This sets a tragic tone to the story whereby the disciples' lapse and abandonment is much stronger than in any other Passion narrative.

The Mount of Olives (Mark 14:26–31)

Following the institution of the sacrament, Jesus leaves the Upper Room committed to the necessity that he must suffer and die. Mark notes: "And when they had sung an hymn, they went out into the mount of Olives" (Mark 14:26). Apparently, "the Passover celebration was not confined to a single location. The meal could be eaten in one place, and the recital of prayers, hymns, etc., could be held in another, provided that the company remained together."[37]

The view east from Jerusalem is dominated by the Mount of Olives, the setting of several important stories in both the Old and New Testaments and since then an important Christian site.[38]

After the temple was established in Jerusalem, the ritual of the red heifer was celebrated on the Mount of Olives; leaving the temple by the east gate, the procession led by the high priest crossed the Kidron Valley on a special causeway and climbed to the summit, where the animal was eventually sacrificed (see Numbers 19:1–10; *Mishnah* Parah 3.6).[39]

Mark may have this in mind as he begins his story, which has been described as the "most dramatically articulate part of the Passion narrative."[40]

A Place Called Gethsemane (Mark 14:32–42)

At some point Jesus and the disciples came "to a place which was named Gethsemane" (Mark 14:32) on the Mount of Olives (see Mark 14:26). In a provocative essay, Jerome Murphy-O'Connor identifies a whole series of doublets found here.[41] I will highlight them as we proceed, believing that this literary structure provides a logical way to emphasize certain aspects of the story.

The name *Gat-shemana* means "oil press" and is traditionally placed in the lower part of the Mount of Olives, across the Kidron Valley from the city walls.[42] Today one can visit the "Cave of Gethsemane," which "Byzantine Christians regarded as the place where the disciples rested while Jesus prayed a stone's-throw away." A gutter hints that it may have been used for holding or moving some liquid produced in the cave (from an oil press?).[43]

The land, possibly part of a family estate, may have been owned by someone at least sympathetic to Jesus or someone who was already a disciple. In any case, since olive processing takes place in the fall and Jesus was there in the spring, it might not have caused the owner or caretaker concern if he and his disciples took refuge there. It is even possible that John Mark's family owned both the large Upper Room and an olive grove that contained an olive press. If so, this might explain Mark's appearance in this section (see Mark 14:51–52).

Mark's careful, concise portrayal of the next scene depicts Jesus being abandoned by the disciples in three perceptible steps. First, Jesus moves away from the main body of the disciples who have followed him to Gethsemane; second, he moves from the inner circle of three disciples (Peter, James, and John); and finally, he falls to the earth alone to beseech the Father three times to take the cup from him.

One can imagine the light of the full moon filtering through the olive trees as Jesus tells his disciples: "*Sit ye here,* while I shall pray. And he taketh with him Peter and James and John, and *began to be sore amazed,* and to be very heavy; and saith unto them, My soul *is exceeding sorrowful* unto death: *tarry ye here,* and watch. And he went forward a little, and fell on the ground, and *prayed that, if it were possible,* the hour might pass from him. And he said, Abba, *Father, all things are possible* unto thee; take away this cup from me: nevertheless not what I will, but what thou wilt. And he cometh, and *findeth them sleeping,* and saith unto Peter, Simon, sleepest thou? couldest not thou watch one hour? Watch ye and pray, least ye enter into temptation. The spirit truly is ready, but the flesh is weak. And again he went away, and prayed, and spake the same words. And when he returned, he *found them asleep* again, (for their eyes were heavy,) neither wist they what to answer him. And he cometh the third time, and saith unto them, Sleep on now, and take your rest: it is enough, the hour is come; behold, *the Son of man is betrayed into the hands of sinners.* Rise up, let us go; lo, he that *betrayeth me is at hand*" (Mark 14:32–42; emphasis added).

Several observations are necessary at this point. First, the five sets of doublets found here are italicized. The consistent use of these structural doublets, in some cases using nearly exact words, seems to highlight and intensify the story being told.[44]

Second, the echo of Psalm 42 can be heard in Jesus' words, "My soul is exceeding sorrowful unto death." Two passages from Psalms seem to parallel this saying: "O my God, my soul is cast down within me. . . . Why art thou cast down, O my soul? and why art thou disquieted within me?" (Psalm 42:6, 11).

Third, since Mark's telling of the story is based on Peter's memoirs, we may be seeing a word-picture based on Peter's recollections. If so, we can appreciate the frank portrayal presented here, which is particularly critical of Peter himself. Remember that Peter's real name is Simon. Jesus renamed him Peter (from Greek or Latin), or Cephas (from Hebrew or Aramaic), a name that means "rock or stone." In Mark he is always referred to by this new name Jesus gave to him until this point, when Jesus says, "*Simon*, sleepest thou?" (Mark 14:37; emphasis added). I believe Jesus' use of *Simon* instead of *Peter* is significant and may reveal that he has not become the *rock* yet.

Fourth, Jesus finding the disciples asleep three times may well be related to Peter's triple denial later in the story. Matthew seems to pick up on this cue in his Passion narrative, since he suggests that Jesus' accusation against Peter for sleeping was really directed toward all the disciples (see Matthew 26:40–41).

Finally, Jesus is in some way fully aware that the cup he is drinking from is part and parcel of his mission, that his suffering and death is a final and extreme act of service to his Father and for us.

Jesus' Agony (Mark 14:33–36)

Recalling Jesus' experience at the Mount of Transfiguration (see Mark 9:2–8) may help us visualize his experience here on the Mount of Olives in a singular way. One account highlights him glorified, whereas the other preserves the story of the very darkest moment of his life.[45]

Mark, more than the other Gospel authors, portrays Jesus' agony in Gethsemane in clear and moving language, revealing "the starkness of the event, the reality of the suffering."[46] Jesus is God's son, yet because he is endowed with the human will to live he does not want to die. The name that Jesus uses in his cry to God, "Abba"

(Father), heightens the pathos of this tragic scene. Another Bible translation offers wording that may help us not only to feel what the scriptures say but also to understand them better: "He took with him Peter, James and John, and began to be horror-stricken and desperately depressed. 'My heart is breaking with a death-like grief,' he told them. 'Stay here and keep watch.' Then he walked forward a little way and flung himself on the ground, praying that, if it were possible, the hour might pass him by. 'Dear Father,' he said, 'all things are possible to you. Let me not have to drink this cup! Yet it is not what I want but what you want" (Mark 14:33–36, Phillips's Translation).[47]

What is Mark trying to describe? "In short," Jerome Murphy-O'Connor opines, "Jesus began to be filled with appalling dread."[48] Why? Another thoughtful commentator, Elder Neal A. Maxwell, writes: "The suffering Jesus began to be 'sore amazed' (Mark 14:33), or, in the Greek, 'awestruck' and 'astonished.'

"Imagine, Jehovah, the Creator of this and other worlds, 'astonished'! Jesus knew cognitively what He must do, but not experientially. He had never personally known the exquisite and exacting process of an atonement before. Thus, when the agony came in its fulness, it was so much, much worse than even He with his unique intellect had ever imagined!"[49]

One is reminded of the passage in Hebrews: "Who in the days of his flesh, when he had offered up prayers and supplications with strong crying and tears unto him that was able to save him from death, and was heard in that he feared; though he were a Son, yet learned he obedience by the things which he suffered" (Hebrews 5:7–8). A marginal note in the Joseph Smith Translation indicates that verses seven and eight refer to Melchizedek, but the parallel to Jesus seems probable.[50]

Despite Jesus' awful agony on that night, the author of Hebrews concludes: "And being made perfect, he became the author of eternal salvation unto all them that obey him" (Hebrews 5:9). While the early Saints learned that Jesus' suffering was terrible, they also learned that he prevailed as he integrated this moment into his overall surrender to his Father, thus demonstrating both his absolute loyalty to God and his service to humanity.

Mark's description is softened by the shorter Luke version. Additionally, John's later account emphasizes Jesus' power and authority. Following their lead, later Christians deemphasized the importance of Jesus' humanity and chose rather to focus on the risen Christ's glory. Today, "contemporary theologians probably err in the other direction, overemphasizing Jesus' humanity in a well-intentioned effort to make him seem more relevant."[51]

Jesus' Betrayal and Arrest (Mark 14:43–52)

Mark continues his story, announcing the arrival of the arresting party: "And immediately, while he yet spake, cometh Judas, one of the twelve, and with him a great multitude with swords and staves, from the chief priests and the scribes and the elders. And he that betrayed him had given them a token, saying, Whomsoever I shall kiss, that same is he; take him, and lead him away safely. And as soon as he was come, he goeth straightway to him, and saith, Master, master; and kissed him. And they laid their hands on him, and took him" (Mark 14:43–46).

"The *kiss* was a disciple's usual greeting of a teacher" during this period.[52] Mark portrays Judas' action with the use of the emphatic form of the Greek verb *to kiss*, allowing us to translate the passage as: "Rabbi, rabbi; and ardently kissed him."[53] Apparently, like our customs today, various types of physical contact in the ancient world had increasing senses of obligations, moving from a simple handshake to an embrace and finally to a kiss. These acts demonstrate varying degrees of intimacy and fidelity.

The original audience would be aghast at Judas' act. As one writer notes: "For if, in that ancient Mediterranean world, to betray *after* a kiss was shameful, to betray *with* a kiss was infamous."[54]

And now one sees clearly Jesus' threefold prophecy beginning to be fulfilled about the "Son of man" being delivered "into the hands of men." What seems to be perfectly clear is that in Judas' baleful action, and similar actions by both Jewish leaders and Pilate himself, Judas is caught up, although unwittingly, in the Father's saving event—the focus of the plan of salvation.

Mark is careful to reveal that Jesus did nothing to escape a violent death: "And they laid their hands on him, and took him. And one of them that stood by drew a sword, and smote a servant of the high priest, and cut off his ear. And Jesus answered and said unto them, Are ye come out, as against a thief, with swords and with staves to take me? I was daily with you in the temple teaching, and ye took me not: but the scriptures must be fulfilled" (Mark 14:46–49).

Jesus' question and retort, "Are ye come out, as against a thief [robber], with swords and with staves to take me? I was daily with you in the temple teaching, and ye took me not," reveals that we should not understand the word *thief* in the usual way. Rather, Josephus and others use this same Greek word to indicate a type of robber who would violently take from the socially privileged (see discussion on Barabbas below). In all likelihood, when he asked them if they were searching for a "robber," Jesus is referring to those roving bandits which "formed much of the fighting force in the early stages of the anti-Roman revolt, and it was they who coalesced with other groups eventually to form the Zealot party after the anti-Roman revolt broke out" in A.D. 66.[55]

Apparently, the arresting party expects a fight from Jesus' followers, hence the "swords and staves" noted by Mark. Malina and Rohrbaugh add: "Since social bandits commonly hid in caves and remote wadis, Jesus points out that he has not been hiding but has been daily in the Temple, where he could have been arrested with little difficulty."[56] John's additional mention of lanterns and torches (see John 18:3) only confirms this view.

The disciples at first stand in firm opposition to Jesus' arrest, but finally they all forsake him and flee. Mark's account emphasizes everyone's complete abandonment of Jesus: "And they all *forsook him, and fled*" (Mark 14:50; emphasis added). He then adds one unique insight: "And there followed him a certain young man, having a linen cloth cast about his naked body; and the young men laid hold on him: and he left the linen cloth, and fled from them naked" (Mark 14:51–52).

As noted earlier, some propose that the unnamed disciple is John Mark, the author of the Gospel narrative. The fact that the young man had a "linen cloth" suggests that he was from a wealthy family. If it was John Mark, he may have either followed Jesus to the

Mount of Olives, followed Judas, or ran ahead of the arresting party when they came looking for Jesus at the Upper Room first. Is it possible that he went to warn Jesus? Unfortunately, Mark did not leave clues for answering such questions of interest to the modern reader, including the identity of this disciple and his reason for being there.

Mark's possible reasons for recording the story originally seem clear, however. First, Mark demonstrates the fulfillment of Jesus' earlier saying, "the sheep shall be scattered" (Mark 14:27). Secondly, associated with the first point, Jesus is in fact totally alone, an excruciatingly painful state of affairs. Finally, it contrasts the disciples' actions at the beginning of the Gospel with this scene at the end. Mark began with the first disciples being called to leave all (nets, work, and family) and follow Jesus (see Mark 1:18, 20). Later we learn that some left everything (see Mark 10:28). Now these disciples, who at first sought to follow Jesus, ultimately leave everything to get away from him.

Over the years I have struggled to understand exactly what happened on this night. What did the disciples feel and what were the motives for fleeing? I have become persuaded that their loss of nerve is not the same as a loss of faith in Jesus. Nevertheless, this cannot minimize the abandonment Jesus certainly felt—not just physically, but emotionally—for the events reveal betrayal by one of his own and the vain attempt by another to return evil for evil with a sword.

Before the Chief Priests and Elders (Mark 14:53–72)

The story continues as the multitude leads "Jesus away to the high priest: and with him were assembled all the chief priests and the elders and the scribes" (Mark 14:53). Is this group the Sanhedrin described in later Jewish sources? The text is not clear, and scholarly opinion on the subject is divided. One commentator opines: "The confusion concerning the number and character of the sanhedrin(s) is related to uncertainty about the structure and leadership of 1st century Jewish society in Palestine."[57]

One may assume that "the chief priests and the elders and the scribes" were more like a privy council, handpicked for their loyalty and commitment to the appeasement achieved with Rome. For several centuries before this time, Rome had spread its power and influence over the Mediterranean world by ruthless military conquest, political domination, and annexation. The very threat of the Roman legions kept most cities and territories cooperative or passive to Rome's demands. Nothing had changed by the time of Jesus.

Jewish Palestine and the region immediately east of it remained vitally important to the Roman empire. It was first of all a strategic border between the Romans and their enemies in the east, the Parthians. Second, the region was an important center of trade, as demonstrated by the numerous Roman roads crossing the land. Goods from further east made their way towards Rome via Jewish Palestine. Exports from Jewish Palestine itself—such as balsam, grapes, olive oil, and wine—were valued throughout the empire. Third, during this period some areas in Jewish Palestine were among the most densely populated regions of the entire Mediterranean world. Finally, the magnificent buildings and other public construction projects dating from this period in places like Caesarea, Jerusalem, Tiberias, and Sepphoris demonstrate the vitality and importance of the region at the time.

Any Jewish leader opposed to this compact with Rome was quickly disposed of, and most likely those who replaced him agreed with the compact, at least in principle. It must be remembered that the Roman imperial system, well established in Judea, gave the emperor power to appoint the prefect, who had power to appoint the high priest, who gathered around him a privy council. These men, acting in concert with the Romans, also served as "a kind of *consilium iudicum* which did the investigation of the case (*cognitio*) and prepared the accusation (*accusatio*) for the court of the prefect, . . . [fitting] the legal situation in a Roman province of that time."[58]

For some time, largely based on late nineteenth century Protestant writers, it was assumed that Jesus' trial before the Jewish body was illegal.[59] Today, many scholars debate this finding, primarily because sources concerning Jewish jurisprudence are found in late second- and early third-century rabbinic writings. This makes it nearly impossible to be certain which principles and procedures were enforced more than one hundred and fifty years earlier and, if they were, which were observed rigorously at the time.[60] When trying to reconstruct the hearing (trial) before the Jewish leaders, many commentators assume that these Jewish sources represent the reality of first-century practice.

The fact that Mark did not note any of the supposed illegal actions by the Jewish leaders (except attempting to find false witnesses) suggests that, for the most part, the Jewish laws and procedures usually cited by authors to highlight the assumed illegality of the hearings were established after Jesus' death.

Even Pilate does not call into question the legality of their inquiry. He may have used such as a pretext, if it had existed, to stop judicial proceedings against Jesus.

The second- and third-century authors and compilers of these sources claim to report earlier practice as a means of obtaining a seal of approval for their contemporary thought. It should be noted that the *Mishnah* is actually the codification of the Pharisees' oral law, but the Gospels clearly indicate that the Sadducee priests, not the Pharisees, dominated the Jewish council that interrogated Jesus. It seems improbable that the Sadducees, who categorically rejected the oral law, would allow the Pharisees to control the procedures in their jurisdiction. I will discuss Pharisee participation in the hearings in the review of John's Passion narrative.

The Gospels, which are first-century documents, reveal the common practice in the Roman empire of allowing local leaders some measure of local consultation on important questions. It is entirely possible that Pilate was aware of Jesus' activities in advance and authorized the Jewish leaders to take him into custody to interrogate him. While Pilate eventually rejected their decision, he may well have initiated the process.

Like other aspects of the Passion narratives, each Gospel author differs on the sequence of events related to his appearances before the Jewish and Roman authorities and places different emphases on those aspects.

Mark informs us that Peter followed Jesus "afar off, even into the palace of the high priest: and he sat with the servants, and warmed himself at the fire" in a courtyard (Mark 14:54). Nights can be cold in March and April in Jerusalem, located 2,600 feet in the mountains above the Mediterranean.

And while Peter follows Jesus and sits to watch the end, yet Mark contrasts Jesus' actions with those of Peter: Jesus is questioned in the palace, and Peter is questioned in the courtyard (see Mark 14:53–72).

Mark continues: "And the chief priests and all the council sought for witness against Jesus to put him to death; and found none. For many bare false witness against him, but their witness agreed not together. And there arose certain, and bare false witness against him, saying, We heard him say, I will destroy this temple that is made with hands, and within three days I will build another made without hands. But neither so did their witness agree together" (Mark 14:55–59). Mark portrays a group of leaders with their minds already made up. However, it should be noted that Mark also tells us that "Joseph of Arimathæa, an honourable counsellor" was among them (see Mark 15:43; cf. Luke 23:51). While it seems that the majority of the group wanted Jesus out of the way, it is impossible to determine how many sincerely religious men opposed the action. Only one thing do we know: there were those among them who voted against handing Jesus over to the Romans.

For understandable reasons, many Jewish scholars today argue that the Gospel narratives are not historically reliable. They argue that the Jewish leadership was not involved or had minimum responsibility in handing Jesus over to the Romans. However, this does not correspond to "early Jewish tradition [which] freely admits responsibility for 'hanging' Jesus on the eve of Passover because 'he seduced Israel, leading her astray' (Babylonian Talmud, *Sanhedrin* 43a)."[61]

Paul wrote about Jewish involvement in the earliest New Testament document available, usually dated in the early 50s (see 1 Thessalonians 2:14–15). Again, context is essential. Paul is not confused in the details—he, like Peter and others, knew that Jesus was executed by the Romans, but he lays the blame at the feet of those who handed him over to be executed, indicating that they had "killed" him by their actions (see Acts 2:23; see also Peter's statement in 3:13–15).

Only after centuries of persecution from Christians and public pronouncements by famous theologians—like Augustine, John Chrysostom, Thomas Aquinas, and Martin Luther—that it was the "Christian duty to hate or punish the Jews because they killed the Lord" do some feel impelled to distance the Jewish leadership from responsibility in Jesus' death.[62] In the wake of the Holocaust, this effort finds a more receptive audience and ardent advocates, among both Jews and Christians. As already noted, personal responsibility is held by individuals, not ethnic or social groups nor nationalities.

Christian (New Testament), Roman, and Jewish sources all tell the same story that Mark outlined: Jesus was brought before a group of Jewish leaders who judged him guilty of death and then handed him over to the Gentiles to be executed.

One thing that seems obvious from a brief review of world history is that religious opposition often leads to physical violence. And while it is hard for us to understand this, it is nevertheless true of almost all societies and time periods. Again, it is imperative as we discuss the abuse heaped upon Jesus to focus on the individuals involved. We cannot allow ourselves to become angry and hostile against Jews from reading the Passion narratives without proper context and without putting the story into its larger context—the proclamation of the Good News.

Christ, the Son of the Blessed (Mark 14:60–65)

Mark continues his story: "And the high priest stood up in the midst, and asked Jesus, saying, Answerest thou nothing? what is it which these witness against thee?" (Mark 14:60). The high priest (presumably Caiaphas) is not specifically identified in Mark.[63] Mark notes Jesus' response: "But he held his peace [i.e., remained silent; kept quiet], and answered nothing. Again the high priest asked him, and said unto him, Art thou the Christ, the Son of the Blessed? And Jesus said, I am: and ye shall see the Son of man sitting on the right hand of power, and coming in the clouds of heaven" (Mark 14:61–62)—another allusion to the Hebrew scriptures (see Psalm 110:1; Daniel 7:13).

Jesus' affirmation gives the Jewish leaders the needed pretext to bring a charge of treason against him, a charge that could then be dealt with by Roman law and power, just as the Jewish leaders expected it to be. However, the claim to be the Messiah was not a capital crime under the law of Moses, so Jesus' answer must have implied something more significant.

New Testament scholar Joel Marcus argues that there must have been something different about Jesus' claim to be the Messiah: "Why should Jesus' claim to be 'the Messiah, the Son of God' [Mark 14:61, KJV: 'the Christ, the Son of the Blessed'] be considered blasphemous if 'Son of the God' is merely a synonym for 'Messiah'? . . . One searches Jewish literature in vain for evidence that a simple claim to be the Messiah would incur such a charge."[64] Mark's report of the first trial indicates that Jesus' claim to be God's literal son is more crucial and controversial for the Jewish leaders than his claim to be the Davidic Messiah. Marcus believes that this claim is "understood in a quite realistic, almost biological sense" by the Jewish leaders.[65] The Messiah-kingship issue is simply a ruse to get the Romans to take care of Jesus. In fact, the main aspect of the hearing narratives before the Jewish leadership in all three synoptic Gospels is Jesus' identity and activity.

Mark reveals that Jesus was taunted and manhandled by the guards and members of the council itself: "And some began to spit on him, and *to cover his face*, and to buffet him, and *to say unto him, Prophesy*: and the servants did strike him with the palms of their hands" (Mark 14:65; emphasis added). As Messiah, Jesus is expected to prophesy without the aid of eyesight: "And shall make him of quick understanding in the fear of the Lord: and *he shall not judge after the sight of his eyes*, neither reprove after the hearing of his ears" (Isaiah 11:3; emphasis added).

Ironically, at the very moment when Jesus is mocked by the council's challenge to prophesy, his prophecies are coming true—in particular, Peter's denial, but also Judas' earlier betrayal.

Peter's Threefold Denial (Mark 14:66–72)

Peter's denial is the one aspect of the Passion narrative in which all four Gospels are the closest in content and description. There are minor differences, however.[66] It is also an account that many agree demonstrates the faithfulness of the Gospel writers in telling the story, despite any negative reflections upon particular individuals. This possibility has not been lost on others. Origen (A.D. 185–254) spoke of it in this way when he debated Celsus, an anti-Christian, in A.D. 248.[67]

Remember that this story was not intended to record a final judgment of Peter's discipleship.[68] And like other accounts that reveal Peter's struggles (see Mark 8:32–33; 14:37–41), the story suggests the challenges of discipleship.

What may be surprising to the reader is that Peter followed Jesus in the first place, since, according to Mark, the disciples fled from Gethsemane (see Mark 14:50). Mark clearly informs us, however, that Peter followed. Significantly, he did so at a *distance* (KJV, "afar off").

One New Testament scholar captures what well may be the essence of the statement: "*Quod sequitur, amoris est, quod e longo, timoris,*" that is, Peter followed out of love, but at a distance out of fear.[69] This reminds us of John's statement about all the disciples, including Peter, a few days later: "Then the same day at evening, being the first day of the week, when the doors were shut where the disciples were assembled *for fear of the Jews*" (John 20:19; emphasis added). It is not hard to believe that Peter was fearful at the time, particularly once he found himself in the compound and was confronted by a relative of the man he attacked during the commotion of the arrest (see John 18:26). The semantic debate on the difference between *cowardice* and *fearfulness* is not important to Mark and in one way diverts our attention from the story itself.

Mark offers a unique insight about the palace—it was at least a two-story structure: "And as Peter was *beneath* in the palace, there cometh one of the maids of the high priest" (Mark 14:66; emphasis added). Mark continues: "And when she saw Peter warming himself, she looked upon him, and said, And thou also wast with Jesus of Nazareth. But he denied, saying, I know not, neither understand I what thou sayest. And he went out into the porch; and the cock crew. And a maid saw him again, and began to say to them that stood by, This is one of them. And he denied it again. And a little after, they that stood by said again to Peter, Surely thou art one of them: for thou art a Galilean, and thy speech agreeth thereto. But he began to curse and to swear, saying, I know not this man of whom ye speak. And the second time the cock crew" (Mark 14:67–72).

While it is undoubtedly possible to interpret the account differently, the most natural reading suggests that the denial recorded here is really threefold and mounts in intensity. Peter at first pretends he does not understand what he has been asked, thus avoiding the issue. Next he endeavors to get away from the courtyard; unable to leave, he then denies his status as a disciple—in other words, he lies. Finally, with two intensifying actions Peter "began to *curse* and to *swear*" (Mark 14:71; emphasis added). What Mark intends here is debatable by knowledgeable Greek New Testament scholars, but most likely means that "Peter cursed Jesus and took an oath that he had no personal acquaintance with him."[70]

If we take Mark literally, this story reveals a tragic low point in Peter's efforts to take up his cross and follow Jesus. Given an opportunity to confess his discipleship, Peter does not. What is painfully obvious to the original audience of Saints in Rome is that the one who *became* the rock and a pillar of the Church had earlier at least denied he was a disciple of Jesus and at worst cursed his Master in a moment of trial (KJV, "temptation").

Granted the severity of Mark's description, it is not surprising that there was a move among later Christians to temper it. In fact, the process of modifying Mark's hard-hitting account began very early, as is evidenced in Luke's treatment of the story (see Luke 22:56–60; see particularly verse 60 where he softens the account).[71]

If we are right about the authorship and setting of Mark's Gospel, then Peter himself provided the details of this incident. If so, there may be no need to defend Peter, because we should let him tell his story his way. In other words, this is not what someone else says about Peter but rather Peter's own painful revelation about events only he and Jesus knew of at the time.

It is difficult for many of us to imagine Peter acting in this way because of what we know about his *later* ministry as a courageous martyr for the gospel. There are those who cite Peter's defense of Jesus against the arresting party to argue for a different interpretation (only John reveals the identity of the individual who struck the high priest's servant during the brief scuffle at Jesus' arrest). Yet we may miss the subtlety of Mark's account if we fail to recognize that the disciples indeed were willing to defend and if necessary die with Jesus in Jerusalem *until* Jesus forbids resistance and surrenders himself (see also JST, John 11:16).

How many of us have helped, supported, or defended someone, only to give up and wash our hands of the situation when we discover that the person is unwilling to help, support, or defend himself? Often in such situations a resignation falls upon us and we simply walk away. Granted, we cannot compare Jesus' actions here with any other person because his response, as all the Gospels stress, demonstrates that he embraced death of his own free will and as a voluntary act to reconcile the world to his Father. We must assume that Peter and the other disciples did not at this moment grasp what he was doing—they saw only that their Master surrendered and left them leaderless. In that very moment their commitment lapsed and all their good intentions vanished as they fled into the night.

Peter's attempt to defend Jesus is an important aspect of the story, but we must remember that while he testified that Jesus was the Christ at Caesarea Philippi (see Mark 8:27–29), he *did not understand* what kind of Messiah Jesus was—the Son of Man who returned in glory *after* suffering, as described in the book of Daniel (see Daniel 7–9), and Isaiah's Suffering Servant (see Isaiah 52:13–53:12). This is clear from what follows Peter's declaration (see Mark 8:31–34).

More specifically Mark's frank report must be put into a larger context if we are to discover Mark's possible intent in telling the story as he has. First, it is possible that reporting the event demonstrates to the original audience the fulfillment of Jesus' words as noted above—his ultimate abandonment by all his disciples, including Peter.

Second, from a literary standpoint, Mark seems to use the story to focus on something much more important—the stories present a model for the lives of the original readers. If one sees the story's structure as part of a larger framework, then it is possible to compare and contrast Peter and Jesus, which I believe was Mark's (and Peter's) intent from the beginning. The first section of the story begins when Peter follows Jesus into the courtyard of the high priest (see Mark 14:54). The next section of the story begins and ends as a complete unit: Jesus is accused before the high priest, and during the hearing he does not deny who he is before them (see Mark 14:55–65). The third section begins when Peter is accused in the courtyard of the high priest: unlike Jesus, Peter denies who he is three separate and distinct times (see Mark 14:66–72).

Recall that Peter is the first and last disciple named in this Gospel narrative (see Mark 1:16; 16:7). Peter is the first to come forward and testify of Jesus (see Mark 8:29). When the other disciples flee Gethsemane, Peter follows Jesus, true to his bold commitment: "Although all shall be offended, yet will not I" (Mark 14:29). Jesus warned Peter, along with James and John, before his arrest, "Watch ye and pray, lest ye enter into temptation [trial]," because they were not yet ready to face the test that awaited them (Mark 14:38). Additionally, Peter did not yet understand Jesus' earlier words: "Whosoever will come after me, let him deny himself, and take up his cross, and follow me" (Mark 8:34).

When we also consider the historical setting of the Gospel's composition, the message seems clear. As noted earlier, it was written during a particularly difficult period and was based on Peter's teachings and sermons. For Christians under attack by the state and experiencing economic, social, and political instability, Peter's story gives hope to those who did not always live up to the ideal model of discipleship. Peter's experience would very much echo their own, and he therefore becomes the hopeful model: failings such as Peter's were not unforgivable.

In the end, Peter "called to mind the word that Jesus said unto him, Before the cock crow twice, thou shalt deny me thrice. And when he thought thereon, he wept" (Mark 14:72). Mark's oblique reference to what happened immediately before Peter began to cry has been discussed by many competent scholars. The King James Version's translation is good, "he thought thereon," but many other possibilities exist. An alternative translation reads: "A second time a rooster crowed. And remembered Peter the word as spoke to him— Jesus: Before a rooster crows twice, three [times] you will deny me. And *having broken down* he was crying."[72]

The mention that it was at the very moment when the rooster

crows suggests *exact* fulfillment of Jesus' prophecies, and we are informed by Mark that Peter recalled *exactly* what Jesus said earlier.

Interestingly, the Joseph Smith Translation changes the verse to read: "And Peter called to mind the words which Jesus said unto him, Before the cock crow twice, thou shalt deny me thrice. And he went out, and fell upon his face, and wept bitterly" (JST, Mark 14:72). Like Matthew and Luke, the Joseph Smith Translation reveals that Peter *wept bitterly* (see Matthew 26:75; Luke 22:62).

The word *wept* is usually associated with "lamentation, crying, and mourning."[73] In the New Testament itself, more than half the times it is used it specifically refers to the mourning process and therefore connotes a highly emotional experience that was part of the ancient culture and therefore distant from our modern experiences with death, especially as many Latter-day Saints confront death and dying today.

Some have suggested that Jesus' prophecy regarding Peter's threefold denial was actually a commandment intended to preserve Peter's life from those who would kill him as well as his Master. In this way, Peter was showing ultimate faith rather than human weakness in his denials. Personally, I am at a loss to explain Peter's bitter weeping *if* he did only what he had been *commanded* to do. This, along with the resurrected Christ's threefold question about Peter's love for him in John 21, which led Peter to feel hurt, leads me to believe that Peter knew he had failed in some way and *wept bitterly* because he knew Jesus knew also.[74]

In the end Jesus' prophecies and not Peter's prediction proved to be true. His repartee to Jesus' prophecy that *all* would be offended (scandalized) is now understood for what it really was—a sincere desire that did not reflect reality. Peter's only consolation in all of this is that Jesus' other prophecies would also come true, including: "I have prayed for thee, that thy faith fail not: and when thou art converted, strengthen thy brethren" (Luke 22:32).

In this sense then, Peter's weeping may have eventually been tempered by the fact that Jesus announced his care and concern for Peter while at the same time acknowledging Peter's denial of him. Mark's account of the first interrogation ends at this point, and the second interrogation begins.

Jesus Stands Before Pilate (Mark 15:1–15)

Following the interrogation at the palace of the high priest somewhere in the upper city, the Jewish leaders hand Jesus over to the Romans for trial in the morning: "And straightway in the morning the chief priests held a consultation with the elders and scribes and the whole council, and bound Jesus, and carried him away, and delivered him to Pilate" (Mark 15:1). The Greek verb for *delivered* is *paradidōnai* ("handing over"), a term deeply charged with doctrinal significance in the gospel tradition. We are introduced to Pilate for the first time in this verse.[75]

Pontius Pilate was Rome's fifth governor of Judea (*Pontius Pilatus Praefectus Iudaeae*), appointed in A.D. 26 or 27 and suspended from office shortly before the death of Tiberius in A.D. 37.[76] From the end of Herod's son's (Archelaus) reign in A.D. 6, Judea and Samaria were ruled directly by the Romans, except for a brief period during the reign of the Jewish king Agrippa, A.D. 41–44. The earliest Roman governors, from A.D. 6 to 41, were called *prefects*, a military title originally. From 44 on, they were called *procurators*, a title designating "a financial office representing the emperor on an estate or in a senatorial province."[77]

In the New Testament Pilate is called *hēgemōn* (Latin *praeses*), "a title most properly used for a senatorial governor."[78] Interestingly, as is the case with another leader involved with Jesus' death whom we will discuss later, archeologists discovered an artifact linked directly to Pilate from the first century. A battered stone, now on display at the Israel Museum, was found in 1961 by Italian archeologists excavating in Caesarea near the Roman theater. The limestone block measures 32 inches high, 27 inches wide, and 8 inches thick with four lines of engraving still intact, which includes Pilate's name, one of the few attestations of his existence outside the New Testament.[79]

Like his predecessors, Pilate was directly responsible for all aspects of Roman administration in the province, including serving as the head of its judicial system. Pilate was also responsible for collecting taxes and tributes; distributing funds for official provincial business; and sending revenues and administrative reports to the imperial capital in Rome. The Roman legate in Syria was in charge of the army in case of serious military needs. Pilate did have troops at his disposal, but they acted more like police units. Mark portrays Jesus as standing before the man who has "power even to execute."[80]

In the Gospel of Luke, reference is made to Pilate on another occasion (see Luke 13:1). Apparently a riot broke out in the temple, and Pilate, faced with the possibility of political agitation during the feasts, used deadly force to quell the disturbance—he required that his soldiers kill Galilean pilgrims to the feast. This was the man to whom Jesus was sent.

No Gospel writer claims that any of Jesus' disciples were present during the legal proceedings against Jesus before Pilate. However, as Raymond Brown argues, "it is absurd to think that some information was not available to them about" those proceedings.[81]

G. W. H. Lampe suggests that "it is probable that an official record of the trial of Jesus before Pilate was made at the time and preserved. . . . We do not know, however, whether the prefect of Judæa would have sent a copy of the record to Rome, but that he should have reported the trial and execution of Jesus to Tiberius seems inherently probable, especially in view of the fact that it was the general belief in antiquity not only that Pilate would have done this but that his *acta* must be extant in the archives of the imperial government."[82] We may assume that a record was made, and, if so, that people talked about it. There were apparently attempts to produce forged records which purported to be copies of the original record.[83]

Characteristically, Mark reports the events with a few vivid words and without elaborating the detail: "And Pilate asked him, Art thou the King of the Jews? And he answering said unto him, Thou sayest it. And the chief priests accused him of many things: but he answered nothing. And Pilate asked him again, saying, Answerest thou nothing? behold how many things they witness against thee. But Jesus yet answered nothing; so that Pilate marvelled. Now at that feast he released unto them one prisoner, whomsoever they desired" (Mark 15:2–6).

While it may seem that Jesus' first response, "Thou sayest it," means nothing more than "The terms are yours, not mine," the

Joseph Smith Translation adds: "And Jesus answering said unto him, I am, even as thou sayest" (JST, Mark 15:2). This provides a totally different interpretative framework.

At the conclusion of this section, the people, at the behest of the chief priest, asked Pilate to release Barabbas, apparently a revolutionary (see Mark 15:7–11). When questioned what should be done to Jesus the crowd responded: "Crucify him" (Mark 15:13). Should we expect that everyone among the large crowds in attendance at the Passover feast stood before Pilate and demanded Jesus' death? We probably should be careful to distinguish this crowd from those who had hailed Jesus when he arrived in the city a day earlier. There may have been some in both groups, but the text does not explicitly indicate that they were identical. Mark informs us that the chief priests were afraid of the general population all along the way. The Gospels tell us of a variety of responses to Jesus' ministry, ranging from some who simply ignored him to others who believed and followed to some, as in this case, who wanted to kill him.

When Jewish disciples of Jesus—like Mark, Matthew, and John—use the term *Jews* they mean "those *other* Jews who do not believe." Only when the Roman Empire became Christian and the Church was primarily composed of Gentiles does the term *Jews* clearly mean a distinct and separate people. This is not the case for the first-century Church, no matter how polemical it may sound.[84]

The quick pace of events highlights the grim fact that "the point of [Roman] crucifixion was precisely the fear of its sudden, merciless application; it was one of the purest forms of official, governmental violence."[85] Mark's presentation of the events after the second trial is painful, albeit succinct and unadorned. "And so Pilate, willing to content the people, released Barabbas unto them, and delivered Jesus, when he had scourged him, to be crucified" (Mark 15:15). The brutalization of Jesus is nowhere more poignant than during this episode.

Mark portrays Pilate as one who knows Jesus is innocent but nevertheless hands him over to be crucified to please the crowd. This is apparently not the whole story, as insights found in the other Passion narratives seem to indicate. Some scholars suggest the portrayal of Pilate found in the Gospels "is exactly the opposite of what we know about him" from other ancient sources, in particular Jose-phus.[86] While this may be generally true, the same can be said of other historical figures discussed by Josephus. It is not unreasonable to suppose that Josephus provides the stereotype instead of the com-plex view of Pilate. For many thoughtful scholars, the New Testa-ment's portrayal of Pilate adds to our view from other sources, thus giving us a fuller picture.

Although we may feel sympathetic towards Pilate from reading Mark's account, we should also understand quite clearly that Jesus' death came as "a result through some conjunction of imperial and sacerdotal authority."[87] In this sense Ramón Trevijano argues: "The canonical gospels agree on the fact that, although P[ilate] recog-nized Jesus' innocence, he committed a judicial crime to satisfy the people."[88]

Jesus Is Scourged and Mocked (Mark 15:15–20)

During the first century, scourging or flogging was a common and legal but brutal form of punishment. The *flagrum* (whip) was a dangerous weapon usually made of a wooden handle and leather thongs with a variety of items interwoven in the leather. There is evidence of at least four types: first, a chain and knuckle-bones; sec-ond, leather thongs; third, leather and knuckle-bones; and finally, leather and lead shot.[89] The victim was stripped naked and bound to a pillar, then soundly beaten by two soldiers, one positioned to cover the entire back, buttocks, and legs. While it is true that the Jews limited the number of stripes to a maximum of forty (thirty-nine in case of a miscount), the Romans recognized no such limitation. Vic-tims often did not survive this punishment.[90] Ironically, while scourging resulted in significant loss of blood, execution by crucifix-ion was a relatively bloodless procedure. According to Mark, Jesus' state following the scourging was at least serious and probably criti-cal. He survives, but only to be executed.

Mark continues: "And the soldiers led him away into the hall, called Prætorium; and they call together the whole band. And they clothed him with purple, and platted a crown of thorns, and put it about his head. And began to salute him, Hail, King of the Jews!

And they smote him on the head with a reed, and did spit upon him, and bowing their knees worshipped him. And when they had mocked him, they took off the purple from him, and put his own clothes on him, and led him out to crucify him" (Mark 15:16–20). The use of *Prætorium* is one of the Latinisms often cited by scholars to suggest a western Roman Empire, probably Rome itself, origin for the Gospel.

Note that Pilate did not have at his disposal Rome's most disciplined soldiers, but the five cohorts consisted of auxiliary troops from the local region, many of whom were probably apathetic towards Jews at best and rabid anti-Jewish at worst.

The interrogation, scourging, and mocking probably took place in Herod's palace, on the northwestern edge of the city. When the Romans assumed direct control in Judea in A.D. 6, the Emperor's representative, who lived in Caesarea, used the palace as his Jerusalem residence. To suggest that Herod's sons continued control of the site following Rome's assumption of direct authority in Judea may be simplistic. Pilate lived in Herod's palace at Caesarea, and no record suggests otherwise. The Roman administrative site would have afforded Pilate easy entrance and exit from the city in addition to access to other comforts expected for Rome's representative. The palace contained rooms for a hundred guests, numerous banquet halls, patios, gardens, ponds, groves, and cloisters.[91] Today the only remains of the magnificent palace and towers are found in the Citadel, just south of the Jaffa Gate.

In this brief but important scene Mark portrays the mocking of Jesus. The soldiers placed a crown of thorns on his head. Generally identified as *Ziziphus spina-christi* (Christ Thorn), the generic terms apply to small spiny or prickly shrubs and vines that thrive "along roadsides and in neglected areas" throughout the Holy Land.[92] No one can be sure what plant was used. In all likelihood, the emphasis was intended to be on the royal mockery of Jesus, not on the pain we so commonly associate with the crown today. Mark continues: "And when they had mocked him, they took off the purple from him, and put his own clothes on him, and led him out to crucify him" (Mark 15:20).

There is a possible parallel in Zechariah's prophecy to Jesus' mockery here: "And he shewed me Joshua the high priest standing before the angel of the Lord, and Satan standing at his right hand to resist him. And the Lord said unto Satan, The Lord rebuke thee, O Satan; even the Lord that hath chosen Jerusalem rebuke thee: is not this a brand plucked out of the fire? Now Joshua was clothed with filthy garments, and stood before the angel. And he answered and spake unto those that stood before him, saying, Take away the filthy garments from him. And unto him he said, Behold, I have caused thine iniquity to pass from thee, and I will clothe thee with change of raiment. And I said, Let them set a fair mitre upon his head. So they set a fair mitre upon his head, and clothed him with garments" (Zechariah 2:1–5).

There are two important points highlighted in this passage from Mark. First, Romans generally stripped the individuals for scourging and then led them away to the site of execution naked. Apparently in Judea they adjusted their procedures to accommodate Jewish abhorrence of public nudity, so they "put his own clothes on him, and led him out" to be crucified (see Mark 15:20). Second, Mark might have had in mind a deeper significance when he informs us that they "led him out" of the city to be crucified.

Jesus Is Led Out to Golgotha (Mark 15:21–22)

As noted earlier, the site of the ritual of the red heifer was beyond the walls of the temple and city. Mark may have connected the phrase "led him out [*exagein*]" with the red heifer being slaughtered outside (*exō*) the camp (see Numbers 19:2–3). The author of Hebrews relates the suffering of Jesus also in this way (see Hebrews 13:11–13). The red heifer was slaughtered and burned to make ashes that were used to purify individuals and objects that had been polluted by human corpses, which was considered the "father of all pollutions."[93]

Mark continues: "And they compel one Simon a Cyrenian, who passed by, coming out of the country, the father of Alexander and Rufus, to bear his cross. And they bring him unto the place Golgotha, which is, being interpreted, The place of a skull" (Mark 15:21–22). The Joseph Smith Translation renders Matthew's version

of this verse: "And when they were come unto a place called Golgotha, that is to say, a place of *burial*" (JST, Matthew 27:35; emphasis
added). We will discuss the implications later.

Via Dolorosa *and* Sacra Via

In a thought-provoking essay, Thomas Schmidt attempts to
show how a first-century Roman audience may have read Mark's
Passion narrative.[94] He argues that the Gentile audience may well
have thought of "a kind of Roman triumphal march, with
Jerusalem's Via Dolorosa replacing the Sacra Via of Rome."[95]

In fact, he suggests that Paul had this in mind when he wrote:
"Christ always leads us in triumphal procession, and through us
spreads in every place the fragrance that comes from knowing him.
For we are the aroma of Christ to God among those who are being
saved and among those who are perishing" (New Revised Standard
Version, 2 Corinthians 2:14–15).

After reviewing the features of the Roman triumphal march, details with which the first-century Roman audience would have been
familiar, Schmidt identifies possible parallels with Mark's narrative:
"Mark's crucifixion narrative contains a number of striking parallels
to the Roman triumph. While the cumulative force of the comparison is significant, the most obvious allusions are made at the beginning of the narrative, perhaps signaling to Mark's audience that
there is more to come for those 'on the inside.' "[96]

Schmidt summarizes his findings: "The prætorian guard gathers
early in the morning to proclaim the triumphator. They dress him in
the purple triumphal garb and place a crown of laurel on his head.
The soldiers shout in acclamation of his lordship . . . and perform
acts of homage to him. They accompany him through the streets of
the city. The sacrifice walks alongside a person who carries the im-
plement of the victim's death. The procession ascends to the place
of the (death's) head, where the sacrifice is to take place. The triumphator is offered ceremonial wine. He does not drink it but pours
it out on the altar at the moment of sacrifice. Then, at the moment
of being lifted up before the people, at the moment of the sacrifice,
the triumphator is again acclaimed as lord, . . . and his viceregents

appear with him in confirmation of his glory. The epiphany of the triumphator is accompanied by divine portents . . . , confirming that he is one with the gods."[97]

How do we explain these parallels, taking for granted that the Gospel narrative is *history remembered* and not *parallels historicized*, meaning that the allusions used in earlier scriptural text were used here to create parallels of non-historical events. It may be one of the vagaries of history, but to "an audience prepared by the context of Mark's gospel to look for double meanings, it would be a glaring and meaningful coincidence."[98]

Mark may reveal to his Roman audience that Jesus' crucifixion is an "anti-triumph," demonstrating that his march to a Roman cross was actually his coronation as the true triumphator. Comparing Caesar, who proclaimed himself a god, with Christ, Mark suggests how fruitless and banal emperor worship was in light of the testimonies of Jesus, both human and divine, that "truly this man was the Son of God" (Mark 15:39).

A Hill Far Away (Mark 15:21–22)

The visual image of a "green hill" is not based on the text. Rather, it is a notion popularized in a beautiful and reverential hymn written in the nineteenth century by Cecil Frances Alexander, "There Is a Green Hill Far Away."[99] Rather, the terrain surrounding the city of Jerusalem is stony and hard. Mark's account does not give directions to the hill where Jesus was executed but merely states that he was brought "unto the place Golgotha" (Mark 15:22).

Three sites are identified as possible locations for Golgotha in Jerusalem today, two of which are heavily visited by tourists and pilgrims. First, the long-standing traditional site for many Christians is located in the Church of the Holy Sepulchre.[100] The Church of the Holy Sepulchre is found within the Christian Quarter in the Old City, occupied by Latin Catholics, Greek Orthodox, Armenians, Syrians, Copts, and Ethiopians. Tradition also holds that this may have been the place of Jesus' tomb. Apparently, at the beginning of the first century, the site was a disused quarry outside the ancient city walls. In light of Mark's later report, "And with him they crucify two thieves; the one on his right hand, and the other on his left" (Mark 15:27), it seems impossible that three individuals could have been executed on this site, a rocky protrusion to the right of the present entrance to the Church of the Holy Sepulchre.

Second, the most popular alternative site to this spot is near the Garden Tomb, north of Damascus Gate between Nablus Road and Salah-ed-Din Street. Brought to the attention of the world in 1883 by General Charles Gordon, the Garden Tomb and the nearby hill just behind a modern Arab bus depot have become very popular for many Protestants and Latter-day Saints. Here many people see two side-by-side caves, which combine with fissures in the rock to resemble a gigantic skull, especially when viewed from the top of the Old City's walls.[101] Joseph Smith changed the phrase "Golgotha, that is to say, a place of a skull" to "a place of burial" (JST, Matthew 27:33); in light of that change, it seems likely the skull-like appearance of the rock was not the original emphasis intended by the author.

The third and less well-known site is located near the traditional site of the Church of the Holy Sepulchre.[102]

It is impossible to know exactly what people living in Rome during the first century, Mark's original audience, thought as they read his account of the crucifixion. One thing is certain, their mental image of crucifixion was *not* based on the modern paintings, movies, and sculptures to which we are exposed—and which often have aspects that definitely fall under the heading of artistic license.

Sometimes in order to distinguish Jesus from the two other men being crucified, artists and film directors depict the other men tied, not nailed, to their crosses. While history contains examples of victims being tied to a cross in order to lengthen the process of death, nothing in the New Testament indicates that such was the case. If Jesus was nailed, we should assume that the two criminals executed with him were also nailed.

Another frequent image is the piercing of Jesus' feet, generally the right foot placed over the left, with one nail penetrating them both. Reportedly Helena, the mother of Constantine, found three nails with the cross she found, thought to be the original.[103] That number therefore became standard, necessitating that only one nail be used for his feet in most Christian art thereafter.

Another common feature is the size, shape, and construction of the cross. Again, artistic developments over the centuries have shaped our present mental images. The depiction and use of the cross (or crucifix), not the doctrine of the cross, was a late development in Christianity. The cult of the cross developed after the dedication of the Constantinian basilica of the Holy Sepulchre in A.D. 325, giving rise to iconographic depictions to which almost all modern representations owe their development, including Protestant.[104]

The oldest Christian example of a depiction of the crucifixion appeared in the last half of the fifth century. Now housed in the British Museum, on the top left panel of the wooden doors from St. Sabina Church, Jesus is depicted without clothing on a cross. By the next century, clothing and other symbolic items were added to the representations. While the Protestant Reformation rejected the long historic use of the crucifix, it retained the use of a simple cross as part of its iconographic tradition. When depicting Jesus' execution, most modern artists retain the sixth century development in Christian art by portraying him clothed with a loin cloth.

While it seems nearly impossible for us to get beyond these modern images as we think about the crucifixion, a recent archeological discovery near Jerusalem of a crucified man dating from about the time of Jesus gives us pause. Despite the abundance of literary sources attesting to the frequency of crucifixion in the ancient world, this was the first direct anthropological evidence discovered revealing in such a dramatic way this cruel form of punishment, eventually abolished by Constantine in the fourth century. (Although apparently the Nazis used this form of punishment at several death camps during World War II.)

Since the publication of the photographic image showing a large iron nail piercing the heel bone of the man, scholars have been busy reinterpreting the literary evidence, resulting in a much clearer picture of this form of execution.[105]

The Crucifixion (Mark 15:24–37)

Jesus' crucifixion is the one prominent feature of the Gospel accounts not challenged by most scholars since several independent

New Testament sources—Paul, Mark, Acts, and John—agree on this point.[106] Added to this are the Gospel narratives of Matthew and Luke (which scholars believed used Mark as a source). Josephus also refers to Jesus' crucifixion.[107]

.   Mark, like the other Gospel writers, tells us little about the details of this form of state-sponsored terrorism. As LDS biblical scholar Richard Lloyd Anderson noted some time ago: "The four gospels relate Jesus' execution with marked terseness; ancient readers were familiar with the grim procedures of death on the cross. Thus modern readers must revisit ancient literature to picture what was taken for granted and not described by New Testament authors."[108] (There may be an additional reason for the brevity in the account which we will discuss below.) It should be noted that crucifixion was not rigidly administered the identical way in every case; room must be left for significant variations depending on local and individual circumstances of a particular execution. Nevertheless, we can reconstruct a general outline of the procedure.

Crucifixion inflicted unspeakable pain and physical suffering on the condemned. Unfortunately, sometimes we do not "see this oppressive, genocidal, imperial mode of torture for what it was."[109] The stench, screams, and horrible sights of the public place of execution on the outskirts of Jerusalem offered a grotesque counterimage to the elegance and architectural splendors of the magnificent Herodian Temple and the Roman streets, palaces, pools, and plazas in the largest city in the Roman province of Judea.

In particular, the Romans used this means of execution in Jewish Palestine for robbers, revolutionaries, and insurrectionists.[110] From King Herod's time (37 B.C.) until the destruction of Jerusalem in A.D. 70, the Romans crucified thousands in Jewish Palestine. These executions were carried out publicly as a deterrent so that as many people as possible could see and be moved by fear of it. Thus, no less than the other powerful forms of visual communication used by the Romans, crucifixion was meant to convey a message.[111] The crosses planted outside the city walls of Jerusalem, like other Roman cities throughout the empire, warned potential rebels, runaway slaves, and rebellious prophets of what could happen to them.

Additionally, by publicly displaying a naked victim at a promi-nent place such as a crossroads, a crowded highway, a theater, or high ground, the Romans also ensured the condemned would suffer uttermost humiliaton. Many Jews were particularly averse to this punishment in light of Deuteronomy 21:23, which specifically pro-nounces God's curse on anyone hung on a tree.

The process of crucifixion was described in detail by Roman writers such as Cicero, Livy, Tacitus, and Seneca the Younger. Ci-cero noted in particular that it was an "extreme and ultimate pun-ishment of slaves; . . . the cruelest and most disgusting penalty."[112] The first-century Jewish historian Josephus, who witnessed several crucifixions as an adviser to Titus during the siege of Jerusalem, tersely describes this form of Roman punishment as "the most wretched of deaths." He reports that a threat by the Roman be-siegers to crucify a Jewish prisoner caused the garrison of Machaerus to surrender in exchange for safe conduct.[113]

The Romans, however, did not introduce crucifixion among the Jews. The Jews employed this form of punishment before the time of Jesus; indeed, it had a long history in Jewish Palestine, probably im-ported during Persian times (559–330 B.C.). Apparently the Has-monean king Alexander Janneus (103–76 B.C.) and other Jewish rulers in power hung men and women on *trees*, a noun interchange-able with *cross*. I will briefly review this event in the discussion of John's Passion narrative.[114] For some Jews, however, such actions were "unjust, grotesque, and unforgivable."[115]

Roman crucifixion usually consisted of three distinct elements: scourging, carrying the cross to the execution grounds, and nailing and lifting. A board (*titulus*) covered with gypsum and inscribed with black letters specifying the crime was either carried by the con-demned person or carried before the procession. Two main types of crosses were apparently used by the Romans at the time: T-shaped and dagger-shaped. In either case, the upright beam was planted in a fixed position, and the crossbar (*patibulum*) was carried by the vic-tim. Additionally, the executioners could use either a low cross (*crux humilis*), on which the feet of the condemned were from ten to eigh-teen inches above the ground, or the high cross (*crux sublimis*), where the feet of the person were about three feet above the ground. A peg (*sedecula*) or short crossbar forming a narrow seat could be added to allow the condemned to half sit while dying on the cross.

The victim's hands or wrists were either bound to the rough wooden cross beam with ropes or affixed there with tapered iron spikes measuring between five and seven inches long. The crossbar, with the condemned hanging from it, was then lifted by means of two poles (*forcillae*) ending with a Y-shaped fork or by ladders. The crossbar was secured on top of the upright for a T-shaped cross or in a mortise of it in the case of a dagger-shaped cross. The victim's were either left hanging loose or nailed to the upright beam.

Death by crucifixion was not meant to be quick. The victim might agonize for days. It generally transformed anyone branded as an enemy of the Roman order from a living, breathing person into a bruised corpse. Seneca the Younger vividly described this process: "Can any man be found willing to be fastened to the accursed tree, long sickly, already deformed, swelling with ugly tumours on chest and shoulders, and draw the breath of life amid long-drawn-out agony? I think he would have many excuses for dying even before mounting the cross!"[116] Apparently such a long drawn-out death was one of the main goals of Roman execution in that it not only punished the intended victim but simultaneously served as a warning to those observing it.

Roman soldiers were present at the execution and following it, thus ensuring that family members did not take the victim down *before* death occurred. Additionally, the soldiers prevented friends and family from taking the body *after* death for a private burial, thus depriving them a place to visit, mourn, and remember the dead. The Romans were masters of depriving these privileges, so important in the ancient world to their enemies, through "three supreme penalties of being burned alive, cast to the beasts in the amphitheater, or crucified."[117]

Crucifixion, as with the other two forms of execution, involved pitiless maltreatment, public abasement, and lack of burial. The impossibility of burial resulting from the first two modes of execution are self-evident; in the third it is assumed that the body was left on the cross so the dead and rotting flesh became meat for birds and animals. In nearly all Roman executions, carrion birds and animals of prey were normal concomitants of the scene.

The Roman Army (Mark 15:16)

The Roman army consisted of large units, called legions, of approximately 5,000 soldiers each. These were divided into cohorts of 480 each, supplemented by smaller calvary units. The cohorts were divided into 6 "centuries" composed of 80 soldiers each, rather than 100 as the name implies. The centurions commanded the centuries and were more professional than the senior officers, who were from the upper ranks of society and served mostly for short periods of time. The centurions who were especially effective in training and organizing soldiers would be transferred to more prestigious legions. For security and efficiency reasons, soldiers were not usually stationed in the territories where they had originated. In the lifetime of Jesus, four of these legions were on permanent assignment in Syria-Palestine.

The Parting of His Garments (Mark 15:23–27)

As noted above, Mark does not describe the ghastliness of crucifixion because the original audience was fully aware of this prolonged and horrible form of punishment. Another, and maybe more fundamental, reason for the meager description is theological. The lack of details of the actual crucifixion process stand in contrast to Mark's discussion of other details connected with the execution. This can only be explained when one realizes that Mark is not interested in recording the historical events simply to preserve a story; rather, he is much more interested in the narrative's doctrinal significance. In a similar vein, later Christian tradition attempted to provide a name for those left nameless in the Passion narratives, including those crucified with Jesus. Thus, the names of Pilate's wife, the centurion, those crucified with Jesus, and the officer in charge of the watch at the tomb are most likely late apocryphal additions to the story with no basis in historical fact.[118] Mark's emphasis is placed on those details that reveal prophetic fulfillment and provide understanding of Jesus' suffering.

Mark adds: "And they gave him to drink wine mingled with myrrh: but he received it not. And when they had crucified him, they parted his garments, casting lots upon them, what every man should take. And it was the third hour [nine o'clock in the morning], and they crucified him. And the superscription of his accusation was written over, THE KING OF THE JEWS. And with him they crucify two thieves [robbers]; the one on his right hand, and the other on his left" (Mark 15:23–27). Here again Mark provides another allusion to the Old Testament (see Psalm 22:18), which we will discuss in Matthew's Passion narrative.

As noted earlier, Roman authorities generally stripped victims of their clothing, forcing them to march naked to the execution site. Apparently, Jesus was allowed to wear his clothing to Golgotha, but once there was humiliated by its removal. When Mark notes that "they parted his garments, casting lots upon them, what every man should take," he probably meant that the soldiers parted his garments; that is, they tossed their dice, with the winner of each toss taking the article of clothing that he wanted. Like military personnel throughout the empire, Roman soldiers generally carried dice to divert themselves when off duty. Roman dice were usually made of bone and marked like our modern dice.[119]

Abused and Mocked Again (Mark 15:29–32)

Mark's story continues as Jesus' opponents appear before him, gloating and making derogatory remarks: "And they that passed by railed on him, wagging their heads, and saying, Ah, thou that destroyest the temple, and buildest it in three days, save thyself, and come down from the cross" (Mark 15:29–30). The scene continues as the Jewish leadership mock him with the ironic taunt: "He saved others; himself he cannot save" (Mark 15:31). The chief priests and the scribes challenge: "Let Christ the King of Israel descend now from the cross, that we may see and believe" (Mark 15:32). The scene finally ends as "they that were crucified with him reviled him" too (Mark 15:32).

Mark is clear that Jesus was mocked while upon the cross. One commentator suggests that some of the Jewish officials may have been "repeating the charges of the trial, [trying] to urge Jesus to confess his sins and publicly deny his claim to be the Son of God."[120] According to the *Mishnah*, "the confession, with the petition that God may reckon the death penalty as atonement for the committed sin, gives the criminal the chance to obtain a share in the world to come."[121]

Last Words (Mark 15:33–41)

Mark continues: "And when the sixth hour was come, there was darkness over the whole land until the ninth hour. And at the ninth hour Jesus cried with a loud voice, saying, Eloi, Eloi, lama sabachthani? which is, being interpreted, *My God, my God, why hast thou forsaken me?* And some of them that stood by, when they heard it, said, Behold, he calleth Elias. And one ran and filled a spunge full of vinegar, and put it on a reed, and gave him to drink, saying, Let alone; let us see whether Elias will come to take him down. And Jesus cried with a loud voice, and gave up the ghost" (Mark 15:33–37; emphasis added). Another allusion to the Old Testament is found in Jesus' cry: "My God, my God, why hast thou forsaken me?" (See Psalm 22:1).

The story preserved here of Jesus' last moments reveals in a significant way the point made in the preface about audience. There are two different sayings reported to be Jesus' last words: "Father, into thy hands I commend my spirit" (Luke 23:46); and "It is finished" (John 19:30). Here in Mark we only have: "And Jesus cried with a loud voice" (Mark 15:37), leaving us with no specific words at all. The Joseph Smith Translation provides these words from the Gospel of Matthew: "Jesus, when he had cried again with a loud voice, *saying, Father, it is finished, thy will is done,* yielded up the ghost" (JST, Matthew 27:50; emphasis added), giving us an additional version of Jesus' last words.

If we had access to an audio recording of Jesus' last words, we would hear him speaking Aramaic. Most people would need someone trained in ancient languages to provide a translation of what they would hear on the tape. What we would likely discover is that during the last hour of his life, Jesus said (in Aramaic) the words noted above. Nevertheless, which were his last words? There must be, by definition, last words. Each Gospel writer chose the appropriate last words for his audience, omitting others he felt unnecessary for the specific needs of those people who read or heard these testimonies in the first place. This demonstrates the importance of understanding the original audience, the author's original purpose, and the historical setting in order to fully appreciate each Gospel narrative.

The historical setting helps us more than anything else to understand why Mark, more than the other Gospel authors, left such a shocking, harsh, and severe description of the crucifixion. Mark's audience needed encouragement as they witnessed family and fellow Christians betrayed, arrested, tried, and brutally martyred under Nero Caesar, the young, spoiled, self–centered emperor of the Roman world. For them, suffering and death under his authority was not defeat but became an example of taking up the cross and following Jesus.

Mark's story of brutality ends with the veil of the temple being "rent in twain from the top to the bottom" (Mark 15:38), a final act of disorder in a violent scene in which Jesus is put to death at the hands of ruthless men agitated by a frenzied crowd incited by their leaders.

Mark writes: "And when the centurion, which stood over against him, saw that he so cried out, and gave up the ghost, he said, *Truly this man was the Son of God*" (Mark 15:39; emphasis added). In capturing the centurion's confession, Mark presents Jesus' execution—the moment of his greatest suffering and humiliation—as both literally and figuratively a triumph. The scene changes as Mark describes the careful watch kept by some of Jesus' faithful disciples, which provides comfort to the reader while ending the description of violent abuse directed at their Master: "There were also women looking on afar off: among whom was Mary Magdalene, and Mary the mother of James the less and Joses, and Salome; (Who also,

when he was in Galilee, followed him, and ministered unto him;)
and many other women which came up with him unto Jerusalem"
(Mark 15:40, 41).

Jesus' Burial (Mark 15:42–46)

A commandment from the Old Testament requires the burial of
a crucified individual by sunset: "And if a man have committed a sin
worthy of death, and he be to be put to death, and thou hang him
on a tree: his body shall not remain all night upon the tree, but thou
shalt in any wise bury him that day; (for he that is hanged is accursed of God;) that thy land be not defiled, which the Lord thy
God giveth thee for an inheritance" (Deuteronomy 21:22–23). The
LDS edition footnote for this passage states: "According to Rabbinical commentaries, to leave a body hanging was a degradation of the
human body and therefore an affront to God, in whose image man's
body was made" (Deuteronomy 21:23, note a).

The Old Testament provides several examples of this principle
being implemented (for example, see Joshua 8:23, 29; 10:5, 26–27).
Many argue that these passages refer to hanging on a tree *after* death,
that is, the victim was already dead before being crucified. Regard-
less of how the Israelites conducted crucifixions, for the Romans one
main purpose of a *live* crucifixion was to prolong death, making the
execution a torturous experience for the victim and a ghastly re-
minder to those witnessing it of Rome's willingness to enforce *Pax
roma* (Roman peace) by violent force.[122]

Therefore, it seems that removing the body of a crucified victim
before sunset (that is, while people could still see the agonized body)
circumvented one of the main goals of Roman execution. This is not
a clearcut issue, however. For example, Josephus observed, in com-
menting on the brutal activities of the rebels in Jerusalem during the
first Jewish revolt (A.D. 66–70): "They actually went so far in their
impiety as to cast out the corpses [of the murdered high priests]
without burial, although the Jews are so careful about funeral rites
that even malefactors who have been sentenced to crucifixion are
taken down and buried before sunset."[123] However, some scholars
believed that Josephus's statement is a polemic against the Zealots

and therefore is not helpful in determining the actual situation at the time. They cite the fact that in the literally thousands of crucifixions mentioned by Josephus, only this once does he mention anything about victims being taken down before sunset.[124]

While admitting the possibility that Jesus was an exception to the rule of leaving a victim's body on the cross until there was nothing left, some argue that the Romans may have buried crucified dead in a mass grave speedily and indifferently. Burial in a shallow, mounded grave with a little lime at best, and dogs at worst, balanced their goals (denying a place to remember, mourn, and visit) and Jewish sensibilities (disposing of the body before sunset). The fact that among countless victims of crucifixion only one executed individual's remains have been discovered seems to demonstrate that Roman methods and goals generally prevailed, even in Judea.

Whatever the situation was at the time, Mark reveals that in the case of Jesus, someone asked for his body before sunset in order to bury him in a private tomb. Mark notes: "And now when the even was come, because it was the preparation, that is, the day before the sabbath, Joseph of Arimathæa, an honourable counsellor, which also waited for the kingdom of God, came, and went in boldly unto Pilate, and craved the body of Jesus" (Mark 15:42–43).

Another interesting subtle historical detail is Mark's statement: "And Pilate marvelled if he were already dead: and calling unto him the centurion, he asked him whether he had been any while dead" (Mark 15:44). As noted earlier, because crucifixion was not only a means of execution but also of torture, death was meant to be prolonged. Pilate's surprise at the quick death of Jesus is therefore totally within the parameters of what we know about the first century.

The story ends: "And [Joseph] bought fine linen, and took him down, and wrapped him in the linen, and laid him a sepulchre which was hewn out of a rock, and rolled a stone unto the door of the sepulchre" (Mark 15:46). While many scholars have been skeptical of the historical value of this passage, assuming that the Romans either denied burial altogether or bodies were consigned to a mass grave, archeological discoveries in Jerusalem from the first century now prove that sepulchres as described by Mark were not unheard of and therefore confirm the importance of using the Gospels as a historical record.[125] It is certain that bribery, mercy, or indifference may have played a role in allowing Joseph to remove the body for private burial.

The Place of Burial (Mark 15:46–47)

The Garden Tomb, located north of the Old City Wall in East Jerusalem, is the site many Protestants and Latter-day Saints visit to celebrate Jesus' resurrection. This tomb in a quiet garden generally conforms to the expectation of many who seek a place to pray, read, meditate, and ponder the events associated with Jesus' passion and resurrection. Almost all who visit this tranquil place just beyond the noisy and congested Nablus Road are renewed as they worship in this peaceful spot. It is hard not to feel something special when spending time there, and the piece of fresh rosemary available to all visitors as they leave the garden helps to remind them of their experience. The spirit of the place confirms the reality of the posted sign on the modern wooden door of the tomb itself, "He is not here!"

Like all sites on the itineraries of travel groups to the Holy Land, visitors are cautioned to celebrate the holiness of the events mentioned in scripture instead of worshiping the place itself. It takes some time to train most people on travel study programs to focus more on the event than on the place. It seems many want to know the exact spot. When we look beyond the modern churches, highways, homes, or dump heaps, we can usually connect with the event and thus gain from visiting the place associated with the story.

While the vast majority of scholars generally reject the Garden Tomb as being genuine, it still has its supporters; the original burial place may indeed be near this site if it is not the exact tomb.[126] A soon-to-be published report argues that a first-century Jewish-Christian Synagogue was located near the site. If so, this may demonstrate an earlier tradition of veneration here than at the Church of the Holy Sepulchre.[127]

Unlike the Garden Tomb, the traditional site at the Church of the Holy Sepulchre is dark, cramped, noisy, ornate, and often busy. Yet there is also a certain spirit of peace here as one imagines the millions of believers who have come to this site for nearly two thousand years, affirming their belief in the resurrection of Jesus. Walking in the footsteps of those pilgrims can give one a sense of his influence upon humanity. Some argue that first-century tombs typical of the Herodian period are found in the west wall of the rotunda.[128] However, there is one argument against this site that rises to the surface when examining a map of the distribution of tombs around Jerusalem in the Herodian period.[129]

Jerusalem's necropolis, or cemetery, forms a belt about two miles wide around the ancient city walls. Because there was a prohibition against burials west of the temple, some argue that tombs found there are older than the first century or are located more than three thousand feet from the Temple Mount. It appears from literary sources and archeological data that the first half of the first century precluded burials west (windward) of the Temple Mount. If this is the case, then Jesus' burial could not have taken place at the site of the Church of the Holy Sepulchre, which is almost exactly due west of the Holy of Holies.

For Mark, the story of Jesus' suffering and death does not close with his burial in a new tomb on Friday afternoon, but with his resurrection on Sunday morning. The end therefore is not the end, but the beginning.

NOTES

1. For an excellent overview on Mark, see S. Kent Brown, "The Testimony of Mark," in *Studies in Scripture: Volume 5, The Gospels*, Kent P. Jackson and Robert L. Millet, eds. (Salt Lake City: Deseret Book Company, 1986), 61–87.

2. Eusebius, *Historia Eccles*. III.39.15; see "The Church History of Eusebius," in *A Select Library of Nicene and Post-Nicene Fathers of the Christian Church*, 14 vols. (Grand Rapids, Michigan: Wm. B. Eerdmans Publishing Company, 1978), 1:171–73.

3. Some credited Mark with inventing the new literary genre of *the Gospel*; see discussion of this point in Frank Kermode, "Introduction to the New Testament," *Literary Guide to the Bible*, ed. Robert Alter and Frank Kermode (Cambridge, Massachusetts: Harvard University Press, 1987),

375–86; for an alternative view see Raymond E. Brown, *A Crucified Christ in Holy Week* (Collegeville, Minnesota: The Liturgical Press, 1986), 9. From an LDS perspective, Peter might be more accurately credited with the structure and content than Mark; see S. Kent Brown, "Testimony of Mark," 73.

4. S. Kent Brown, "Testimony of Mark," 71.

5. W. H. C. Frend, *The Rise of Christianity* (Philadelphia: Fortress Press, 1984), 109.

6. *Tacitus,* trans. John Jackson, 5 vols. (Cambridge, Massachusetts: Harvard University Press, 1981), 5:283–84.

7. Samuel Sandmel, *A Jewish Understanding of the New Testament* (Cincinnati: Hebrew Union College Press, 1956), 134.

8. This once popular idea was first announced in 1896 by Martin Kahler; see David L. Barr, *New Testament Story: An Introduction*, 2nd edition (New York: Wadsworth Publishing Company, 1995), 229.

9. John Dominic Crossan, *Who Killed Jesus? Exposing the Roots of Anti-Semitism in the Gospel Story of the Death of Jesus* (San Francisco: Harper-Collins, 1996), 67.

10. Roger R. Keller, "Mark and Luke: Two Facets of a Diamond," in *The Lord of the Gospels: The 1990 Sperry Symposium on the New Testament,* Bruce A. Van Orden and Brent L. Top, eds. (Salt Lake City: Deseret Book Company, 1990), 86.

11. For a complete discussion of this point see Richard Neitzel Holzapfel, "The 'Hidden Messiah,' " *A Witness of Jesus Christ: The 1989 Sperry Symposium on the Old Testament,* Richard D. Draper, ed. (Salt Lake City: Deseret Book Company, 1989), 80–95.

12. Edward Schillebeeckx, *Jesus: An Experiment in Christology* (New York: The Crossroad Publishing Company, 1981), 298.

13. Ibid.

14. For a survey of this subject, see Martin Hengel, *Crucifixion in the Ancient World and the Folly of the Message of the Cross* (Philadelphia: Fortress Press, 1977).

15. Schillebeeckx, *Jesus,* 299.

16. See Otto Betz, "Jesus and the Temple Scroll," *Jesus and the Dead Sea Scrolls,* James H. Charlesworth, ed. (New York: Doubleday, 1992), 75–103.

17. See Anthony J. Saldarini, "Pharisees," in *The Anchor Bible Dictionary,* 6 vols. (New York: Doubleday, 1992), 5:289–303.

18. Schillebeeckx, *Jesus,* 300.

19. Ibid.

20. Bruce J. Malina and Richard L. Rohrbaugh, *Social Science Commentary on the Synoptic Gospels* (Minneapolis: Fortress Press, 1992), 152.

21. For a detailed discussion of the story itself, see Jeni Broberg Holzapfel and Richard Neitzel Holzapfel, *Sisters at the Well: Women and the Life and Teachings of Jesus* (Salt Lake City: Boockraft, 1993), 135–39.

22. William F. Arndt and F. Wilbur Gingrich, *A Greek-English Lexicon of the New Testament and Other Early Literature* (Chicago: The University of Chicago Press, 1957), 97.

23. Malina and Rohrbaugh, *Social Science Commentary*, 153.

24. See Bargil Pixner, "Church of the Apostles Found on Mount Zion," *Biblical Archæology Review* 16 (May-June 1990): 16–35, 60.

25. Martin Hengel, "Luke the Historian and the Geography of Palestine in the Acts of the Apostles," *Between Jesus and Paul* (Philadelphia: Fortress Press, 1983), 97–128, 190–210; F. Mussner, *Apostelgeschichte* (Neue Echter Bible NT 5; Regensburg, Germany, 1984), 18.

26. See Pixner, "Church of the Apostles."

27. For an alternative view see Rainer Riesner, "Jesus, the Primitive Community, and the Essene Quarter of Jerusalem," in *Jesus and the Dead Sea Scrolls*, 198–234.

28. Max Zerwick and Mary Grosvenor, *A Grammatical Analysis of the Greek New Testament* (Rome: Biblical Institute Press, 1981), 155.

29. Arndt and Gingrich, *A Greek-English Lexicon of the New Testament*, 779.

30. Ibid.

31. For a detailed discussion see Richard Neitzel Holzapfel, *The Exodus Story: Ancient and Modern Parallels* (Salt Lake City: Bookcraft, 1997), 37–48.

32. See Raymond E. Brown, *The Anchor Bible: The Gospel According to John*, 2 vols. (Garden City, New York: Doubleday, 1970), 2:934.

33. Howard Clark Kee, Eric M. Meyers, John Rogerson, and Anthony J. Saldarini, *The Cambridge Companion to the Bible* (New York: Cambridge University Press, 1997), 305.

34. Schillebeeckx, *Jesus*, 303.

35. Ibid., 304.

36. C. S. Mann, *Mark: A New Translation with Introduction and Commentary* (Garden City, New York: Doubleday, 1986), 586.

37. Ibid., 581.

38. See Jerome Murphy-O'Connor, *The Holy Land: Oxford Archaeological Guides* (New York: Oxford University Press, 1998), 122.

39. *Mishnah* (Parah 3.6); see Herbert Danby, trans., *The Mishnah* (New York: Oxford University Press, 1983), 700.

40. Albright and Mann, Matthew, 587.

41. See Jerome Murphy-O'Connor, "What Really Happened at Gethsemane?" *Bible Review* 14 (April 1998): 30–32.

42. For an interesting alternative reconstruction of the meaning of Gethsemane, see John J. Rousseau and Rami Arav, *Jesus & His World: Archaeological and Cultural Dictionary* (Minneapolis: Fortress Press, 1995), 110; for an interesting examination of symbolic interpretations of the place, see Truman G. Madsen, "The Olive Press: A Symbol of Christ," in *The Allegory of the Olive Tree: The Olive, the Bible, and Jacob 5*, Stephen D. Ricks and John W. Welch, eds. (Salt Lake City: Deseret Book Company and FARMS, 1994), 1–10.

43. Murphy-O'Connor, *The Holy Land*, 131–32.

44. Murphy-O'Connor believes that this demonstrates Mark's dependence upon two earlier sources; see Murphy-O'Connor, "What Really Happened at Gethsemane?", 32. New Testament scholar Raymond E. Brown, however, rejects this conclusion; see Raymond E. Brown, *The Death of the Messiah: From Gethsemane to the Grave*, 2 vols. (New York: Doubleday, 1994), 1:54–55.

45. Robert L. Millet provides an overview of this story and some thoughtful insights from all four Gospels; see Robert L. Millet, "Treading the Winepress Alone," in *Studies in Scripture: Volume 5, The Gospels*, Kent P. Jackson and Robert L. Millet, eds. (Salt Lake City: Deseret Book Company, 1986), 430–39.

46. David L. Barr, *New Testament Story: An Introduction*, 2nd ed. (New York: Wadsworth Publishing Company, 1995), 315.

47. J. B. Phillips, *The New Testament in Modern English* (New York: Macmillan, 1972).

48. Murphy-O'Connor, "What Really Happened at Gethsemane?", 36.

49. Neal A. Maxwell, in Conference Report, April 1985 (Salt Lake City: The Church of Jesus Christ of Latter-day Saints, 1985), 92.

50. See Robert J. Matthews, *Joseph Smith's Translation of the Bible: A History and Commentary* (Provo: Brigham Young University Press, 1985), 384.

51. Kathleen Norris, *Amazing Grace: A Vocabulary of Faith* (New York: Riverhead Books, 1998), 198.

52. M. Jack Suggs, Katharine Doob Sakenfeld, and James R. Mueller, eds., *The Oxford Study Bible* (New York: Oxford University Press, 1992), 1299–1300.

53. *Interlinear Greek-English New Testament* (Milford, Michigan: Mott Media, 1981), 185.

54. Crossan, *Who Killed Jesus?*, 72.

55. Malina and Rohrbaugh, *Social Science Commentary*, 158.

56. Ibid., 157.

57. Anthony J. Saldarini, "Sanhedrin," in *The Anchor Bible Dictionary*, 6 vols. (New York: Doubleday, 1992), 5:975.

58. Betz, "Jesus and the Temple Scroll," 88.

59. An example of such an approach is Dale Foreman's *Crucify Him: A Lawyer looks at the Trial of Jesus* (Grand Rapids, Michigan: Zondervan Books, 1990), especially 113–26.

60. Terrence Prendergast, "Trial of Jesus" in *The Anchor Bible Dictionary*, 6 vols. (New York: Doubleday, 1992), 6:660–63.

61. R. E. Brown, *A Crucified Christ in Holy Week*, 13.

62. Ibid., 15.

63. S. Kent Brown suggests: "Mark spoke simply of the high priest or chief priests without identifying anyone by name, a further indication that Mark's readers knew who they were." See S. Kent Brown, "Testimony of Mark," 66.

64. Joel Marcus, "Mark 14:61: 'Are You the Messiah-Son-of-God?' " *Novum Testamentum* 31 (April 1989): 127.

65. Ibid., 140.

66. See comparative chart in Raymond E. Brown, *The Death of the Messiah: From Gethsemane to the Grave*, 2 vols. (New York: Doubleday, 1994), 1:590–91.

67. Origen, Contra Celsum 2.15; see *The Anti-Nicene Fathers* (Grand Rapids, Michigan: Wm. B. Eerdmans Publishing Company, 1951) 4:437-38.

68. See Bruce R. McConkie, *Doctrinal New Testament Commentary: Volume 1, The Gospels* (Salt Lake City: Bookcraft, 1965), 770, 794, 863.

69. Alfred Plummer, *A Critical and Exegetical Commentary on the Gospel According to Luke* (Edinburgh: T. & T. Clark, 1896), 515.

70. R. E. Brown, *Death of the Messiah*, 1:605.

71. For an alternative interpretation of the story see Andrew C. Skinner, "The Arrest, Trial, and Crucifixion," in *Studies in Scripture: Volume 5, The Gospels*, 441–42. Skinner uses some important and thoughtful questions raised by President Spencer W. Kimball about the story as a launching pad for his articulate retelling of the story; see Spencer W. Kimball, "Peter My Brother," *Speeches of the Year* (Provo: Brigham Young University Publications, 1971), 1–8.

72. *The New Greek-English Interlinear New Testament* (Wheaton, Illinois: Tyndale House Publishers, Inc., 1990), 184–85.

73. Arndt and Gingrich, *A Greek-English Lexicon of the New Testament*, 433.

74. This interpretation is suggested by President David O. McKay; see David O. McKay, "Christ, the Light of Humanity," *Improvement Era* 71 (June 1968):5.

75. For a brief and nontechnical introduction to the Romans in the East, see Roberta L. Harris, *The World of the Bible* (New York: Thames and Hudson, 1995), 118–21.

76. See Daniel R. Schwartz, "Pontius Pilate," in *The Anchor Bible Dictionary*, 6 vols. (New York: Doubleday, 1992), 5:395–401.

77. Kee, Meyers, and Rogerson, *Cambridge Companion*, 384.

78. Ibid.

79. Alan Millard, *Discoveries from the Time of Jesus* (Batavia, Illinois: Lion Publishing Corporation, 1990), 66–67.

80. Josephus, *Jewish Wars* 2.8.1; see H. St. J. Thackeray, trans., *Josephus II: The Jewish Wars, Books I-III* (Cambridge, Massachusetts: Harvard University Press, 1926), 367.

81. R. E. Brown, *The Death of the Messiah*, 1:14.

82. G. W. H. Lampe, "The Trial of Jesus in the *Acta Pilati*," in *Jesus and the Politics of His Day*, Ernst Bammel and C. F. D. Moule, eds. (New York: Cambridge University Press, 1984), 173.

83. Ibid., 175.

84. The same is true when United States citizens make critical statements about American society or culture. No one misunderstands their meaning: they know they do not mean *every* American, but only those who act or think differently from themselves. The term *American* takes on new meaning, however, when a citizen from another nation uses the term as an outsider.

85. Richard A. Horsely and Neil Asher Silberman, *The Message and the Kingdom: How Jesus and Paul Ignited a Revolution and Transformed the Ancient World* (New York: Grosset/Putnam, 1997), 86.

86. Crossan, *Who Killed Jesus?*, 111.

87. John Dominic Crosson, *The Cross That Spoke: The Origins of the Passion Narrative* (San Francisco: Harper & Row, 1988), 405.

88. Ramón Trevijano, "Pilate," in *Encyclopedia of the Early Church*, 2 vols. (New York: Oxford University Press, 1992), 2:687.

89. Ben Witherington III, *The Acts of the Apostles: A Socio-Rhetorical Commentary* (Grand Rapids, Michigan: William B. Eerdmans Publishing Company, 1998), 676.

90. See G. E. M. de Ste. Croix, *The Class Struggle in the Ancient Greek World* (Ithaca, New York: Cornell University Press, 1981), 472–73.

91. Mark's use of *aul* tends to confirm this since Josephus uses the same Greek word when he describes Herod's Palace and uses another Greek word when describing the Antonia Fortress.

92. David Darom, *Beautiful Plants of the Bible: From the Hyssop to the Mighty Cedar Trees* (Herzlia, Israel: Palphot Ltd., [n.d.]), 30.

93. See David P. Wright, "Red Heifer," in *The Anchor Bible Dictionary*, 6 vols. (New York: Doubleday, 1992), 3:115–16.

94. Thomas Schmidt, "Jesus' Triumphal March to Crucifixion: The Sacred Way as Roman Procession," *Bible Review* 13 (February 1997): 30–37.

95. Ibid., 30.

96. Ibid., 32.

97. Ibid., 37.

98. Ibid., 34.

99. *Hymns* (Salt Lake City: The Church of Jesus Christ of Latter-day Saints, 1985), no. 194.

100. See Murphy-O'Connor, *The Holy Land*, 45–55.

101. Ibid., 141.

102. See Joan E. Taylor, "Golgotha: A Reconsideration of the Evidence for the Sites of Jesus' Crucifixion and Burial," *New Testament Studies* 44 (April 1998): 180–203.

103. See J. W. Drijvers, *Helena Augusta: The Mother of Constantine the Great and the Legend of Her Finding the True Cross* (Leiden, Netherlands: E. J. Brill, 1991).

104. Vittorino Grossi, "Cross, Crucify," *Encyclopedia of the Early Church*, 2 vols., Adrian Walford, trans. (New York: Oxford University Press, 1992), 1:209.

105. A startling full-page color photograph appears in Hershel Shanks, *Jerusalem: An Archaeological Biography* (New York: Random House, 1995), 178.

106. Several attempts to describe the passion of Jesus Christ from a medical perspective have yielded additional insights beyond the textual descriptions provided by the Gospel writers; see for example William D. Edwards, Wesley J Gabel, Floyd E. Hosmer, "On the Physical Death of Jesus Christ," *The Journal of the American Medical Association* 255 (21 March 1986): 1455–63.

107. Josephus, *Jewish Antiquities* 18.3.3; see Louis H. Feldman, trans., *Josephus IX: Jewish Antiquities, Books XVIII-XIX* (Cambridge, Massachusetts: Harvard University Press, 1926), 49–51.

108. Richard Lloyd Anderson, "The Ancient Practice of Crucifixion," *Ensign* 5 (July 1975), 32.

109. Horsely and Silberman, *The Message and the Kingdom*, 85.

110. See Hengel, *Crucifixion in the Ancient World*, 33–35.

111. The following summary is based on Rousseau and Arav, *Jesus and His World*, 75.

112. As cited in Anderson, "The Ancient Practice of Crucifixion," 32.

113. Josephus, *Jewish Wars* 7.7.4; see H. St. J. Thackeray, trans., *Josephus III: The Jewish Wars, Books IV-VII* (Cambridge, Massachusetts: Harvard University Press, 1926), 563.

114. See M. Wilcox, "Upon the Tree—Deut. 21:22–23 in the New Testament," *Journal of Biblical Literature* 96 (1977):85–99.

115. Joe Zias and James H. Charlesworth, "Crucifixion and the Dead Sea Scrolls," in *Jesus and the Dead Sea Scrolls*, 278.

116. Seneca the Younger, *Epistles*, 101.14.

117. Crossan, *Who Killed Jesus?*, 161.

118. See Bruce M. Metzger, *New Testament Studies: Philological, Versional, and Patristic* (Leiden, Netherlands: Brill, 1980), 23–24.

119. Rousseau and Arav, *Jesus and His World*, 326.

120. Betz, "Jesus and the Temple Scroll," 89.

121. Ibid.

122. For a comparison between the two alternatives, Roman peace and the Gospel of Jesus Christ, see Klaus Wengst, *Pax Romana and the Peace of Jesus Christ* (Philadelphia: Fortress Press, 1987).

123. Josephus, *Jewish Wars* 4.5.2; see H. St. J. Thackeray, trans, *Josephus III: The Jewish Wars, Books IV-VII* (Cambridge, Massachusetts: Harvard University Press, 1928), 93.

124. See John Dominic Crossan, *Who Killed Jesus?*, 166.

125. See Joseph Zias and Eliezer Sekeles, "The Crucified Man from Giivtar: A Reappraisal," *Israel Exploration Journal* 35 (1985):22–27.

126. See Jeffrey Chadwick, "In Defense of the Garden Tomb," *Biblical Archæology Review* 12 (August 1986): 16–17.

127. Conversation with Jeffrey R. Chadwick in Jerusalem, 18 June 1998.

128. See Murphy-O'Connor, *The Holy Land*, 45–55.

129. See John J. Rousseau and Rami Arav, *Jesus and His World: Archaeological and Cultural Dictionary* (Minneapolis: Fortress Press, 1995), 164–69, especially 168.

$\mathcal{M}$ATTHEW'S PASSION NARRATIVE

From earliest times, Matthew's Gospel was the Catholic church's favorite because it is the only one to mention a church and has always been printed first in Christian Bibles.[1] Additionally, some have argued for it being awarded the pride of place as the first Gospel of the New Testament because it was "the most widely used by early Christians interested in knowing about the birth, life, death, and resurrection of Jesus."[2]

While Matthew may be the best known and most widely quoted gospel of the three synoptics, scholars generally assume that Matthew used Mark's account as an important source in compiling his narrative. In many places they are identical, leading one to believe that there is a close relationship between the two accounts. I do not deny the possibility that both writers could have been inspired by the Holy Spirit to produce the same material. This is certainly a possibility to seriously consider. I do not, however, see any doctrinal reason for rejecting the proposal that the texts are related. While I do not accept all of the conclusions or reasoning of biblical scholars on this particular subject, I think that several arguments proposed not only make practical sense but also strengthen the doctrinal framework of the New Testament.

Although Matthew was a member of the Twelve, his reliance on Mark's account is understandable, especially if we assume that it contains Peter's memoirs. This would be particularly true for those events that involved Peter personally but of which Matthew may not have had personal knowledge. Matthew's Gospel (1,068 verses) apparently quotes some 80 percent (606 verses) of Mark's 661 verses.

There are a few commentators who believe Matthew to be the oldest of the Gospels, basically accepting in a modified format the Griesbach hypothesis, first postulated in 1789.[3] Their rationale often includes the assumption that since Mark is the shortest of the three synoptic gospels, it is an abbreviation of Matthew.

The Greek text demonstrates how closely Matthew followed Mark. In some cases it appears there is no major difference between them. In several others it appears that Matthew clarifies Mark's passages. There appears to be two reasons for these clarifications: first, some passages may have been misunderstood by later readers; and second, Matthew seems to be cleaning up the Greek in Mark. It seems much more difficult to explain why Mark would change Matthew rather than vice-versa. Nevertheless, the relations between the synoptic Gospels have not yet been resolved, and this proposal is still a matter of hypothesis.

There are some 200 verses which do not occur in Mark but are found in both Matthew and Luke, often with a striking or even word-for-word similarity. Generally, scholars explain this phenomena by suggesting they used another source, identified as "Q" (from the German word *Quelle*, which means "source"). This explanation is now almost universally accepted despite uncertainties as to the scope of its content. Nevertheless, "Q" remains a hypothetical source.

It seems reasonable that the early disciples recorded Jesus' sayings and that such a document was a welcomed source for anyone wishing to prepare a narrative of Jesus' deeds, supplemented with his sayings. A similar process occurred in the Restoration when Joseph Smith began to write his own history in the 1830s and 1840s. Though an eyewitness, the Prophet used diaries, journals, newspaper clippings, and writings of others as he carefully prepared his own account, incorporating material from these other sources.[4]

Finally, Matthew used his own unique source—himself. Matthew was a disciple of Jesus and is identified as one of the Twelve Apostles (Mark 3:18; Matthew 10:3; Luke 6:15; and Acts 1:13). The Greek name found in the Gospels (*Matthaios* or *Maththaios*) is derived from the Hebrew or Aramaic *Mattiyah*, *Mattiya'* or *Matta'i*, meaning "Gift of Yahweh" or "Gift of God."[5] Apparently, he was also known as Levi (see Mark 2:14; Luke 5:27).

Many commentators believe the numerous "fulfillment citations" (as many as 60 quotations from the Old Testament) make it
likely that Matthew wanted to show how Jesus fulfilled Hebrew
prophecy.[6] His audience was, therefore, most likely Jewish, the only
ones who would care about his particular issue. Because of this belief, some have even suggested that Matthew originally wrote his
Gospel account in Hebrew or Aramaic. Modern translations, including the King James Version, are based on Greek manuscripts.

Fulfilling the Scriptures

As noted above, Matthew often quotes passages from the Hebrew scriptures and then shows how Jesus fulfilled these prophecies.
In his Passion narrative, Matthew cites eleven specific Old Testament scriptures:

Zechariah 11:12	Matthew 26:15	"Thirty pieces of silver"
Zechariah 13:7	Matthew 26:31	"I will smite the shepherd, and the sheep of the flock will be scattered"
Psalm 42:6, 11	Matthew 26:38	"My soul is exceeding sorrowful, even unto death"
Psalm 110:1; Daniel 7:13	Matthew 26:64	"Hereafter shall ye see the Son of man sitting on the right hand of power, and coming in the clouds of heaven"
Zechariah 11:13; Jeremiah 18:2–12; 19; 32:6–9	Matthew 27:5–9	"Cast it unto the potter"
Exodus 9:12 (Greek Septuagint); Psalm 69:3	Matthew 69:3	"My throat is dried"

Psalm 22:18	Matthew 27:35	"They parted my garments among them, and upon my vesture did cast lots"
Psalm 22:7; 109:25	Matthew 27:39	"They that passed by reviled him, wagging their heads"
Psalm 22:8	Matthew 27:43	"He trusts in God; let him deliver him now, if he will have him: for he said, I am the Son of God"
Psalm 22:1	Matthew 27:46	"My God, my God, why hast thou forsaken me?"
Psalm 69:21	Matthew 27:48	"In my thirst they gave me vinegar to drink"

In many of the allusions to the psalms it should be noted that the righteous one does not just suffer, but does so specifically because of his faithfulness to God's will.

The Final Conflict (Matthew 26:3–5)

In Matthew, the Passion narrative (see Matthew 26:1–27) begins with a conspiratorial meeting of high priests and elders in Caiaphas's house: "Then assembled together the chief priests, and the scribes, and the elders of the people, unto the palace of the high priest, who was called Caiaphas, and consulted that they might take Jesus by subtilty, and kill him. But they said, Not on the feast day, lest there be an uproar among the people" (Matthew 26:3–5).

In this passage the reader is introduced to Caiaphas for the first time, something Mark does not do in his Passion narrative, most likely because the Roman audience would not care to know the specific name of the high priest. Joseph Caiaphas was the high priest from A.D. 18 through 36. His eighteen years of service is significantly longer during a century when the average high priest served only four years at best. His service overlaps with that of Pilate, who was appointed Roman prefect of Judea from A.D. 26 through 36. Interestingly, and probably very significantly, they both were dismissed about the same time in late A.D. 36 and early 37. Josephus notes, "[The Syrian governor, Vitellius] ordered Pilate to return to Rome to give the emperor his account of the matters with which he was charged, . . . [and] he removed from his sacred office the high priest Joseph surnamed Caiaphas."[7] We should assume from the literary evidence that Pilate and Caiaphas worked well together in their efforts to continue the pact between Rome and the Jews in Judea. This is a fundamental and important observation which places the arrest, hearings or trials, and condemnation into its proper historical setting.

In the Jerusalem Peace Forest in North Talpiyot, south of the Old City, a tomb complex dating from this period was discovered in November 1990. It contained twelve ossuaries (depositories for the bones of the dead), two found in their original positions in the southern chamber of the tomb. One of these is very ornate, identified as number six, with an Aramaic inscription *Yehosef bar Qafa*, probably meaning "Joseph of Caiaphas."[8] This ossuary, which is currently on display at the Israel Museum in Jerusalem today, contained partial remains of six individuals, including a 60-year-old male, perhaps Joseph, nicknamed Caiaphas—the high priest the year Jesus was executed, as noted in John and Matthew.

Standing before the ossuary in the archeological section of the museum can create for the onlooker an odd sensation while gazing in utter astonishment at the ancient name etched on the stone box. The discovery of this artifact from the past is one of the vagaries of archeological work in the Holy Land and, ironically, brings the story very much to life.

While Matthew's portrayal highlights the deadly opposition to Jesus from those most intimately involved at the highest levels of Jewish social, political, economic, and religious life, he also reveals Jesus' popularity among the *'am ha'aretz*, the "people of the land." Population figures for antiquity are notoriously difficult to ascertain. Most scholars believe there were roughly four to five million Jews in the Roman Empire at the time. As Ferderick J. Cwiekowski notes, "The Jews of the diaspora outnumbered by far those who lived in the homeland."[9] In Jewish usage, *diaspora*, a Greek word meaning "scattered abroad," sometimes translated as dispersion, is used to refer to Jews who lived outside the land of Israel after the destruction of Solomon's Temple in 586 B.C. and the Babylonian exile.

During the Roman period one could find Jewish communities throughout the empire and beyond in the East. Some studies estimate the Jewish population in Jewish-Palestine as somewhere between a half and three-quarters of a million people, a small percentage of the four to five million total. The population of the largest city in Judea, Jerusalem, was estimated to range between thirty and sixty thousand. A great range, but considering the difficulty ancient demographic studies encounter, it at least gives us a general idea.

LDS New Testament scholar Stephen E. Robinson outlines this little-discussed issue against the social setting of the Gospels: "The vast majority of the population in Jewish Palestine did not go to church, that is, they did not have an active affiliation with any of the Jewish sects. Most people accepted the views of the Pharisees on the interpretation of the law, but few actually became Pharisees. . . . They made up probably 90 percent of the crowds and multitudes to which John the Baptist and Jesus preached."[10]

In our discussion of Mark's use of the term *Jews* we made some observations. It is necessary to review the issue again because Matthew, in addressing a Jewish-Christian audience, is more open about Jewish crowds and groups, realizing that his original audience understood what he meant by these terms. As noted earlier, the fact that Matthew is a Jewish author, writing to a Jewish audience, helps us appreciate Matthew's account by placing it into a proper context.[11]

This is very similar to the experience of families, clubs and em-
ployees of a particular organization. With insiders (members of the
same group) we are often frank, personal, and less cautious in our
conversation about the group or particular members of the group
(positive or negative). When in discussions with those who are not
insiders, we are often more circumspect. Family ties and organiza-
tional bonds often dictate a reserved discussion of intimate and personal issues. In a sense Matthew's Gospel represents an insider discussion of the family (Jewish), which may never have been intended
to be scrutinized by outsiders (Gentiles). We cannot be sure whether
Matthew ever anticipated that his reading audience would eventually develop into a totally gentile membership, often hostile to Jews
and unable to place the in-house harsh and frank discussion within
a proper context.

Here at the beginning of the Passion narrative Matthew highlights Jesus' popularity with the people, the *'am ha'aretz*, mentioned
by Robinson. This is an important counterbalance to such statements as, "They all say unto him, Let him be crucified" (Matthew
27:22), and, "Then answered all the people, and said, His blood be
on us, and on our children" (Matthew 27:25). The broad condemnation of the Jews by Matthew, who is Jewish, and for his audience,
who is apparently Jewish, should be only understood in light of
Jesus' own words at the Last Supper: "For this is my blood of the new
testament, which is shed for many for the remission of sins"
(Matthew 26:28; cf. 1 Timothy 2:6). The power of his atoning blood
is in no way diluted by one segment of the Jewish population's willingness to shed innocent blood.[12]

Anointing for Burial (Matthew 26:6–13)

The scene shifts to Bethany: "Now when Jesus was in Bethany,
in the house of Simon the leper, there came unto him a woman having an alabaster box of very precious ointment, and poured it on his
head, as he sat at meat. But when his disciples saw it, they had in-
dignation, saying, To what purpose is this waste? . . . When Jesus understood it, he said unto them, Why trouble ye the woman? for she
hath wrought a good work upon me. . . . For in that she hath poured

this ointment on my body, she did it for my burial" (Matthew 26:6–13).[13] Here again the point seems obvious, "Jesus knows already that he will die, and knows also that he will be buried without the customary anointing."[14]

The Price of a Slave (Matthew 26:14–16)

Judas Iscariot was a disciple, even though Matthew notes that he "also betrayed him" (see Matthew 10:4), a comment that may have been a result of hindsight. The passion drama continues: "Then one of the twelve, called Judas Iscariot, went unto the chief priests, And said unto them, What will ye give me, and I will deliver him unto you? And they covenanted with him for thirty pieces of silver. And from that time he sought opportunity to betray him" (Matthew 26:14–16). Apparently, thirty pieces of silver was the common price of a slave.[15] As Michael Macrone so aptly notes: "If there's a more infamous sum in literature, I don't know of it. The $24 paid for Manhattan and Michael Milken's $550 million income don't even come close."[16]

Matthew is rich in its intratextual connections. Here one is reminded of Judas' avarice against Jesus' command to his disciples to take no silver (see Matthew 10:9). Additionally, Judas is linked with the Roman soldiers who took silver as part of the conspiracy to hide the fact of the Resurrection (see Matthew 28:11–15). Finally, his question, "What will you give me?" contrasts with the other disciples' question, "Where wilt thou that we prepare for thee to eat the passover?" (Matthew 26:17).

The Last Supper (Matthew 26:17–30)

The story then turns to the preparation for the Passover, Jesus' last among his disciples: "Now the first day of the feast of unleavened bread the disciples came to Jesus, saying unto him, Where wilt thou that we prepare for thee to eat the passover? And he said, Go into the city to such a man, and say unto him, The Master saith, My time is at hand; I will keep the passover at thy house with my disciples. And the disciples did as Jesus had appointed them; and they made ready the passover. Now when the even was come, he sat down [reclined] with the twelve" (Matthew 26:17–20).

The disciples' response here may remind us of Exodus 12:28, and Matthew probably intended his audience to make the connection as part of his theme of a new exodus. Matthew describes in Roman tradition the preparation on Thursday during the day and the meal on Thursday evening as taking place within the one day. According to Jewish tradition, in which a new day began at sunset, the preparation falls on Nisan 14 and the evening meal on Nisan 15, because it was considered a new day.

As noted earlier, the dinner itself may be a Passover *seder* (meal) itself. Those who reconstruct this meal as a *seder* do so on the assumption that the *Mishnah* is a safe guide to Passover practices of some 150 years earlier. So with the legal principles and practices discussed earlier in Mark's Passion narrative, we have to be careful when using second-century and third-century sources to reconstruct events during the first half of the first century.

During the dinner Jesus identifies the betrayer and institutes the Lord's Supper: "Now when the even was come, he sat down with the twelve. And as they did eat, he said, Verily I say unto you, that one of you shall betray me. And they were exceeding sorrowful, and began every one of them to say unto him, Lord, is it I? And he answered and said, He that dippeth his hand with me in the dish, the same shall betray me. The Son of man goeth *as it is written* of him: but woe unto that man by whom the Son of man is betrayed! it had been good for that man if he had not been born. Then Judas, which betrayed him, answered and said, Master, is it I? He said unto him, Thou hast said" (Matthew 26:20–25; emphasis added). Important to Matthew's purpose is the fact that Jesus' death is a fulfillment of scriptures: "as it is written."

According to Malina and Rohrbaugh, "Judas proves his total lack of shame by brazenly asking whether Jesus knew it was he who was part of the secret plan; Jesus informs him that he is in on the secret (v. 25) and carries on as usual, as befits a man of honor."[17]

Despite the steadily escalating sense of foreboding, Jesus wants to eat with them: "And as they were eating, Jesus took bread, and blessed it, and brake it, and gave it to the disciples, and said, Take, eat; this is my body. And he took the cup, and gave thanks, and gave it to them, saying, Drink ye all of it; for this is my blood of the new testament, which is shed for many for the remission of sins. But I say unto you, I will not drink henceforth of this fruit of the vine, until that day when I drink it new with you in my Father's kingdom" (Matthew 26:26–29). The synoptic Gospels all discuss the introduction of the sacrament. Matthew's original audience would likely be aware of how sacrificial blood acted as the seal of a covenant (see Exodus 24:8).

The betrayal is only one aspect of the story—the betrayed Jesus will atone for the sins of mankind. In this salvific act, Jesus offers his life willingly to inaugurate a new covenant (or testament). Instead of recounting the last event in Jesus' ministry, Matthew's portrayal of the Last Supper is more a celebration of the beginning of the new symbol of deliverance—the sacrament.

The transition from the Passover to the Last Supper completed, Jesus and the disciples sing a hymn (see Matthew 26:30). It is natural for us to immediately think of hymns familiar to us. However, the singing mentioned here would be quite unfamiliar to the modern reader. Many have tried to identify the hymn as part of the Passover liturgy and therefore identify several possible Psalms, including the second half of the Hallel (Psalms 113–18).[18] The uncertainty of how many hymns are to be understood here comes from the Greek word *hymnein,* which indicates one hymn or more.

The Flock to Scatter (Matthew 26:31–34)

Either in the Upper Room or on the way to Gethsemane, Jesus speaks again about the disciples' reaction to the evening's coming events: "Then saith Jesus unto them, All ye shall be offended because of me this night: for it is written, I will smite [hit or slay] the shepherd, and the sheep of the flock shall be scattered abroad" (Matthew 26:31). The scripture quoted comes from Zechariah (see Zechariah 13:7).

Peter responds to Jesus' prophecy: "Though all men shall be offended because of thee, yet will I never be offended" (Matthew 26:33). This rebuttal reminds the reader of a similar one recorded earlier in Matthew: "From that time forth began Jesus to shew unto his disciples, how that he must go unto Jerusalem, and suffer many things of the elders and chief priests and scribes, and be killed, and be raised again the third day. Then Peter took him, and began to rebuke him, saying, Be it far from thee, Lord: this shall not be unto thee" (Matthew 16:21–22).

In both instances Peter is unwilling to accept prophetic utterances, one from Jesus himself and the other from the scriptures. However, in the latter, Peter seems to be concerned with the *all* of the prophecy since he apparently accepts the inevitability of the event, *"Though all men shall be offended"* (Matthew 26:33; emphasis added). He nevertheless argues for personal exclusion.

As he did earlier, Jesus challenges Peter's unwillingness to accept his prophetic ability: "Jesus said unto him, Verily I say unto thee, That this night, before the cock crow, thou shalt deny me thrice" (Matthew 26:34). Thirty-one times in Matthew's Gospel does Jesus use the solemn intensifier *verily* to introduce one of his sayings. Similarly, the Greek word *aparnesthai* (deny) is strong and means to "disown, deny having anything to do with one."[19] In the New Testament it implies "a previous relationship of obedience and fidelity. It can take place only where there has first been acknowledgment and commitment."[20] This fits well with Peter's wholeheartedness to follow Jesus and confess that he was God's Son (see Matthew 4:18–20; 16:16).

Gethsemane (Matthew 26:36–45)

Following the revelations of denial and abandonment, Jesus goes to Gethsemane. Which way he traveled with the disciples can only be a learned guess. We will propose one, however, in our discussion on John's Passion narrative. It was most likely a narrow steep descent to the Kidron from the Upper Room.

More than any other place in Matthew's Gospel one may see how he used Mark's Passion narrative. A careful examination reveals numerous correspondences and several changes which in effect elucidate Mark's account through ommissions and minor additions.[21] For example, Mark says: "And *they* came to a place which was named Gethsemane" (Mark 14:32; emphasis added). *They* is ambiguous for one has to know that *they* includes Jesus, whom Mark does not explicitly mention. Matthew, however, introduces the story in much the same way but clarifies Mark's account by identifying Jesus specifically: "Then cometh *Jesus* with them unto a place called Gethsemane" (Matthew 26:36; emphasis added).

The sky was illuminated by a full or nearly full moon. Upon arriving at Gethsemane Jesus "saith unto the disciples, Sit ye here, *while I go and pray yonder*" (Matthew 26:36; emphasis added; see also JST, Matthew 26:36). Again, perhaps Matthew is clarifying Mark's account, which might suggest that Jesus would pray nearby: "And they came to a place which was named Gethsemane: and he saith to his disciples, Sit ye here, while I shall pray" (Mark 14:32).

Mark's account next reads: "And he taketh with him Peter and James and John, and began to be sore amazed, and to be very heavy; and saith unto them, My soul is exceeding sorrowful unto death: tarry ye here, and watch" (Mark 14:33–34). Matthew seems to smooth it out and reports: "And he took with him Peter and the two sons of Zebedee, and began to be *sorrowful* and very heavy. Then saith he unto them, My soul is exceeding *sorrowful*, even unto death: tarry ye here, and watch with me" (Matthew 26:37–38; emphasis added). Matthew changes Mark's word *amazed* to *sorrowful*, thus matching Jesus' own description (see D&C 19:15–18). An alternative translation from the Greek for *sorrowful* and *very heavy* is "distressed and troubled."[22]

Matthew continues his portrayal of Jesus' agony in Gethsemane: "And he went a little further, and fell on his face, and prayed, saying, O my Father, if it be possible, let this cup pass from me: nevertheless not as I will, but as thou wilt. And he cometh unto the disciples, and findeth them asleep, and saith unto Peter, What, could ye not watch with me one hour? Watch and pray, that ye enter not into temptation: the spirit indeed is willing, but the flesh is weak" (Matthew 26:39–41). Here is another example of Matthew's efforts to avoid confusion; he edits Mark to clarify the story for *his* readers. Mark's account says that Jesus addressed Peter with the name *Simon*. Mark's original audience may well have been familiar with Peter, so this presented no problem for them. However, Matthew changed it because someone in his audience might not know that Simon and Peter are the same person.

Additionally, Matthew apparently changes Mark's descriptions of what happened to Jesus: "And he went forward a little, and *fell on the ground*, and prayed that, if it were possible, the hour might pass from him" (Mark 14:35; emphasis added). Matthew's Jewish audience would appreciate his emphasis: "And he went a little further, and *fell on his face*" (Matthew 26:39), since falling on one's face is a typical Israelite posture for prayer (see Genesis 17:3; Judges 13:20).

Both Mark and Matthew specifically inform us that Jesus prayed three separate times. Matthew records: "He went away again the second time, and prayed, saying, O my Father, if this cup may not pass away from me, except I drink it, thy will be done. And he came and found them asleep again: for their eyes were heavy. And he left them, and went away again, and prayed the third time, saying the same words" (Matthew 26:42–44). Interestingly enough, Matthew's account of Jesus' prayer is shorter then Mark's. For those who argue for Matthew's priority based on the assumption that Mark is a truncated version of Matthew, this may present a problem. Suggesting that Mark expanded Matthew's account seems to put them at odds with their original argument. Why did Matthew shorten Mark's account? It seems reasonable to assume that Matthew wanted to once again eliminate what might be misunderstood in Mark's account.

In Mark, Jesus prays that "if it were possible, the hour might pass from him. And he said, Abba, Father, *all things* are possible unto thee" (Mark 14:35–36; emphasis added). Matthew's account avoids what may be construed as a contradiction by recording the substance of Jesus' prayer in this way: "O my Father, if it be possible, let this cup pass from me: nevertheless not as I will, but as thou wilt" (Matthew 26:39).

Finally, after the third time, he returns to find the disciples asleep and says to them: "Sleep on now, and take your rest: behold, the hour is at hand, and the Son of man is betrayed into the hands of sinners" (Matthew 26:45).

Judas' Kiss (Matthew 26:46–56)

In Matthew's account, Jesus begins his prayer sorrowful, troubled, and prostrate, but ends on his feet, resolutely facing the mob that has approached. Jesus commands his disciples, "Rise, let us be going; behold, he is at hand that doth betray me" (Matthew 26:46). The scene continues: "And while he yet spake, lo, Judas, one of the twelve, came, and with him a great multitude with swords and staves, from the chief priests and elders of the people. Now he that betrayed him gave them a sign, saying, Whomsoever I shall kiss, that same is he: hold him fast" (Matthew 26:47–48).

Judas, the traitor, greets Jesus, "Hail, master," and then kisses him (Matthew 26:49). By using a kiss to show whom the soldiers should arrest, Judas perverts a gesture of the close friendship he has had with his former Master. Matthew includes "Hail" to the salutation as a further example of Judas' falseheartedness. Matthew's audience may well have recalled this verse from Proverbs 27: "Faithful are the wounds of a friend; but the kisses of an enemy are deceitful" (v. 6).

"And Jesus said unto him, Friend, wherefore art thou come? Then came they, and laid hands on Jesus, and took him. And, behold, one of them which were with Jesus stretched out his hand, and drew his sword, and struck a servant of the high priest's, and smote off his ear. Then said Jesus unto him, Put up again thy sword into his place: for all they that take the sword shall perish with the sword. Thinkest thou that I cannot now pray to my Father, and he shall presently give me more than twelve legions of angels? But how then shall the scriptures be fulfilled, that thus it must be?" (Matthew 26:50–54).

Jesus demonstrates his willingness to fulfill the divine plan, even though he could have asked his Father to "give [him] more than twelve legions." An infantry brigade, or legion, numbered about five thousand soldiers.

After this brief skirmish, "all the disciples forsook him, and fled" (Matthew 26:56).

A Jewish audience, including Matthew himself, may have recalled the words found in Proverbs, "Faithful are the wounds of a friend; but the kisses of an enemy are deceitful" (Proverbs 27:6), when the story was told. To speculate on Jesus' precise thoughts at the very moment of betrayal seem fruitless without more textual evidence.

Parallels Between David and Jesus

The story presented by Matthew might have reminded his first-century Jewish audience of King David's own experience. Apparently Matthew intends that the reader sees the parallel between the story of Ahithophel and David and that of Judas and Jesus.

In both stories an intimate and faithful friend turns traitor: "And Absalom sent for Ahithophel the Gilonite, David's counsellor, from his city, even from Giloh, where he offered sacrifices. And the conspiracy was strong; for the people increased continually with Absalom. . . . And one told David, saying, Ahithophel is among the conspirators with Absalom. And David said, O Lord, I pray thee, turn the counsel of Ahithophel into foolishness" (2 Samuel 15:12, 31).

Second, both David and Jesus cross the Kidron Valley and ascend up the Mount of Olives: "And all the country wept with a loud voice, and all the people passed over: the king also himself passed over the brook Kidron, and all the people passed over, toward the way of the wilderness. . . . And David went up by the ascent of Mount Olivet" (2 Samuel 15:23, 30).

Third, in both stories both David and Jesus pray during their struggles: "And [David] wept as he went up, and had his head covered, and he went barefoot: and all the people that was with him covered every man his head, and they went up, weeping as they went up" (2 Samuel 15:30).

Fourth, another possible parallel is between Ittai the Gittite and Peter: "And Ittai answered the king, and said, As the Lord liveth, and as my lord the king liveth, surely in what place my lord the king shall be, whether in death or life, even there also will thy servant be" (2 Samuel 15:21).

Fifth, another possible parallel is the request of David's and Jesus' prayer for the will of God to be accomplished: "And the king said unto Zadok, Carry back the ark of God into the city: if I shall find favour in the eyes of the Lord, he will bring me again, and shew me both it, and his habitation" (2 Samuel 15:25).

A sixth possible parallel is the soldiers that accompany both Ahithophel and Judas: "Moreover Ahithophel said unto Absalom, Let me now choose out twelve thousand men, and I will arise and pursue after David this night: and I will come upon him while he is weary and weak handed, and will make him afraid: and all the people that are with him shall flee; and I will smite the king only: and I will bring back all the people unto thee: the man whom thou seekest is as if all returned: so all the people shall be in peace" (2 Samuel 17:1–3).

Finally, another parallel is made explicit in Matthew concerning the death of Judas and Ahithophel: "And when Ahithophel saw that his counsel was not followed, he saddled his ass, and arose, and gat him home to his house, to his city, and put his household in order, and hanged himself, and died, and was buried in the sepulchre of his father" (2 Samuel 17:23).

Matthew's repeated use of the Old Testament provides a clue to his unique purpose, namely, demonstrating the fulfillment of God's purposes in and through Jesus. Matthew seems more interested in themes than in the details of historical narrative; the most superficial examination of his Gospel from a purely historical point of view reveals that a disproportionate amount of attention is devoted to the Passion narrative.

Thus Old Testament quotations in the Passion narrative combined with Matthew's familiar formula "that it might be fulfilled which was spoken by the prophet" (Matthew 27:35), the Gospel of Matthew reemphasizes God's salvation proclaimed from the beginning of time. The emphasis on the Messiah is his redemption from the captivity of sin, not from military power as expected by the Jews.

Peter Follows (Matthew 26:58)

Matthew, like Mark before, tells us: "But Peter followed him afar off unto the high priest's palace, and went in, and sat with the servants, *to see the end*" (Matthew 26:58; emphasis added). Matthew explicitly tells us something no other author does: Peter followed

Jesus "to see the end." Additionally, the original Jewish audience may have thought about Psalm 38 as they read the story: "My lovers [Hebrew "friends and neighbors"] and my friends stand aloof from my sore; and my kinsmen stand afar off" (Psalm 38:11).

Jesus Stands Alone (Matthew 26:57–68)

Jesus is betrayed by one of his own, abandoned by the remaining disciples, and in the end accused by his own religious leaders. Deserted by his disciples and surrounded by his enemies, Jesus is taken before "Caiaphas the high priest, where the scribes and the elders were assembled" (Matthew 26:57). This is the second and final reference to Caiaphas in Matthew and represents the successful completion of the conspiracy noted at the beginning of the chapter. The exact nature of this meeting is unknown.

Jesus' response to the high priest's question brings the verdict of blasphemy and the attendant condemnation to death: "And the high priest arose, and said unto him, Answerest thou nothing? what is it which these witness against thee? But Jesus held his peace. And the high priest answered and said unto him, I adjure thee by the living God, that thou tell us whether thou be the Christ, the Son of God. Jesus saith unto him, Thou hast said: nevertheless I say unto you, Hereafter shall ye see the Son of man sitting on the right hand of power, and coming in the clouds of heaven. Then the high priest rent his clothes, saying, He hath spoken blasphemy; what further need have we of witnesses? behold, now ye have heard his blasphemy. What think ye? They answered and said, He is guilty of death" (Matthew 26:62–66).

One thinks of Peter's confession: "Thou art the Christ [Messiah], the Son of the living God" (Matthew 16:16). Here the high priest says: "I adjure thee by the living God, that thou tell us whether thou be the Christ, the Son of God" (Matthew 26:63).

Throughout his records, Matthew records various witnesses to Jesus' divine Sonship, including his enemies who grudgingly, indirectly, or ironically announce it: the Father at his baptism (see Matthew 3:17), Satan during the wilderness temptations (see Matthew 4:1–13), townspeople at Nazareth (see Matthew 13:53–58),

Peter at Caesarea Philippi (see Matthew 16:16), the Father again on the Mount of Transfiguration (see Matthew 17:5), during the hearing before the Jewish leaders (see Matthew 26:63), and finally the Roman soldier at the foot of the cross (see Matthew 27:54). This is evidence that Matthew gives his reader to claim Jesus' words and deeds as authoritative.

Matthew continues: "Jesus saith unto him, Thou hast said: nevertheless I say unto you, Hereafter shall ye see the Son of man sitting on the right hand of power, and coming in the clouds of heaven. Then the high priest rent his clothes, saying, He hath spoken blasphemy; what further need have we of witnesses? behold, now ye have heard his blasphemy. What think ye? They answered and said, He is guilty of death. Then did they spit in his face, and buffeted him; and others smote him with the palms of their hands, saying, Prophesy unto us, thou Christ, Who is he that smote thee?" (Matthew 26:64–68).

The Jewish audience probably knew that the penalty for blasphemy was death by stoning as noted in the law of Moses (see Leviticus 24:13–16). Additionally, Matthew's first-century Jewish audience may have recalled the Suffering Servant prophecy from Isaiah as they heard this section read: "I hid not my face from shame and spitting" (Isaiah 50:6).

Scholars are at a loss to explain the grounds on which Jesus is found guilty, since there seems to be no violation of the Mosaic commandments. However, Caiaphas's tearing of his garments supports the reading that a judicial finding is involved as outlined in the *Mishnah:* "When sentence was to be given they did not declare him guilty of death [on the grounds of evidence given] with the substituted name, but they sent out all the people and asked the chief among the witnesses and said to him, 'Say expressly what thou heardest', and he says it; and the judges stand up on their feet and rend their garments, and they may not mend them again."[23]

Peter Wept Bitterly (Matthew 26:69–75)

Matthew tells of Peter's denial, following very close to Mark's account: "Now Peter sat without in the palace: and a damsel came unto him, saying, Thou also wast with Jesus of Galilee. But he denied before them all, saying, I know not what thou sayest. And when he was gone out into the porch, another maid saw him, and said unto them that were there, This fellow was also with Jesus of Nazareth. And again he denied with an oath, I do not know the man. And after a while came unto him they that stood by, and said to Peter, Surely thou also art one of them; for thy speech bewrayeth [reveals] thee. Then began he to curse and to swear, saying, I know not the man. And immediately the cock crew. And Peter remembered the word of Jesus, which said unto him, Before the cock crow, thou shalt deny me thrice. And he went out, and wept bitterly" (Matthew 26:69–75).[24]

Judas' Fate (Matthew 27:3–10)

Matthew now interrupts the story of Jesus' Passion with a discussion of Judas' final fate. The story highlights the irony of the action. Those who care nothing about Jesus' life are anxious about the lawful deposition of the blood money: "Then Judas, which had betrayed him, when he saw that he was condemned, repented himself, and brought again the thirty pieces of silver to the chief priests and elders, saying, I have sinned in that I have betrayed the innocent blood. And they said, What is that to us? see thou to that. And he cast down the pieces of silver in the temple, and departed, and went and hanged himself. And the chief priests took the silver pieces, and said, It is not lawful for to put them into the treasury, because it is the price of blood. And they took counsel, and bought with them the potter's field, to bury strangers in. Wherefore that field was called, The field of blood, unto this day" (Matthew 27:3–8). Matthew sees in this action the fulfillment of another Messianic prophesy (see Matthew 27:9–10; Acts 1:18–19).

Ironically, long associated with the Field of Blood, the Aceldama (Aramaic ḥăqēl dĕma', which literally means "field of blood") is most likely the burial place of the high priest family who ruled in Judea during this period and played a role in Jesus' interrogations before his execution.[25] Located about one half mile south of the Old City of Jerusalem at the southeastern end of the Hinnom Valley, the site contains more than 80 burial caves, dating from the Herodian period (37 B.C. to A.D. 70). The most ornate of them probably belongs to the leader of the high priest Annas' family, which played such a leading role in the New Testament period (see the discussion regarding Annas in John's Passion narrative discussion).

The Jewish council takes Jesus finally to the Gentiles for trial, mockery, and execution. In spite of these trials, Jesus is self-composed when he confronts the Roman governor, who can decree his death.

Barabbas (Matthew 27:15–23)

Like the other Gospel authors, Matthew informs us of the custom of releasing a prisoner at the feast, thus giving Pilate a possible escape clause. "Now at that feast the governor was wont [accustomed] to release unto the people a prisoner, whom they would [desired]. And they had then a notable [notorious] prisoner, called Barabbas. Therefore when they were gathered together, Pilate said unto them, Whom will ye that I release unto you? Barabbas, or Jesus which is called Christ? For he knew that for envy they had delivered him" (Matthew 27:15–18).

Another of Matthew's insights is the account of Pilate's wife, who as a Gentile recognizes Jesus' innocence and seeks his release, while the Jewish leaders work the crowd to have the notorious Barabbas released and Jesus crucified. "When he was set down on the judgment seat, his wife sent unto him, saying, Have thou nothing to do with that just man: for I have suffered many things this day in a dream because of him. But the chief priests and elders persuaded the multitude that they should ask [request] Barabbas, and destroy Jesus. The governor answered and said unto them, Whether of the twain will ye that I release unto you? They said, Barabbas" (Matthew 27:19–21).

Like Mark, Matthew introduces a scene full of irony, except that Matthew's account is all the more poignant. Some important manuscripts of Matthew's Gospel compare Barabbas and Jesus in a unique way, for they phrase Pilate's question in 27:17 as: "Whom do you want me to release to you, *Jesus* Barabbas or Jesus called Christ?" (Emphasis added). Respected New Testament textual scholar Bruce

Metzger states, "A majority of the [Editorial Committee of the United Bible Societies' Greek New Testament] was of the opinion that the original text of Matthew had the double name in both verses [27:16–17] and that [Jesus] was deliberately suppressed in most witnesses for reverential considerations."[26] Since "Barabbas" might mean "Son of the Father," it would be a fascinating irony for Pilate to have faced two accused men named Jesus, one "Son of the Father," the other "Son of God."

The Passion narratives inform us that Barabbas was most likely a rebel, an insurgent freedom fighter who opposed Roman occupation of Judea. Matthew calls him "a notable prisoner" (see Matthew 27:16) while John identifies him as a robber or bandit (see John 18:40, where the Greek word is *lēstēs*, which can be correctly translated as either). As legal historian John W. Welch notes, given the political environment, "that one word [bandit] alone speaks volumes about why a crowd of people could possibly have expressed their preference in favor of such a figure, a bandit, and consequently against Jesus."[27]

Mark and Luke say Barabbas was arrested for insurrection and murder (see Mark 15:7; Luke 23:19). These identifications have led some to suggest that he was of the "party of Zealots, who desired to throw off the Roman yoke" by armed resistence.[28] LDS biblical scholar Kent P. Jackson correctly notes that there were at least "five distinctive groups of revolutionaries" mentioned in Josephus, our only substantial source on this particular subject.[29] So while it might be impossible to correctly identify to which group Barabbas belonged, he was apparently part of those who most likely opposed the status quo in Roman-occupied Judea.

Presented with the choice between the two (an unarmed Savior and a formally-armed rebel), the Jewish crowd seeks the release of the one who in their eyes was most actively engaged in bringing them freedom. Matthew informs the reader that, ironically, the Jews chose the wrong person to release from a religious point of view; that is, they chose the wrong "Son of the Father." The Romans, on the other hand, chose the wrong person to crucify from a political point of view, since Barabbas represented those forces which would eventually ignite the Jewish Revolt in A.D. 66. The resultant loss of taxes, tolls, rents, and tribute was immense, for added to the cost of funding the war in terms of lives, supplies, and time, was the disruption of travel and trade throughout the whole region. It eventually ended in A.D. 73 or 74 when the last pocket of resistance on Masada was finally overwhelmed by Roman forces.

Finally, the scene may reveal one more profoundly ironic moment as Matthew tells us that Jesus, the true Son of God, and Barabbas, the revolutionary, have switched roles.

Motive (Matthew 27:18)

Matthew reveals what motive Pilate ascribed to the Jewish leaders for delivering Jesus to him: "For he knew that for *envy* they had delivered him" (Matthew 27:18; emphasis added). Of course there would have been many others. Each individual involved would have had his own reason for wanting Jesus out of the way. And while they may not have agreed on the reasons or justifications for their action, they did finally come to a consensus about him.

Washed His Hands (Matthew 27:24)

Matthew informs us that when Pilate saw that the people wanted Jesus crucified, he "took water, and washed his hands before the multitude" (Matthew 27:24), as though he could wash himself of Jesus' blood. In the end, Pilate condemns Jesus just as the Jewish leaders had done, and in both cases Jesus is mocked, spat upon, and struck. Finally, Jesus is not given justice by either Romans or Jews.

Jewish Context (Matthew 27:25)

A much misused and incorrectly interpreted passage, I believe, which brought about unspeakable suffering to Jews from the time the Roman Empire became Christian to the present, follows: "Then answered all the people, and said, His blood be on us, and on our children" (Matthew 27:25). Matthew apparently speaks only of those who opposed Jesus and had gathered together before Pilate when he states *all the people*. He does not include himself, Jesus' mother, the large number of Jesus' Jewish disciples, and other Jews living throughout the Roman Empire who could not possibly have consented nor be held responsible for the actions of this one group of people.

It may be helpful to place this harsh critique of the Jews in context. When Matthew wrote his Gospel, the Jewish-Christian Saints were experiencing extreme persecution from their fellow Jews. This opposition to the Church was simply a continuation of the Jewish opposition to Jesus himself. Members of the original opposition to Jesus centered in the temple in Jerusalem and a few synagogues in Galilee. Eventually, followers of Jesus were subjected to excommunication, or exclusion from membership in their Jewish community and from its rights and privileges. Excommunication apparently took three forms of increasing severity in early Judaism.[30]

The mildest form was *nezifah* (rebuke), lasting seven days and consisting merely of social and religious isolation. Following an expression of contrition the person was brought back into activity within the community. The next level of action was *niddui* (banishment), lasting at least thirty days and possibly longer, depending on the person's attitude. During the period of excommunication the individual was completely shut off from social intercourse, except with immediate family members. Their children were at times forbidden to participate in religious duties and practices (circumcision, worship, and education). And finally, the most extreme form was *herem* (ban), lasting an indefinite period. At this point, the individual was completely denied every benefit of social and religious life apart from the barest necessities.

The story found in John 9 provides an explicit reference to the practice of excommunication during Jesus' mortal ministry. Following the healing of a blind man, his parents were called before the Jewish leadership to answer specific questions. They avoided answering the questions by arguing that their son was old enough to answer for himself. We are informed by John: "These words spake his parents, because they feared the Jews: for the Jews had agreed already, that if any man did confess that he was Christ, he should be *put out* of the synagogue" (John 9:22; emphasis added).

It is certain that Jesus and his disciples met opposition in the synagogues and were sometimes handled roughly in the heat of debate (see Luke 4:28–29). Just when formal excommunication occurred is difficult to ascertain, but apparently there was something of this nature going on. By the end of the first century the Jewish-Christians apparently were being forced to choose between continued fellowship in their Jewish circles and acceptance of Jesus as the Messiah with banishment. This was a deliberate effort to exclude Jewish-Christians from the community fold.

Eventually, a curse upon those who followed Jesus was added to synagogue worship. *Minim* is the term used in the Rabbinical sources (*Midrash* and *Talmud*) for heretics. While the etymology is unknown, some believe it is derived from *ma'amin Yeshu notseri* (believers in Jesus the Nazarene). Although the precise meaning of *minim* varied with the circumstances, there is no doubt that it later came to mean Jewish-Christians in particular. "The writings of the *minim*," said Rabbi Tarfon, "deserve to be burned, even though they may contain the name of God, for sectarianism is more dangerous than paganism."[31] A prayer against the *minim*, which was added to the *Amidah*, was composed by Shemu'el ha-Qatan at the request of the *nasi*, Rabbi Gamli'el, as part of the Jewish struggle against Christianity, which at the time was considered a Jewish sect. The wording of the prayer underwent repeated changes for fear of censorship and to obviate anti-Jewish criticism; thus, *malshinim* (informers) was substituted for *minim*. The benediction (*Birkat ha-minim*) was actually a curse concerning *minim*. It constitutes the twelfth of the benedictions of the *Amidah* composed from earlier sources sometime before A.D. 100.

With the introduction of a solemn curse on *minim* into the *Amidah* prayer, the Jewish community finalized its breach with Christianity. Currently the prayer reads: "And for the slanderers let there be no hope; and may all wickedness perish in an instant; and may all Your enemies be cut down speedily. May you speedily uproot, smash, cast down, and humble the wanton sinners—speedily in our days. Blessed are You, HASHEM (LORD), Who breaks enemies and humbles wanton sinners."[32]

Early versions included mention of the *Notserim*, asking God to mark a border between rabbinic and Jewish-Christian communities.

One early version from the Cairo Geniza, a place tourists still visit in Old Cairo, reveals the framework which may have originated during the last three decades of the first century: "And for apostates let there be no hope; and may the insolent kingdom be quickly uprooted, in our days. And may the Nazarenes and the heretics perish quickly; and may they be erased from the Book of Life; and may they not be inscribed with the righteous. Blessed art thou, Lord, who humblest the insolent."[33]

Minim were banned from performing any religious or ritual functions within the community. Apparently, they were treated as though they were dead, so family members were enjoined to mourn for them. Later, in the face of the individual's physical death, family members were barred from participating in any form of mourning. Instead they were to rejoice.[34]

This section of Matthew's Passion narrative ends as Pilate "scourged Jesus, [and] delivered him to be crucified" (Matthew 27:26).

Mocking by the Gentiles (Matthew 27:27–30)

In an act of intense dramatic irony, "the soldiers of the governor took Jesus into the common hall, and gathered unto him the whole band of soldiers. And they stripped him, and put on him a scarlet robe. And when they had platted a crown of thorns, they put it upon his head, and a reed in his right hand: and they bowed the knee before him, and mocked him, saying, Hail, King of the Jews! And they spit upon him, and took the reed, and smote him on the head" (Matthew 27:27–30).

Matthew's original Jewish audience, as during the Jewish hearing, may have easily recalled Isaiah's description of the Suffering Servant: "I gave my back to the smiters, and my cheeks to them that plucked off the hair; I hid not my face from shame and spitting" (Isaiah 50:6). Here an additional description may bear on the account: "But he was wounded for our transgressions, he was bruised for our iniquities: the chastisement of our peace was upon him; and *with his stripes we are healed*" (Isaiah 53:5; emphasis added). Matthew used this same passage, expanding it to include the previous verses from

Isaiah also (see Matthew 8:17), but it seems likely that the latter part of the verse may have evoked recollection of the prophesy. It did for Peter (see 1 Peter 2:24).

While Matthew notes the mocking of Jesus by the Romans, he also reveals to his Jewish audience that when the soldiers mocked Jesus as the King of the Jews, they did so to dishonor the Jews. The mocking, therefore, may have a couple of purposes: first, to demonstrate to the Jews "how Romans would deal with anyone who would try to rule in their place," and second, "it serves to insult the Judeans by portraying their king as a naked slave for all to mock."[35]

From the Jewish leaders' accusations to the Roman condemnation, those who exercised power over Jesus denied him justice, and each physically mistreated him. In the end they all, including Judas, attempted unsuccessfully to deny responsibility for the shedding of innocent blood.

Golgotha (Matthew 27:26, 31–33)

Matthew next describes the action from Jesus' scourging to the place of execution, Golgotha: "Then released he [Pilate] Barabbas unto them: and when he had scourged Jesus, he delivered him to be crucified. . . . And after that they had mocked him, they took the robe off from him, and put his own raiment on him, and led him away to crucify him. And as they came out, they found a man of Cyrene, Simon by name: him they compelled to bear his cross. And . . . they were come unto a place called Golgotha, that is to say, a place of *burial*" (JST, Matthew 27:26, 31–33; emphasis added).

Two Bandits (Matthew 27:38–44)

The Gospels agree that others were executed with Jesus. Matthew states: "Then were there two thieves crucified with him; one on the right hand, and another on the left" (Matthew 27:38). Identified in the King James Version of Matthew as *thieves*, the men in this passage, as in Mark's account, are described as *bandits* or *robbers*, an important difference in first-century usage as noted above. John described Barabbas in this same way (see above). Luke uses the term *malefactors* (Greek *kakourgoi*, meaning "evildoers") to describe the two individuals (see Luke 23:33), whereas John talks only of *others* (see John 19:18).[36]

Ascertaining exactly what Matthew intended by describing these two as bandits is problematic because banditry was a "phenomenon of great complexity which [could] assume various forms, some of which involve[d] resistance against the existing social order."[37] While it is "impossible to distinguish resistance against Rome as the foreign power from resistance against the Jewish ruling class which represented the Roman authority in Judea," many agree that banditry in Judea was motivated more by "ideology and religion" than "economic or antisocial elements."[38]

Again, Matthew and his audience probably saw in this historical incident another fulfilment of ancient prophecy. In fact, Jesus himself quotes Isaiah: "For I say unto you, that this that is written must yet be accomplished in me, And he was reckoned among the transgressors: for the things concerning me have an end" (see Luke 22:37). However, it is more likely the text found in Psalm 22 that came to mind to the original audience of Matthew: "The assembly of the wicked [evildoers] have inclosed me: they pierced my hands and my feet" (Psalm 22:16). As noted earlier, Psalm 22 is full of allusions to Jesus' suffering and death.

Regarding this particular episode the Psalmist wrote: "But I am a worm, and no man; a reproach of men, and despised of the people. All they that see me laugh me to scorn [they taunted me]: they shoot out the lip, they shake the head, saying, He trusted on the Lord that he would deliver him: let him deliver him, seeing he delighted in him" (Psalm 22:6–8).

Now read carefully Matthew's account: "And they that passed by reviled him, wagging [shaking] their heads, and saying, Thou that destroyest the temple, and buildest it in three days, save thyself. If thou be the Son of God, come down from the cross. Likewise also the chief priests mocking him, with the scribes and elders, said, He saved others; himself he cannot save. If he be the King of Israel, let him now come down from the cross, and we will believe him. He trusted in God; let him deliver him now, if he will have him: for he said, I am the Son of God. The thieves also, which were crucified with him, cast the same in his teeth" (Matthew 27:39–44).

Again we discover a play on three—the triple taunting from those that passed by, the Jewish leaders, and the bandits themselves. Luke gives a different insight to the bandits (see Luke 23:39–43).

Jesus' Final Prayer (Matthew 27:46)

Matthew gives us a transliteration of Jesus' Aramaic cry and then a translation of the words in Greek: "And about the ninth hour Jesus cried with a loud voice, saying, Eli, Eli, lama sabachthani? That is to say, My God, my God, why hast thou forsaken me?" (Matthew 27:46). For Matthew these are Jesus' final discernible words (see Matthew 27:50). Mark's rendering of the death cry is: "And at the ninth hour Jesus cried with a loud voice, saying, Eloi, Eloi, lama sabachthani? which is, being interpreted, My God, my God, why hast thou forsaken me?" (Mark 15:34). The variant transliteration of Jesus' words, quoted from Psalm 22:1 (Hebrew or Aramaic version?), probably demonstrates the difficulty the authors had in reproducing Jesus' exact words in a Greek text.

Note that Matthew frames his Passion narrative with two prayers: the first, "O my Father, if it be possible, let this cup pass from me: nevertheless not as I will, but as thou wilt" (Matthew 26:39) and the second, the one noted here (see Matthew 27:46). Matthew uses this literary tool to graphically show Jesus' struggle to accomplish the divine plan.

In these two prayers Matthew provides a warning and a consolation to the reader about the cost of discipleship. First, disciples must accept the Father's will just as Jesus did when in Gethsemane. Second, during our most difficult struggles we might ask God: "Why have you forsaken me?" The answer to this last question is: He has always been there.

Last Words (JST, Matthew 27:50)

The Joseph Smith Translation states: "Jesus, when he had cried again with a loud voice, *saying, Father, it is finished, thy will is done,* yielded up the ghost" (JST, Matthew 27:50).

Poetic Septrain (Matthew 27:51–53)

Matthew continues his account with seven events: "And, behold, the veil of the temple was rent in twain from the top to the bottom; and the earth did quake, and the rocks rent; And the graves were opened; and many bodies of the saints which slept arose, and came out of the graves after his resurrection, and went into the holy city, and appeared unto many" (Matthew 27:51–53).

Reaction (Matthew 27:54)

Matthew adds: "Now when the centurion, and they that were with him, watching Jesus, saw the earthquake, and those things that were done, *they feared greatly*, saying, Truly this was the Son of God" (Matthew 27:54; emphasis added). Like the other Gospel writers, Matthew tells us of the centurion's confession but adds that "*they feared greatly*." This spontaneous praise counterbalances the soldiers' earlier maltreatment of Jesus (see Matthew 27:26–37).

The End and the Beginning

Parallels with the beginning of his Gospel narrative are important and include the following details: dreams (Matthew 1:20; 27:19); gentile witnesses (Matthew 2:1; 27:54); physical phenomena (Matthew 2:2; 27:51); conpiracies (Matthew 2:8; 27:1); opposition from the political leader, chief priests, elders, and scribes (Matthew 2:3–4; 27:1–2); and angelic involvement (Matthew 2:13; 28:2).

Burial (Matthew 27:55–66)

The Pharisees surface again in the narrative as Matthew reveals their efforts, along with the chief priests, to discredit Jesus one more time. This passage probably implicitly demonstrates what John makes explicit (see John 18:3) regarding the Pharisees' actions during the last twenty-four hours: "Now the next day, that followed the day of the preparation, the *chief priests* and *Pharisees* came together unto Pilate, saying, Sir, we remember that that deceiver said, while he was yet alive, After three days I will rise again. Command therefore that the sepulchre be made sure until the third day, lest his disciples come by night, and steal him away, and say unto the people, He is risen from the dead: so the last error shall be worse than the first. Pilate said unto them, Ye have a watch: go your way, make it as sure as ye can. So they went, and made the sepulchre sure, sealing the stone, and setting a watch" (Matthew 27:62–66; emphasis added).

Conclusion

The story of Jesus' suffering, arrest, trial, condemnation, execution, and burial is the central focus of Matthew's entire Gospel narrative. They are in fact the key elements in God's plan for redemption for humankind. Matthew wanted the reader to know the necessity of Jesus' suffering and death (see Matthew 16:21; 17:22–23). And in the end, Matthew records Jesus' command that his disciples must take up the cross and follow him (see Matthew 10:38; 16:24).

NOTES

1. A well-written introduction to Matthew and his Gospel is Robert L. Millet, "The Testimony of Matthew," in *Studies in Scripture, Volume Five: The Gospels*, Kent P. Jackson and Robert L. Millet, eds. (Salt Lake City: Deseret Book Company, 1986), 38–60.

2. Bart D. Ehrman, *The New Testament and Other Early Christian Writings: A Reader* (New York: Oxford University Press, 1998), 9.

3. A prominent contemporary spokesman for Matthew's priority in the Latter-day Saint community is Robert L. Millet; see Millet, "The Testimony of Matthew," 60, endnote 30.

4. See Dean C. Jessee, "Joseph Smith and the Beginning of Mormon Record Keeping," in *The Prophet Joseph: Essays on the Life and Mission of Joseph Smith*, Larry C. Porter and Susan Easton Black, eds. (Salt Lake City: Deseret Book Company, 1988), 138–60.

5. The Aramaic name is built on the Hebrew words *nātan* "he gave," and *Yah(u)*, a shortened form of "Yahweh"; see Dennis C. Duling,

"Matthew" in *Anchor Bible Dictionary*, 6 vols. (New York: Doubleday, 1992), 4:618.

6. Two excellent publications provide a review of Old Testament quotations found in the New Testament: a general and easily accessible one is Robert G. Bratcher, *Old Testament Quotations in the New Testament* (New York: United Bible Societies, 1984), and a more technical effort which includes the Hebrew and Greek texts is Gleason L. Archer and Gregory Chirichigno, *Old Testament Quotations in the New Testament* (Chicago: Moody Press, 1983).

7. Louis H. Feldman, trans., *Josephus*, 10 vols. (Cambridge, Massachusetts: Harvard University Press, 1926), 9:63, 65, 69.

8. Zvi Greenhut, "The 'Caiaphas' Tomb in the North of Jerusalem," *'Atiqot* (English Series), 21 (1992):63–71.

9. Frederick J. Cwiekowski, *The Beginnings of the Church* (New York: Paulist Press, 1988), 37.

10. Stephen E. Robinson, "The Setting of the Gospels," *Studies in Scriptures, Volume 5: The Gospels*, 29.

11. For a slightly different but fundamentally similar response see Anthony J. Saldarini, "Understanding Matthew's Vitriol," *Bible Review* 13 (April 1997): 32–39.

12. See Raymond E. Brown, *The Death of the Messiah: From Gethsemane to the Grave*, 2 vols. (New York: Doubleday, 1994), 1:62.

13. For a discussion of this event, see W. F. Albright and C. S. Mann, *Matthew: A New Translation with Introduction and Commentary* (Garden City, New York: Doubleday, 1986), 314–15.

14. W. F. Albright and C. S. Mann, *The Anchor Bible: Matthew* (Garden City, New York: Doubleday, 1986), 314.

15. Ibid., 316.

16. Michael Macrone, *Brush Up Your Bible!* (San Francisco: Harper-Collins Publishers, 1993), 228.

17. Bruce Malina and Richard L. Rohrbaugh, *Social Science Commentary on the Synoptic Gospels* (Minneapolis: Fortress Press, 1992), 155.

18. See M. Jack Suggs, Katharine Doob Sakenfeld, and James R. Mueller, eds., *The Oxford Study Bible* (New York: Oxford University Press, 1992), 1299.

19. Max Zerwick and Mary Grosvenor, *A Grammatical Analysis of the Greek New Testament* (Rome: Biblical Institute Press, 1981), 87.

20. Gerhard Kittel, ed., *Theological Dictionary of the New Testament*, 10

vols. (Grand Rapids, Michigan: Wm. B. Eerdmans Publishing Company, 1991), 1:470.

21. The following insight gleamed from Jerome Murphy-O'Connor, "What Really Happened at Gethsemane?" *Bible Review* 14 (April 1998): 32–33.

22. See footnote *a* to Matthew 26:37 in the LDS edition of the King James Version of the Bible.

23. *Mishnah* (Sanhedrin 7.5); see Herbert Danby, trans., *The Mishnah* (New York: Oxford University Press, 1983), 392.

24. *Bewrayeth* comes from the verb *bewray* which means: "to reveal, expose, or make known"; see *Oxford English Dictionary*, 2 vols. (New York: Oxford University Press, 1973), 1:222.

25. See Leen and Kathleen Ritmeyer, "Akeldama: Potter's Field or High Priest's Tomb?" *Biblical Archaeology Review* 20 (November/December 1194):22–35, 76.

26. Bruce M. Metzger, *A Textual Commentary on the Greek New Testament* (New York: United Bible Societies, 1971), 67–68.

27. John W. Welch, "Robbers in First-Century Judea," in *Masada and the World of the New Testament* (Provo: FARMS, 1997), 150.

28. P. Parker, "Barabbas," in *The Interpreter's Dictionary of the Bible*, 4 vols. (New York: Abingdon Press, 1962), 1:353.

29. Kent P. Jackson, "Revolutionaries in the First Century," in *Masada and the World of the New Testament* (Provo: FARMS, 1997), 129.

30. Summary based on R. J. Zwi Werbloswky and Geoffrey Wigoder, eds., *The Oxford Dictionary of the Jewish Religion* (New York: Oxford University Press, 1997), 242, 467.

31. As cited in Werbloswky and Wigoder, *The Oxford Dictionary of the Jewish Religion*, 242.

32. *The Complete Art Scroll*, trans. Siddur Rabbi Nosson Scherman (New York: Mesorah Publishers, 1984), 107.

33. As cited in Werbloswky and Wigoder, *The Oxford Dictionary of the Jewish Religion*, 467.

34. Ibid.

35. Malina and Rohrbaugh, *Social Science Commentary*, 164.

36. Welch, "Robbers in First-Century Judea," 149–50.

37. Benjamin Isaac, "Banditry," in *The Anchor Bible Dictionary* (New York: Doubleday, 1992), 1:575.

38. Ibid., 578.

*L*UKE'S PASSION NARRATIVE

L uke, also known as Lucas, is generally identified as the "beloved physician" and coworker of Paul (see Colossians 4:14; 2 Timothy 4:11; Philemon 1:24).[1] Many scholars believe he was a gentile convert and the author of a unified literary work, the longest in the New Testament, of two parts (namely, Luke and Acts).[2] The introductory note in both Luke and Acts indicates that the writings of Luke are dedicated to "the most excellent Theophilus" and may have been intended for a gentile Christian audience (see Luke 1:1–4; Acts 1:1). As one scholar notes, "these two books were originally written as a single, linked, two-volume work so divided because each part filled a standard scroll. The end of the [Gospel of Luke] leaves the readers hanging for the start of the [Acts of the Apostles]."[3]

The Gospel of Luke was probably written sometime in the 60s or early 70s; like Matthew, Luke apparently used Mark's Gospel as one of the important sources in writing his story. Unlike Matthew, however, Luke (1,149 verses) reproduces just over half of Mark (about 65 percent), or about 350 of Mark's 661 verses.[4] Luke probably used the collection of sayings designated "Q" as did Matthew; from these and other sources (see Luke 1:1–4) he wrote his own distinctive portrayal of Jesus. The basic story line of this Gospel is similar to those of Mark and Matthew, yet Luke adds significant details to the Passion narrative.

The Final Section of the Gospel

Following his discussion of Jesus' ministry in Jerusalem during the final week, Luke commences another important section of the story. In this distinct division of the Gospel narrative, Jesus comes to the climax of his "departure," mentioned in Luke 9:31 as the exodus, as he begins his ascent to his Father. The ascent begun in Luke's Passion narrative (see Luke 22:1–23:56) will be completed in the final division of the book, known as the Resurrection narrative (see Luke 23:56–24:53). Luke begins his Passion narrative with Judas' betrayal of Jesus, the Last Supper, and the farewell discourse (see Luke 22:7–38).

The Last Supper (Luke 22:14–20)

Only Luke preserves this particular statement by Jesus: "And when the hour was come, he sat down, and the twelve apostles with him. And he said unto them, *With desire I have desired to eat this passover with you before I suffer:* For I say unto you, I will not any more eat thereof, until it be fulfilled in the kingdom of God. And he took the cup, and gave thanks, and said, Take this, and divide it among yourselves: for I say unto you, I will not drink of the fruit of the vine, until the kingdom of God shall come" (Luke 22:14–18; emphasis added). Jesus' statement: *"With desire I have desired to eat this passover with you before I suffer"* reveals the importance he attached to the meal.

The Joseph Smith Translation adds to verse 16: "For I say unto you, I will not any more eat thereof, until it be fulfilled *which is written in the prophets concerning me. Then I will partake with you,* in the kingdom of God" (JST, Luke 22:16; emphasis added).

Variant manuscripts preserve two principal forms of this passage: first, "the longer, or traditional, text of cup-bread-cup," and second, "the shorter, or Western, text . . . omits verses 19b and 20 . . . , thereby presenting the sequence of cup-bread."[5] While some modern translations prefer the shorter version, the majority of the United Bible Societies' Greek New Testament committee, "impressed by the overwhelming preponderance of external evidence supporting the longer form, explained the origin of the shorter form as due to some scribal accident or misunderstanding."[6]

Luke continues: "And he took bread, and gave thanks, and brake it, and gave unto them, saying, This is my body which is given for you: this do in remembrance of me. Likewise also the cup after supper, saying, This cup is the new testament [covenant] in my blood, which is shed for you" (Luke 22:19–20).

Jesus Announces Judas' Betrayal (Luke 22:21–22)

In a unique transposition of Mark's order of the story, Luke shifts the prophecy of Judas' betrayal to the end of the meal (see Luke 22:13–22). While not strictly in the chronological order, Luke's desire may have been to intensify the tragedy of the moment: betrayal comes from the very one who has participated in the Passover meal of Jesus' *new* family.

Jesus Announces Peter's Denial (Luke 22:31–39)

Luke preserves additional information about Jesus' announcement of Peter's denial. In this material we learn that Jesus' interprets what is about to happen in light of a passage from Isaiah: "Therefore will I divide him a portion with the great, and he shall divide the spoil with the strong; because he hath poured out his soul unto death: and *he was numbered with the transgressors*; and he bare the sin of many, and made intercession for the transgressors" (Isaiah 53:12; emphasis added).

Luke records: "And the Lord said, Simon, Simon, behold, Satan hath desired you, that he may sift the children of the kingdom as wheat: But I have prayed for you, that your faith fail not: and when you are converted, strengthen your brethren. And he said unto him, being aggrieved, Lord, I am ready to go with you, both into prison and unto death. And the Lord said, I tell you, Peter, that the cock shall not crow this day, before that you will thrice deny that you know me. And he said unto them, When I sent you without purse, and scrip, and shoes, lacked ye any thing? And they said, Nothing. Then said he unto them, I say unto you again, he who hath a purse, let him take it, and likewise his scrip: and he who hath no sword, let him sell his garment, and buy one. For I say unto you, this that is written must yet be accomplished in me, *And he was reckoned among the transgressors*: for the things concerning me have an end. And they said, Lord, behold, here are two swords. And he said unto them, it is enough" (JST, Luke 22:31–38; emphasis added).

Notice that the Joseph Smith Translation stated that Peter was "aggrieved." Why? First of all the word means "to cause grief, to inflict injury on: wrong."[7] It may be that Peter is unwilling to accept the scenario just announced by Jesus (see Luke 22:31–33). Additionally, he feels he has been judged wrongly by Jesus, thus he protests the accusation. The text seems to support this interpretation.

Luke provides a transition to the next scene: "And he came out, and went, as he was wont, to the mount of Olives; and his disciples also followed him" (Luke 22:39).

At the Mount of Olives (Luke 22:40–45)

Luke's account of the drama on the mount is marked by delicacy and tenderness. He seems unable to bring himself to report some details which seem too distressing: for example, Luke does not say that Jesus was scourged nor that Judas actually kissed Jesus. He does, however, make us aware of the magnitude of the terrible struggle between Jesus and the powers of evil. The Passion is the last decisive contest. Jesus comes out of it as victor through his patience—a word that is not a good rendering of the Greek hypomonē, which suggests the attitude of the believer enduring blows in his trial as he is sustained by God.[8]

The decisive struggle occurs in "the place" at the Mount of Olives. Luke does not provide his gentile audience the name Gethsemane as it was his practice to avoid Semitic names and expressions. Here in great agony, the Lord began his great atoning rite: "And when he was at the place, he said unto them, Pray that ye enter not into temptation. And he was withdrawn from them about a stone's cast, and kneeled down, and prayed, saying, Father, if thou be willing, remove this cup from me: nevertheless not my will, but thine, be done" (Luke 22:40–42).

Then, comforted by God through an angelic messenger, Jesus emerges victorious (see Luke 22:43). Now at peace, held in his Father's arms, he can be wholly reconciled to his God.

Luke uses the Greek agōnia in 22:44 to indicate Jesus' intense anxiety over what will happen to him. The Greek meaning of agōnia is the "athlete's state of mind before the contest, agony, dread."[9] As a result, Luke reports, Jesus "prayed more earnestly: and his sweat was as it were great drops of blood falling down to the ground" (Luke 22:44). Although some ancient manuscripts omit 22:43–44 (Codex Vaticanus), it "was known to Justin Martyr, Irenaeus, Tatian, and Hippolytus in the second century."[10] Restoration scriptures confirm this view (see D&C 19:18).

Luke again softens Mark's frank portrayal of the disciples. Here, instead of explaining that they fell asleep while their Master went-through his most terrible suffering, Luke says: "And when he rose up from prayer, and was come to his disciples, he found them *sleeping for sorrow*" (Luke 22:45; emphasis added).

As we conclude this section, we should note that "several elements in this scene are reminiscent of the Lord's prayer (e.g. vv. 40, 42, 46)."[11] Luke recorded earlier: "And it came to pass, that, as he was praying in a certain place, when he ceased, one of his disciples said unto him, Lord, teach us to pray, as John also taught his disciples. And he said unto them, When ye pray, say, Our Father which art in heaven, Hallowed be thy name. Thy kingdom come. Thy will be done, as in heaven, so in earth. Give us day by day our daily bread. And forgive us our sins; for we also forgive every one that is indebted to us. And lead us not into temptation; but deliver us from evil" (Luke 11:1–4).

Judas and the Arresting Party (Luke 22:47–51)

Events happen swiftly now in Luke's account. Judas arrives with his newfound allies and attempts to salute Jesus. Jesus reminds Judas that it is the Son of man whom he thus betrays. One of the disciples (we learn from John that it was Peter), anxious to do something, smites off the ear of the high priest's servant. Jesus "touched [the servant's] ear, and healed him" (Luke 22:51; see verses 47–51). He helps his opponent, even in the midst of his own danger. The physician Luke most likely sees Jesus as the greatest healer. Whether for friend or foe, Jesus' mission is one of reconciliation and healing, and while this may be the last physical healing mentioned in the Gospel, it is not the last of Jesus' healing activity.

Jewish Leadership (Luke 22:52)

Luke's writings reveal more than any other Gospel author the close relationship between Annas and Caiaphas, Jewish leaders during this period (see Luke 3:2; Acts 4:6). What we learn from Luke is that Annas's influence lasted far longer than his appointment as high priest from A.D. 6–15. Through five sons, apparently a son-in-law, Caiaphas, and a grandson who all served as high priests during the first century, Annas influenced Jewish religious affairs for nearly forty years.

Caiaphas was involved with Jesus' interrogation, and one of Annas's sons (Annas the younger) purportedly accused James, Jesus' brother and leader of the Church in Jerusalem, and delivered him up to be stoned shortly before A.D. 70.[12] In fact, the first three Christian martyrs were probably executed under the tenure of this family (see Acts 6–7; 12). Nonetheless, for Luke, the focus of the proceedings is on the group of high priests—except for three verses (see Luke 3:2; 22:50, 54), the noun always appears in the plural in Luke when speaking of the authorities questioning Jesus, emphasizing the organization rather than individuals such as Annas or Caiaphas.[13]

Jesus Before Pilate (Luke 23:1–5)

Luke identifies the charges against Jesus: "We found this fellow perverting the nation, and forbidding to give tribute to Caesar, saying that he himself is Christ a King" (Luke 23:2), making the charges against Jesus quite clear: he is accused of opposing the payment of Roman taxes and claiming to be king. Both actions are seditious. Earlier in Luke's narrative, he provides the reader information to refute these charges (see Luke 20:20–26).

In the course of the hearing, Pilate announces Jesus' innocence on three separate occasions (see Luke 23:4, 14, 22). After the first pronouncement, the Jewish leaders "were the more fierce, saying, He stirreth up the people, teaching throughout all Jewry, beginning from Galilee to this place" (Luke 23:5). Here one sees the impact and consequence of Jesus' ministry.

John P. Meier observed: "Herod Antipas, Pontius Pilate, the

high priest and the Sadducean party, the scribes, and the pious lay movement of Pharisees all had their varied reasons for being opposed to Jesus—and, unlike the Pharisees, the other individuals or groups had ways of getting rid of him legally. Moerover, in the great festal crowds of Passover, there was always the possibility of lynch-mob justice or assassination."[14]

Jesus Before Herod Antipas (Luke 23:6–12)

The next scene is found only in Luke: "When Pilate heard of Galilee, he asked if the man were a Galilæan. And as soon as he knew that he belonged unto Herod's jurisdiction, he sent him to Herod, who himself also was at Jerusalem at that time" (Luke 23:6–7). The Herod mentioned here is Herod Antipas, the son of Herod the Great. Luke continues his story by outlining what took place when Jesus appeared before Antipas (see Luke 23:8–11). While subtle, this passage suggests that Jesus was subjected to mockery rather than violent abuse by Herod's men.

Luke highlights the immediate impact of these political leaders coming into contact with Jesus: "And the same day Pilate and Herod were made friends together: for before they were at enmity between themselves" (Luke 23:12). This reminds us of Jesus' healing the ear of one among the party who arrested him in Gethsemane (see Luke 22:51) and prepares us for Jesus' contact with the "malefactor" on the cross (see Luke 23:39–43). Luke, the beloved physician, is interested in the immediate benefits (physical, emotional, and spiritual) emanating from Jesus, who in this case heals a human relationship as he moves between Herod and Pilate, supplanting discord with harmony.

Condemning an Innocent Man (Luke 23:4–23)

As noted, the reader is told explicitly in three different passages that Pilate believed Jesus innocent of any crime worthy of death: (1) "Then said Pilate to the chief priests and to the people, *I find no fault in this man*" (Luke 23:4; emphasis added). (2) "And Pilate, when he had called together the chief priests and the rulers and the people, said unto them, Ye have brought this man unto me, as one that per-

verteth the people; and, *behold, I, having examined him before you,
have found no fault in this man* touching those things whereof ye accuse him: No, nor yet Herod: for I sent you to him; and, lo, nothing
worthy of death is done unto him. I will therefore chastise him, and
release him. (For of necessity he must release one unto them at the
feast.)" (Luke 23:13–17; emphasis added). (3) "And he said unto
them the third time, Why, what evil hath he done? I have found no
cause of death in him: I will therefore chastise him, and let him go"
(Luke 23:22).

Like Mark before, Luke tells of the twice-repeated shouts of the
people, "Crucify him, crucify him" (Luke 23:21); "they were instant
[urging] with loud voices, requiring [demanding] that he might be
crucified" (Luke 23:23). Luke ends his description with the pithy yet
trenchant phrase, "and the voices of them and of the chief priests
prevailed" (Luke 23:23).

A Great Multitude of People (Luke 22:27–31)

Luke again provides important information about the crowds. In
a unique scene Luke tells us about Jesus' statements on the way to
Calvary. He reports: "And there followed him a great company of
people, and of women, which also bewailed and lamented him. But
Jesus turning unto them said, Daughters of Jerusalem, weep not for
me, but weep for yourselves, and for your children. For, behold, the
days are coming, in the which they shall say, Blessed are the barren,
and the wombs that never bare, and the paps which never gave suck.
Then shall they begin to say to the mountains, Fall on us; and to the
hills, Cover us. For if they do these things in a green tree, what shall
be done in the dry?" (Luke 22:27–31).

In addition to the allusion to Hosea, "The high places also of
Aven, the sin of Israel, shall be destroyed: the thorn and the thistle
shall come up on their altars; and they shall say to the mountains,
Cover us; and to the hills, Fall on us" (Hosea 10:8), Luke informs us
of a "great company" which followed Jesus, among them women
"which also bewailed and lamented him" (Luke 23:27). This may
well support our earlier argument that we should be careful in distin-
guishing between groups mentioned in the Passion narratives (see
page 56).

The Place Called Calvary (Luke 23:26–48)

As Jesus is led away to be crucified, "they laid hold upon one Simon, a Cyrenian, coming out of the country, and on him they laid the cross, that he might bear it after Jesus" (Luke 23:26). Omitting the names of Simon's sons indicates that Luke's audience did not know them. However, highlighting the fact that Simon followed Jesus might indicate that he was one of Jesus' disciples.

Luke's narrative continues with what might be one of the most beautiful verses of scripture and found only in his narrative: "And when they were come to the place, which is called Calvary, there they crucified him, and the malefactors, one on the right hand, and the other on the left. Then said Jesus, Father, forgive them; for they know not what they do" (Luke 23:33–34). The Joseph Smith Translation reads at this point: "Then said Jesus, Father, forgive them; for they know not what they do (Meaning the soldiers who crucified him,)" (JST, Luke 23:34).

Bent in torment on the cruel cross of Calvary—the most powerful visual symbol of imperial Roman tyranny and callous disrespect for human life—Jesus, who offered forgiveness throughout his mortal ministry, now pleads for those dutifully and almost mechanically performing their task: executing another victim of Roman justice. The original audience already knew that Jesus preached, "Love your enemies, do good to them which hate you, bless them that curse you, and pray for them which despitefully use you" (Luke 6:27–28). Here in a dramatic way, he practices what he preached. While giving up his life on the cruel cross, Jesus prays to his Father to forgive them.

While our King James Version provides the traditional place-name for the site as Calvary (see Luke 23:33), the Greek text simply identifies it with the Greek word for skull (*kranion*) instead of the Semitic word used by the other Gospel authors. From this Greek word we derive our modern term *cranium* (the part enclosing the brain). Calvary, derived from the Latin *calvaria* (skull), has been popular in English since John Wycliff's translation of the New Testament appeared in 1382.

Luke continues: "And the people stood beholding. And the rulers also with them derided him, saying, He saved others; let him save himself, if he be Christ, the chosen of God. And the soldiers also mocked him, coming to him, and offering him vinegar [probably a sedative mixed with wine], and saying, If thou be the king of the Jews, save thyself. And a superscription also was written over him in letters of *Greek*, and *Latin*, and *Hebrew*, THS IS THE KING OF THE JEWS" (Luke 23:35–38; emphasis added).

For Luke, the proclamation in the two major languages of the Empire (Greek and Latin), along with the one in the language of the Jews (Hebrew) announces Jesus' universal kingship. He continues: "And it was about the sixth hour, and there was a darkness over all the earth until the ninth hour. And the sun was darkened, and the veil of the temple was rent in the midst. And when Jesus had cried with a loud voice, he said, Father, into thy hands I commend my spirit: and having said thus, he gave up the ghost" (Luke 23:44–46).

The tearing of the temple veil just before Jesus' death is another feature in which Luke departs from the other Gospels. Though the synoptic Gospels agree on the reality of this event, Matthew and Mark place it after Jesus' death (see Matthew 27:51; Mark 15:38).

After the curtain is rent, Jesus addresses God: "Father, into thy hands I commend my spirit" (Luke 23:46). This action symbolizes Jesus' communing with the Father, who may have been present in the temple at the last moment before his death.

The cry that Jesus utters on the cross is not a scream of human suffering before death; rather it is the evening prayer known to every Jew: "Into thy hands I commend my spirit." Jesus, however, prefaces it with the term that marks his unparalleled intimacy with God: "Father" (see Luke 23:46). Jesus dies in peace, at one with God.

The crucifixion itself is the last violent act by men in the life of him who promised them life after death. Yet Jesus' promise to the thief and to all of us is not one of mere survival after death, but more accurately a glorious future beyond death (see Luke 23:43).

Luke records the fact that the Roman centurion under the cross commented on Jesus death: "Certainly this was a righteous man" (Luke 23:47). While Luke's statement does not match Mark's, "Truly this man was the Son of God" (Mark 15:39) or Matthew's, "Truly this was the Son of God" (Matthew 27:54), it seems likely that his rendering reflects the basic idea for his gentile audience. While we cannot be certain of the exact words, we can assume that the Gospel authors captured the essence of what the centurion said on this occasion.

The Disciples (Luke 23:49)

Luke records the presence of disciples at the place of execution: "And all his acquaintance, and the women that followed him from Galilee, stood afar off, beholding these things" (Luke 23:49). Beginning with the arrest and ending with the violent death on the cross, the disciples are confronted with the decision whether to embrace Jesus' path of suffering as an essential part of the Father's plan and whether they are ready to do as he said earlier: "If any man will come after me, let him deny himself, and take up his cross daily, and follow me" (Luke 9:23). What seems to be clear is that the final decision will come only after the Resurrection when they come to a fuller understanding of the Passion.

Jesus' Burial (Luke 23:50–56)

Luke ends his Passion narrative: "And, behold, there was a man named Joseph, a counsellor; and he was a good man, and a just: (The same had not consented to the counsel and deed of them;) he was of Arimathæa, a city of the Jews: who also himself waited for the kingdom of God. This man went unto Pilate, and begged the body of Jesus. And he took it down, and wrapped it in linen, and laid it in a sepulchre that was hewn in stone, wherein never man before was laid. And that day was the preparation, and the sabbath drew on. And the women also, which came with him from Galilee, followed after, and beheld the sepulchre, and how his body was laid. And they returned, and prepared spices and ointments; and rested the sabbath day according to the commandment" (Luke 23:50–56). Note that the "women delay the burial anointing because the sabbath has begun and work must be postponed (Deut. 5:12–14)."[15]

While technically this ends the narrative of Jesus' passion, in many ways the climax of the story is found in Luke 24:50–53.

NOTES

1. An excellent introductory essay on Luke and his Gospel is Richard Lloyd Anderson, "The Testimony of Luke," in *Studies in Scripture, Volume Five: The Gospels*, Kent P. Jackson and Robert L. Millet, eds. (Salt Lake City: Deseret Book Company, 1986), 88–108.

2. Some believe that Luke is the unnamed disciple who walked with the risen Christ and Cleopas on the road to Emmaus (Luke 24:13–35); see Bruce R. McConkie, *Doctrinal New Testament Commentary: Volume I, The Gospels* (Salt Lake City: Bookcraft, 1965), 850, and *The Mortal Messiah: Book 4* (Salt Lake City: Deseret Book Company, 1982), 275.

3. John Dominic Crossan, *Who Killed Jesus? Exposing the Roots of Anti-Semitism in the Gospel Story of the Death of Jesus* (San Francisco: Harper-Collins Publishers, 1995), 19.

4. Edwin D. Freed, *The New Testament: A Critical Introduction* (Belmont, California: Wadsworth Publishing Company, 1986), 45.

5. Bruce M. Metzger, *A Textual Commentary on the Greek New Testament* (New York: United Bible Societies, 1975), 173–74.

6. Ibid., 176.

7. *The Merriam-Webster Dictionary* (Springfield, Massachusetts: Merriam-Webster, Inc., 1997), 33.

8. Arndt and Gingrich, *A Greek-English Lexicon of the New Testament*, 854.

9. See Max Zerwick and Mary Grosvenor, *A Grammatical Analysis of the Greek New Testament* (Rome: Biblical Institute Press, 1981), 237.

10. G. B. Caird argues, "Its omission is best explained as the work of a scribe who felt that this picture of Jesus overwhelmed with human weakness was incompatible with his own belief in the Divine Son who shared the omnipotence of his Father." G. B. Caird, *The Gospel of St. Luke* (New York: Penguin Books, 1985), 243.

11. M. Jack Suggs, Katharine Doob Sakenfeld, and James R. Mueller, eds., *The Oxford Study Bible* (New York: Oxford University Press, 1992), 1360–61.

12. Josephus, *Antiquities* 20.ix.1 (see lines 198–200); see Louis H. Feldman, trans., *Josephus IX: Jewish Antiquities* (Cambridge, Massachusetts: Harvard University Press, 1965), 9:107

13. See Bruce Chilton, "Caiaphas," *The Anchor Bible Dictionary*, 6 vols. (New York: Doubleday, 1992), 1:804.

14. Raymond E. Brown, *The New Jerome Bible Commentary* (Englewood Cliffs, New Jersey: Prentice Hall, 1990), 1326.

15. Suggs, Sakenfeld, and Mueller, *The Oxford Study Bible*, 1363.

$\mathcal{J}$OHN'S PASSION NARRATIVE

O ne of the most beloved writings of the New Testament, the Gospel of John has long been recognized for its distinctive portrayal of Jesus.[1] Sometimes called the Fourth Gospel, its author is identified as John, a disciple of Jesus and one of the Twelve (see Matthew 10:1–2; Mark 3:14, 17; 14:32–33; Luke 6:13–14; 9:54; John 20:1–2).[2] The Greek name found in the Gospels *Iōannēs* is derived from the Hebrew or Aramaic *Yôhānān*, a name common among the Jews during the Hellenistic period, especially among the priesthood.[3] He is identified as one of the sons of Zebedee and the brother of James. It is clear that he and his father and brother were fishermen (Matthew 4:21–22; Mark 1:19–20; Luke 5:10 adds that James and John "were partners with Simon" Peter).

In ancient documents, the order of names in a list usually suggests age or social standing; therefore, it is assumed that John was younger than James because his name usually appears second. James and John are called *Boanērges*, which Mark translates as "sons of thunder" (Mark 3:17). In all likelihood, his mother was Salome, the sister of Mary, making him Jesus' cousin.[4]

Many have already noticed that "John has some significant stylistic features."[5] These features are important since "John is a Gospel where style and theology are intimately wedded."[6] Writing some sixty years after Jesus' suffering and death, John meditated on the passion for a long time before committing it to writing. Unexpectedly, the oldest textual evidence of the New Testament in existence is a torn papyrus page containing parts of John 18:31–33 on the *recto* (front side) and 18:37–38 on the *verso* (back side).[7] A beautiful photographic copy of the papyrus is reproduced in Allan Millard's *Discoveries from the Time of Jesus*.[8] This papyrus fragment, discovered in the sand of Egypt, is known as the Papyrus Ryland Greek 457 or P52. This small piece measures only 3.5 by 2.3 inches and is generally dated between A.D. 100 and 125. The text preserved is part of John's Passion narrative and brings us very close to the original composition.

In John's Passion narrative (see John 12:1–19:42), he chooses the episodes that have the most significance to the faithful. Additionally, John's Gospel is written on the supposition that the synoptic story of the events is well known.[9]

John informs his ancient readers that Jesus was not suddenly overtaken by events, like members of the Jesus Seminar argue in our popular news magazines today. And for some modern Christians who believe Jesus' death brought salvation to humanity, even though he neither expected nor intended to bring it about, John is clear that the Passion and its effects were totally foreseen by Jesus, that he accepted the will of God, and that he drank "the cup which [his] Father hath given [him]" (John 18:11). Like Restoration scriptures and the teachings of the modern prophets and apostles of this dispensation, John's testimony is clear and certain on this important point. Yet John does not describe Jesus' passion as premeditated to the extent that it looks like suicide. All in all, John's dramatic and revealing narrative tells us how Jesus embraced and interpreted his Passion in advance as a voluntary sacrifice with cosmic significance.

The Son of Man Shall Be Lifted Up
(John 3:14; 8:28; 12:32)

John provides us with three specific statements by Jesus which are necessary to help interpret the events of his suffering and death: (1) "And as Moses lifted up the serpent in the wilderness, even so must the Son of man be lifted up" (John 3:14). (2) "Then said Jesus unto them, When ye have lifted up the Son of man, then shall ye know that I am he, and that I do nothing of myself" (John 8:28). (3) "And I, if I be lifted up from the earth, will draw all men unto me" (John 12:32).

John presents the Passion as Jesus' triumphal progress towards the Father. Jesus is never a fateful victim but is in charge: "Therefore doth my Father love me, because I lay down my life, that I might take it again. No man taketh it from me, but I lay it down of myself. I have power to lay it down, and I have power to take it again. This commandment have I received of my Father" (John 10:17–18).

Additionally stressed over and over again, Jesus knows that he is going to die, he knows what kind of death it will be, and he goes to it freely: "But there are some of you that believe not. For Jesus knew from the beginning who they were that believed not, and who should betray him" (John 6:64). "Jesus answered them, Have not I chosen you twelve, and one of you is a devil? He spake of Judas Iscariot the son of Simon [Judas, son of Simon the Iscariot]: for he it was that should betray him, being one of the twelve" (John 6:70–71).

"For he knew who should betray him; therefore said he, ye are not all clean. . . . I speak not of you all: I know whom I have chosen: but that the scripture may be fulfilled, He that eateth bread with me hath lifted up his heel against me. Now I tell you before it come, that, when it is come to pass, ye may believe that I am he. . . . When Jesus had thus said, he was troubled in spirit, and testified, and said, Verily, verily, I say unto you, that one of you shall betray me" (John 13:11, 18–19, 21). "Now are we sure that thou knowest all things, and needest not that any man should ask thee: by this we believe that thou camest forth from God" (John 16:30). "Jesus therefore, knowing all things that should come upon him, went forth, and said unto them, Whom seek ye?" (John 18:4).

John does not separate death and exaltation in his account but sees them as inextricably intertwined. The lifting of Jesus up on the cross is also the beginning of his ascension into the glory of God, whence he will send the Spirit upon the world (see John 19:30). "I, if I be lifted up from the earth, will draw all men unto me," Jesus declares (John 12:32).

To draw all men to himself is the essence of Jesus' mission, according to John's writings. He anticipates knowingly and accepts willingly death not simply as the consequence of his prophetic calling but as his last service of love. The Passion of Christ is the climax of his ministry, which offers salvation by every action.

The Last Supper (John 13–17)

The account begins: "Now before the feast of the passover, when Jesus knew that his hour was come that he should depart out of this world unto the Father, having loved his own which were in the world, he loved them unto the end" (John 13:1).

Beyond the scope of this study, John provides long extended insights to Jesus' last evening with the disciples. He does not review for us the discussion of the meal itself, since his readers already know the story. He instead chooses to provide the Saints with information not found in the synoptic Gospels. This includes the foot washing at the meal, the commandment of love, consolation for his own, the metaphor of Jesus as the true vine, a discussion of the hatred of the world, and the great intercessory prayer (see John 13–17).

The fundamental theme of these chapters is found in the very first verse of chapter 13, as recited above: "having loved his own which were in the world, he loved them unto the end." In light of the concern he demonstrated for his friends, it is no wonder that he prepares them for the shock of his death by warning them not to fall into despair and disillusion: "A little while, and ye shall not see me: and again, a little while, and ye shall see me, because I go to the Father. . . . Now Jesus knew that they were desirous to ask him, and said unto them, Do ye enquire among yourselves of that I said, A little while, and ye shall not see me: and again, a little while, and ye shall see me? Verily, verily, I say unto you, That ye shall weep and lament, but the world shall rejoice: and ye shall be sorrowful, but your sorrow shall be turned into joy. A woman when she is in travail hath sorrow, because her hour is come: but as soon as she is delivered of the child, she remembereth no more the anguish, for joy that a man is born into the world. And ye now therefore have sorrow: but I will see you again, and your heart shall rejoice, and your joy no man taketh from you. . . . I came forth from the Father, and am come into the world: again, I leave the world, and go to the Father. . . . These things I have spoken unto you, that in me ye might have peace. In the world ye shall have tribulation: but be of good cheer; I have overcome the world" (John 16:16, 19–22, 28, 33).

Table Fellowship

The ritual context of the meal itself is of prime importance to all the Gospel writers, including John. Its significance, however, is often lost to the modern reader who generally is part of the dominant fast-food culture. Anciently, to invite a person to a meal was to extend an honor. It was an offer of peace, trust, brotherhood, and forgiveness; in short, sharing a table meant sharing life.

In Judaism in particular, table fellowship means fellowship before God, for the eating of a piece of broken bread by everyone who shares in the meal brings out the fact that they all have a share in the blessing which the master of the house has spoken over the unbroken bread.

Some background might be helpful to understand the dynamics of John's Last Supper story. The Last Supper in the synoptic Gospels is the Passover dinner (a Passover *Seder*—service), whereas in John it represents the last Passover celebration for Jesus and his disciples under the old covenant, apparently held the day *before* the official Passover.

The original commandment for this celebration is found in Exodus: "And thus shall ye eat it; with your loins girded, your shoes on your feet, and your staff in your hand; and ye shall eat it in haste: it is the Lord's passover" (Exodus 12:11). Additionally, the Lord commanded the Israelites that the Passover dinner was to be celebrated each year after the Israelites entered the promised land: "And it shall come to pass, when ye be come to the land which the Lord will give you, according as he hath promised, that ye shall keep this service" (Exodus 12:25).

By the time Jesus met with his disciples on the momentous evening some two thousand years ago, the Jews no longer stood during the Passover meal. Apparently, since they had achieved their freedom and rest in the promised land, the rabbis taught that the meal should be celebrated reclining, as was the custom of the time. As a symbol of their security and safety in the promised land some adopted the Roman custom of the *triclinium*, a Latin word suggesting "an arrangement of couches on three sides of a central table for the purposes of dining."[10]

For small groups, such as the one meeting in the Upper Room of Mary's home (John Mark's mother), three couches were set around a large table, leaving one side for serving those who were eating. Apparently the custom of the day was that the guest of honor was to sit at the head of the table opposite the door. This setting may help illuminate several pasages of scripture regarding the Last Supper story. First, people reclining to eat in such a setting were in a posiiton to have someone reach their feet easily: "And supper being ended, the devil having now put into the heart of Judas Iscariot, Simon's son, to betray him; Jesus knowing that the Father had given all things into his hands, and that he was come from God, and went to God; he riseth from supper, and laid aside his garments; and took a towel, and girded himself. After that he poureth water into a basin, and began to wash the disciples' feet, and to wipe them with the towel wherewith he was girded" (John 13:2–5).

A second part of the story is found after the foot washing: "When Jesus had thus said, he was troubled in spirit, and testified, and said, Verily, verily, I say unto you, that one of you shall betray me. Then the disciples looked one on another, doubting of whom he spake. Now there was leaning on Jesus' bosom one of his disciples, whom Jesus loved. Simon Peter therefore beckoned to him, that he should ask who it should be of whom he spake. He then lying on Jesus' breast saith unto him, Lord, who is it? Jesus answered, He it is, to whom I shall give a sop, when I have dipped it. And when he had dipped the sop, he gave it to Judas Iscariot, the son of Simon" (John 13:21–26).

One can imagine Jesus reclining at dinner with John on one side and Judas on the other. Apparently, as the treasurer for the Twelve (he had "the bag"; see John 13:29), Judas probably had a place of honor on one side of Jesus; some suggest the left side. John easily, from a reclining position on Jesus' right side, could lay his head onto Jesus' bosom. Peter, however, is far enough away that he has to *nod, signal,* or, as the KJV translates the Greek word used by John, *beckon* to the disciple leaning upon Jesus' breast to obtain information.

Added to the traditional sense of honor, friendship, and service, the ritual aspect of eating with the Lord is noted in Exodus 24: "Then went up Moses, and Aaron, Nadab, and Abihu, and seventy of the elders of Israel: and they saw the God of Israel: and there was under his feet as it were a paved work of a sapphire stone, and as it were the body of heaven in his clearness. And upon the nobles of the children of Israel he laid not his hand: also they saw God, and did *eat and drink*" (Exodus 24:9–11; emphasis added).

Recall that after Jesus' death and resurrection, he met with the disciples and ate with them also (see Luke 24:30; John 21:13; Acts 1:4). Peter made this interesting allusion to eating with the Lord: "And we are witnesses of all things which he did both in the land of the Jews, and in Jerusalem; whom they slew and hanged on a tree: him God raised up the third day, and showed him openly; not to all the people, but unto witnesses chosen before of God, even to us, who did *eat and drink* with him after he rose from the dead" (Acts 10:39–41; emphasis added).

Such ritual meals remind one of the Messianic banquet—a meal to be celebrated when the Messiah comes again as referred to in Isaiah, Ezekiel, Revelation, and the modern scriptures, such as the Doctrine and Covenants. There is also a comment about eating and drinking with the Lord as a sign of salvation in John's book of Revelation: "Behold, I stand at the door, and knock: if any man hear my voice, and open the door, I will come in to him and *will sup* with him, and he with me. To him that overcometh will I grant to sit with me in my throne, even as I also overcame, and am set down with my Father in his throne" (Revelation 3:20–21; emphasis added).

Walking Through the Valley of Death (John 18:1)

John speaks of a journey from the Upper Room to the Mount of Olives: "When Jesus had spoken these words, he went forth with his disciples over the brook Cedron [Kidron], where was a garden, into the which he entered" (John 18:1). The Kidron ravine lies between the Mount of Olives to the east and Mount Moriah to the west. Some scholars suggest that the original meaning of Kidron was "dark" or "shady," suggesting that the "valley was originally quite deep before construction projects in the area began."[11] Apparently, the floor of the valley during the first century was at least 50 feet lower than the present one in many places. Even today, as one walks down from the BYU Jerusalem Center on Mount Scopus or from the ridge of the Mount of Olives nearby to the bottom of the Kidron and then climbs up to the St. Stephen's Gate (the Jewish Lion's Gate or the Arab's Bab el-Ghor Gate) to the Old City, one cannot help but be surprised how steep and rugged the topography is at this point.

The winter-flowing Kidron can be a place of death during flash floods.[12] A walk between the traditional sites of the Upper Room and the Garden mentioned by John generally takes between twenty and forty-five minutes today. While we cannot be certain of the exact route Jesus followed on that particular night, many scholars believe Jesus and his disciples walked down a staired street into the Kidron Valley, still visible in some places near Saint Peter's in Galli-cantu (Saint Peter at the Crowing of the Cock). This main street ran anciently from the top of the southwestern hill to Siloam in the bottom of the valley to connect with the road to Gethsemane. In all likelihood, Jesus climbed these same steps on his return trip to the southwestern part of the city, where he appeared before the Jewish leadership.

One can still retrace ancient paths from the southwestern hill down through the valley and up to the traditional garden at night, recreating a similar journey full of some visual images (olive groves, ancient tombs, topographical features, and a moonlit sky) which Jesus may have witnessed himself. John does not include the place-name *Gethsemane*. The New Testament as it stands now does not contain the common phrase *Garden of Gethsemane*. However, the Joseph Smith Translation adds to Mark's description: "And they came to a place which was named Gethsemane, which was a garden" (JST, Mark 14:36).

As Jesus and his company passed through the city gate, the moonlit night revealed Jerusalem's necropolis (*city of the dead*). The slopes of the Kidron Valley contain literally thousands of tombs. The prophet Joel said that final judgment would begin at the valley of Jehoshaphat (see Joel 3:2, 12; Jehoshaphat means *Jehovah judges*). Zechariah pointed to the Mount of Olives (Zechariah 14:4), and since an early time the Kidron Valley has been identified as the valley of Jehoshaphat.

While tombs existed in this area long before Joel and Zechariah prophesied, their identification of the site as the place of judgment resulted in many more individuals wishing to be laid to rest there so they could be part of the first resurrection.[13]

Three structures presently known as the Tomb of Absalom, the Tomb of Zechariah, and the Tomb of Bene Hezir attract much attention from modern visitors. Each dates from the time before Jesus and are monumental tombs or monuments which can hardly be missed by anyone walking between Jerusalem and the Mount of Olives. On the southern end of the Mount of Olives one can still visit the Tomb of the Prophets. Actually, this is not the burial place of the prophets Haggai, Malachi, and Zechariah, as identified by the sign at the entrance of the tomb complex, but is part of the Jewish cemetery on the Mount of Olives dating from the first century B.C. through A.D. 135. Near the present-day Dominus Flevit ("the Lord wept") Church on the Mount of Olives, one finds similar burial tombs with *kokhim* graves.[14]

All in all it would be virtually impossible for Jesus not to have seen the "city of the dead" as he walked towards the Mount of Olives from the Upper Room. The olive orchards, the deep valley, the city walls, the steep hills, the foreboding tombs, the shadows, and the moonlight all mix to leave a baleful impression. Knowing of his own impending departure, Jesus found himself in the valley of death and may have been visually reminded that night of a freshly cut tomb awaiting him. His violent death was no longer a possibility, but a pending reality.

While Jesus did not fear death, the kind of death he faced may have caused him to examine minutely the significance of the "cup" his Father was about to give him to drink. Near the traditional site of the garden are some ancient steps, located in the gardens of the Russian church of Saint Mary Magdelene, which mark an earlier path.[15] Jesus could easily have taken this way up the hill and into Bethany, making it possible for him to avoid arrest and a torturous death. He had a choice all along, but during this night he came face-to-face with the ultimate decision to accept the cup.

If we eliminate any genuinely free choice on Jesus' part, we turn him into a passive victim whose murder the Father chose to serve for the salvation of mankind. We can only expect that the value of his Passion was deeply determined by Jesus' own free will, no less than by the deliberate choices of other men and the freely adopted divine plan for human salvation.

A Garden (John 18:1–2)

John's story continues as he focuses on the special garden place where he and his disciples "ofttimes resorted" (John 18:2).

The connection between the first garden (Eden) and this garden was perhaps first noted by Cyril of Jerusalem (A.D. c. 315–387) and Cyril of Alexandria (A.D. c. 370–444). BYU Professor Dennis F. Rasmussen drew attention to three gardens: the Garden of Eden, the Garden at the Mount of Olives (Gethsemane), and the Garden Tomb, in a well-written esasy published in 1972.[16] Elder Bruce R. McConkie brought the correlation between the gardens to the attention of the larger Church membership in his final address shortly before his death in 1985.[17]

John began his Gospel by discussing the Creation narrative, alluding to the first garden where the conflict between Adam and Lucifer was played out. Now in a second garden, another conflict between the Savior and the serpent is played out: "where was a garden, into the which he entered, and his disciples. And Judas also, which betrayed him, knew the place: for Jesus ofttimes resorted thither with his disciples" (John 18:1–2).

John does not give us any more information about what happened in the Garden beyond the arrest scene which follows. Perhaps, like other aspects of the Passion narrative, John knew that his readers were by and large familiar with the story and therefore chose not to repeat the agony scene. One New Testament scholar suggests: "John usually does not repeat events that have been adequately described by the other evangelists, but evokes them in a different context by means of a highly specific allusion."[18]

Jesus' Arrest (John 18:3–13)

John continues the drama: "Judas then, having received a band [cohort] of men and officers from the chief priests and Pharisees, cometh" (John 18:3). For the first time in any Passion narrative, John reveals the nature and extent of Roman participation in Jesus' arrest, although the presence of Roman soldiers may be alluded to in Mark 14 with a cryptic reference to "sinners," i.e., Gentiles: "Behold, the Son of man is betrayed into the hands of sinners" (Mark 14:41).

Whether or not the earlier Gospel authors passed over this information to protect Peter's identity or to protect the early Saints from persecution by Rome cannot be determined. When John wrote his Passion narrative there was no reason to protect Peter, who was most likely already dead, executed by Nero in Rome sometime in the 60s during Nero's short but tragic persecution.

The Saints living at the time when John composed his Gospel narrative were experiencing the most intense oppression from Roman authorities experienced yet by believers during the Domitian persecution. Titus Flavious Domintianus (Domitian) was emperor from A.D. 81 through 96 and during his reign attempted to restore the official religion of Rome to its former purity, executing even family members for atheism (practicing Judaism or Christianity).

Domitian's father, Vespasian, rebelled against the imperial family in A.D. 69 and established the Flavian Dynasty in Rome, reigning as emperor from A.D. 69–79. Domitian's brother, Titus, reigned from A.D. 79 through 81. Vespasian and Titus were both instrumental in crushing the Jewish revolt (A.D. 66–70) in Judea. Josephus, a Jewish general during the revolt and later a historian, was captured by Roman forces and eventually became a Roman citizen and pensioner under the patronage of the Flavians (Vespasian, Titus, and Domitian), assuming the name Flavius Josephus. Domitian became emperor upon the sudden death of his brother, Titus.

While Domitian was successful in many endeavors—for example, he completed the now-famous Flavian Amphitheater (the Colosseum in Rome)—his popularity (except among the army) declined. He was stabbed to death just weeks before his forty-fifth birthday on 18 September A.D. 96.

Christian and pagan sources alike reveal the remarkable extent of Domitian's hostility towards the disciples of Jesus, especially during the latter part of his reign. This is the background of John's writings, particularly the book of Revelation.

For whatever reason, John tells of a detachment of soldiers (KJV, "band of men"), literally a "cohort," a term which always refers in the New Testament to Roman soldiers, usually consisting of 600 men, coming out to arrest Jesus. For Mark it was a "crowd," and here we can see how John takes Mark's account and tightens the story by providing this detail.

When John writes, "Judas then, having received a band of men," he does not imply that Judas had any authority, only that he acted as a guide for the group. In charge of the company was a Roman military officer called a tribune (*tribunus militum*, a commander of a cohort of 600 soldiers): "Then the band and the *captain* . . . took Jesus, and bound him, and led him away" (John 18:12–13; emphasis added). Apparently, either Pilate was directly involved in planning Jesus' arrest (because of reports received about his Messianic entrance to the city?) or he placed soldiers at the disposal of the Jewish leadership during the very explosive period of Passover, a nationalistic and religious festival reminding the Jews of their deliverance from bondage in Egypt.[19]

Along with the Roman soldiers was a group of Jewish temple police: "officers [police] from the chief priests" (John 18:3). They are called "the Jewish police" (KJV officers) in John 18:12. Raymond Brown writes: "Such cooperation could have been mutually beneficial if Pilate wanted Jesus temporarily out of the way . . . and if the Sanhedrin wanted Roman support in the event that Jesus' followers caused an uproar over his arrest."[20]

John, along with the other Gospel writers, tells of the prominent role of the chief priests (the incumbent high priest, former high priests still living, and members of the families from whom the high priest was chosen). Additionally, John tells of the presence of Pharisees in the plot to capture Jesus. In all likelihood the political reality of the period required the chief priests to include other important power brokers like the Pharisees in any major decision such as this. Generally the Pharisees had no attachment to Jesus, as the Gospel narratives reveal over and over again, and would have been pleased to have him removed.

As we discovered in our review of the earlier Passion narratives, opposition to Jesus came from the "leading parties in the Sanhedrin [who] were able to come to a common agreement about Jesus, but maybe on very divergent grounds."[21] While these various groups were often divided and disagreed over Jewish doctrine, yet in this one issue they, by majority consensus, agreed together to have Jesus arrested. Later, they agreed to hand him over to the Gentiles on the same basis.

For John, Judas is the tool of Satan. Earlier that evening Judas had gone off into the night, the evil night of which Jesus had warned, the night in which men stumble because they have no light (see John 9:4; 12:35). Perhaps symbolically that is why the Jews with Judas came out with the lanterns and torches: they had rejected the light of the world and so must rely on the aritificial light they carry with them. Even though they came during the nearly full Passover moon, an olive grove could easily provide places to hide, necessitating additional light to secure a prisoner. Additionally, John notes that the large group brought "weapons" with them (John 18:3). In all likelihood the Romans carried swords and the Jewish temple police carried clubs or police batons (see Matthew 26:47; Mark 14:43). If this is true, then both synoptic accounts reveal the presence of Roman and Jewish contingents in their description of weapons.

Now Jesus, totally in control of his fate, leaves the garden to confront the malevolent band before him: "Jesus therefore, knowing all things that should come upon him, went forth, and said unto them, Whom seek ye? They answered him, Jesus of Nazareth. Jesus saith unto them, I am he" (John 18:4–5).[22]

Jesus' simple answer causes this large armed group of Roman soldiers and Jewish temple police to step backwards and fall to the ground (see John 18:6; Psalm 27:2; 35:4). Jesus' adversaries are prostrate before his divine majesty, leaving us little doubt that John intends "I AM" as a divine name (Greek *ego-eimi*).[23]

The Lord told Moses that his people would recognize the name "I AM" as an introduction to his message (see Exodus 3:13–15). It is a name that expresses his character as the faithful God who desires the full trust of his people. Jesus applied the phrase "I AM" to himself earlier (see John 8:58).

John emphasizes that Jesus, as God, has power over the forces of darkness. This statement reinforces our impression that Jesus could not have been arrested unless he permitted it. That belief is further substantiated by Jesus' statement before Pilate, "Thou couldest have no power at all against me, except it were given thee from above" (John 19:11).

While all four Gospel narratives relate the ineffective attempt to save Jesus from arrest by one of his disciples, only John names the participants: "Then Simon Peter having a sword [the Greek connotes a small concealed weapon the size of a knife] drew it, and smote the high priest's servant [not one of the temple police], and cut off his right ear [earlobe]. The servant's name was Malchus. Then said Jesus unto Peter, Put thy sword into the sheath: the cup which my Father hath given me, shall I not drink it?" (John 18:10–11). The "cup" is mentioned in the synoptic Gospel narratives (see Mark 14:36; Matthew 26:39; Luke 22:42) and refers to the cup of suffering.

Jesus Appears Before Annas (John 18:12–23)

Again, those involved in the arrest are identified: "Then the band [cohort] and the captain [tribune] and officers of the Jews [Jewish temple police] took Jesus, and bound him. And led him away to Annas first; for he was father in law to Caiaphas, which was the high priest that same year" (John 18:12–13).

Annas (Ananus or Hanan in many ancient sources), noted in Jewish sources for his greed, wealth, and power, was appointed high priest in A.D. 6 by the Roman prefect Quirinius and deposed in A.D. 16 by Valerius Gratus.[24] He was the head of the priestly family in power during this period, wielding influence through five sons (Eleazar, Jonathan, Theophilus, Matthias, and the younger Annas) and a son-in-law who held the same office. His son-in-law Joseph, nicknamed Caiaphas, served as high priest from A.D. 17 through 36; thus Annas still had significant influence and may have even been the *de facto* leader of the elite family group, who was intimately associated with Roman authority in Judea. The younger Annas is reportedly the high priest who accused James, Jesus' brother and Church leader in Jerusalem, and delivered him up to be stoned shortly before A.D. 70.[25]

Only John tells of this first meeting at Annas's residence, the site of this event is not known. Luke does connect Annas and Caiaphas with Jesus' ministry (see Luke 3:2). Later, Luke notes: "And Annas the high priest, and Caiaphas, and John, and Alexander, and as many as were of the kindred of the high priest, were gathered together at Jerusalem" (Acts 4:6).

Josephus indirectly identifies the location of the high priest's residence as being in the Upper City, the district of Jerusalem where the ruling class and the wealthy lived.[26] One is able to visit some of the homes of the rich in Jerusalem today. A brief description and beautiful color photographs depicting the splendor of the residence are found in numerous books.[27] Martin Goodman provides an intimate portrait of these families in his 1987 book, *The Ruling Class of Judaea*.[28]

The location of the residence of Caiaphas is identified by tradition at two different locations in Jerusalem today.[29] Is it possible that one of these sites may be that of Annas, while the other the location of Caiaphas's residence? If so, the site identified as the high priest residence discovered at St. Peter in Gallicantu (St. Peter of the Cockcrow) may be the location of the interview between Jesus and Annas. It dominates the eastern slope of Mount Zion, which is located on part of the western hill projecting out beyond the south wall of the Old City that was constructed by the Ottoman sultan Suliman the Magnificent some time around 1540.[30] Under the main floor of a fifth-century church is a room surrounded by chambers hewn in the limestone. There are rings on one wall, and in other places various sorts of handles have been cut in the rock. It has been suggested that they were used to tie prisoners while they were scourged or beaten. An underground room with a window overlooking a pit has been interpreted as a guard room.

Additionally, an impressive first-century graded street running from the Tyropoeon Valley up to this area has been identified and is accessible to visitors at the modern Church of St. Peter's in Galicantu. If this site is identified with either Annas or Caiaphas, then Jesus may have walked up these steps as he approached the Jewish leaders for interrogation.

John adds the following to the story: "And Simon Peter followed Jesus, and so did another disciple: that disciple was known unto the high priest, and went in with Jesus into the place of the high priest. But Peter stood at the door without. Then went out that other disciple, which was known unto the high priest, and spake unto her that kept the door, and brought in Peter" (John 18:15–16). Most often, "another disciple" is identified with the "one Jesus loved" because of the passage found in John 20:2. Questions arise on how John knew the high priest, and if it was him, why did John not encounter the same problems that Peter did? A late tradition (c. A.D. 400) suggests that John sold fish from the Sea of Galilee to the high priest family.[31]

There is another possibility, however; this disciple known by the high priest might not be John and should not be identified with the one mentioned in John 20. After introducing Peter, this unknown disciple disappears from the story.

Whoever interceded with the doorkeeper in Peter's behalf, the story quickly focuses on a courtyard where Peter is confronted by an unnamed woman: "Then saith the damsel that kept the door unto Peter, Art not thou also one of this man's disciples? He saith, I am not. And the servants and officers stood there, who had made a fire of coals; for it was cold: and they warmed themselves: and Peter stood with them, and warmed himself" (John 18:17–18). Those who have lived in Jerusalem during March and April have experienced the cold nights and understand the need for the slaves and the Jewish temple police to make a charcoal fire in order to keep warm.

The scene moves from the courtyard into the interior of Annas's residence: "The high priest then asked Jesus of his disciples, and of his doctrine. Jesus answered him, I spake openly to the world; I ever taught in the synagogue, and in the temple, whither the Jews always resort; and in secret have I said nothing. Why askest thou me? ask them which heard me, what I have said unto them: behold, they know what I said. And when he had thus spoken, one of the officers which stood by struck Jesus with the palm of his hand, saying, Answerest thou the high priest so? Jesus answered him, If I have spoken evil, bear witness of the evil: but if well, why smitest thou me?" (John 18:19–23).

John preserves the courtesy title "high priest" for Annas, a well-documented fact from this period because he plainly identifies Caiaphas as the official high priest at the time (see John 18:14). Who is actually present during this interrogation is not mentioned by John, except for slaves and Jewish temple police. Was it a gloomy room in Annas's palace, illuminated by a few torches and perhaps a fireplace? The text does not provide enough help to reconstruct more than a few details of the scene.

The purpose of the interrogation is clear: Annas wants to know about Jesus' disciples and his teachings. Unlike Peter, Jesus stands resolute and answers forthrightly to the questions being posed to him.

Jesus Before Caiaphas (John 18:24)

John continues his narrative: "Now Annas had sent him bound unto Caiaphas the high priest" (John 18:24). In all likelihood, the house of Caiaphas was at the top of the western hill, where luxurious houses of the Herodian period have been found in the courtyard of the Armenian Church of Saint Savior (just beside the Dormition Abbey).[32]

Caiaphas first appears in John's Gospel narrative shortly after the raising of Lazarus: "Then gathered the chief priests and the Pharisees a council, and said, What do we? for this man doeth many miracles. If we let him thus alone, all men will believe on him: and the Romans shall come and take away both our place and nation. And one of them, named Caiaphas, being the high priest that same year [i.e., the year Jesus was killed], said unto them, Ye know nothing at all, nor consider that it is expedient for us, that one man should die for the people, and that the whole nation perish not. And this spake he not of himself: but being high priest that year, he prophesied that Jesus should die for that nation; and not for that nation only, but that also he should gather together in one the children of God that were scattered abroad. Then from that day forth they took counsel together for to put him to death" (John 11:47–53).

The Pharisees (John 18:3)

Unlike the other Gospel narratives, John reveals the presence of the Pharisees in the council that condemns Jesus. As noted earlier, sources seem to confirm the domination of the council by the Sadducees. Some have argued that the Pharisees would not have participated in such a conspiracy because of their aversion to crucifixion. They probably preferred stoning as a means of execution. However, there is one historical precedent that reveals that they were willing to use crucifixion to punish their enemies.

A century earlier the Pharisees became highly influential and politically powerful under the rule of Queen Alexandra Salome, the wife and successor of Alexander Janneus. During this period they persuaded the queen to eliminate prominent members of the Sadducean party; as a result, eighty were executed by crucifixion[33] apparently in retaliation for the execution, also by crucifixion, of revolting Pharisees. This episode demonstrates the Pharisees' willingness to interpret Deuteronomy 21 in relationship to the penalty of crucifixion. Additionally, the use of crucifixion by both the Pharisees and the Sadducees as a punishment of those assumed to be guilty of high treason and blasphemy also demonstrates the futility of excluding Jewish participation in Jesus' trial and death. John's linking the Sadducees and Pharisees highlights the cooperation between both in the death of Jesus.

Purpose and Reasons (John 18:25–27)

John provides insight into some concerns that the Jewish leaders raised about Jesus and his message.[34] At least on one level some were concerned with the potential political consequences of those following Jesus, especially those that acclaimed him king.[35] In all likelihood this group believed that the "compact with Rome, a compact which guaranteed religious autonomy to the Jews as long as the Jews recognized Roman sovereignty" was an important issue.[36] Others were worried about their own economic, political, and social status which was built on the compact with Rome.

These two were interconnected, and it would be difficult to delineate where one ended and the other began. As two New Testament scholars noted: "Piety and righteousness had long since ceased being the main criteria for a High Priest's successful term in office; ever since the deposition of [Herod's son] Archelaus [in A.D. 6], the High Priests had been the de facto representatives of the Judean people to the Roman authorities and they were saddled with the responsibility of maintaining order in Jerusalem."[37] They were apparently paid well for their efforts to maintain *pax Romana* (Roman peace) as is demonstrated by the remarkable remains of the homes and tombs they built in Jerusalem.

Excavations in the Upper City in the 1970s reveal the grandeur and magnificence of the homes of the high-priestly families. An example of what archeologists unabashedly identify as a "palatial mansion" can be seen today at the Wohl Archaeological Museum in the Jewish Quarter of the Old City.[38] Two scholars summarized the process and result of economic advancement among these families of this period: "Ever since the vast expansion of the Temple structures and institutions, these high-priestly families and families of priestly officers in charge of the Temple's treasury, workshops, storerooms, and supply facilities had amassed considerable fortunes, passing down their particular responsibilities and privileges—and wealth—from fathers to sons."[39]

From the story of Zacharias and Elisabeth found in Luke 1, we learn that members of the twenty-four priestly courses (Zacharias was of the course of Abia) lived in villages and towns throughout Judea. The high-priestly families, however, lived in Jerusalem as full-time residents and enjoyed considerable benefits from the flourishing pilgrim donations and revenues.

Most likely, Caiaphas was the one who allowed vendors in the temple and was the greatest beneficiary of the status quo.[40] If so, Jesus' actions against the merchants in the Court of the Gentiles may be one of the issues that separated him from the Jewish leadership (see Matthew 21:12–13; Mark 11:15–17; Luke 19:45–46; John 2:13–17). Jesus was not the only one criticial of practices and policies of the high-priestly families, as many Jews expected God to cleanse the temple and take up residency there.[41]

Again, Simon Peter followed, then "stood and warmed himself. They said therefore unto him, Art not thou also one of his disciples?

He denied it, and said, I am not. One of the servants of the high priest, being his kinsman whose ear Peter cut off, saith, Did not I see thee in the garden with him? Peter then denied again: and immediately the cock crew" (John 18:25–27).

Scholars disagree on John's intent here. Was he speaking of a fowl which according to Jewish tradition was forbidden to be raised in Jerusalem? One writer suggests that it was a Roman signal trumpet (*buccina*), blown at the close of the third watch (between 12:00 midnight and 3:00 A.M.), named "cockcrow." On the other hand, if the prohibition against fowls in the city was not generally observed, one dutiful scholar observed that the natural cockcrow at Jerusalem in March and April occurs most frequently between 3:00 and 5:00 A.M. Another observation suggests three distinct nocturnal cockcrows (about 12:30, 1:30, and 2:30 A.M.).[42]

The Hall of Judgment (John 18:28–40; 19:1–12)

After relating Jesus' trial before Annas and Caiaphas, John tells of Jesus' being brought to the "hall of judgment" to stand before the Roman governor (John 18:28). Along with the other Gospel narratives, John reveals a close relationship between Caiaphas and the Roman administration. Compared to those who were appointed high priests during this period, Caiaphas's eighteen-year reign was an exception revealing the cordial relations implicit within such a distinction.

This section of the story, which includes Jesus' words before Pilate found in John 18:33–37; 19:10–11, may be what Paul alluded to when he wrote from Rome to Timothy: "Christ Jesus, who before Pontius Pilate witnessed a good confession" (1 Timothy 6:13).

In this scene, John provides a mental image of two separate parties standing at a distance from one another. The Jewish leaders remain outside the judgment hall "lest they should be defiled; but that they might eat the passover" (John 18:28). On the other side Jesus stands alone among the Gentiles inside the prætorium. Instead of Jesus being on trial, John dramatically portrays Pilate's trial. He moves back and forth (see John 18:29, 33) between the two who represent opposites: light and darkness, truth and falsehood. By this movement back and forth between the outside and the inside, John highlights the choice Pilate is trying to avoid, yet in the end must make. For John's first-century readers, who were being forced to make a choice between Christ and Caesar during the Domitian persecution, John warns them "that no one can avoid judgment when he or she stands before Jesus."[43]

The story begins at the "early hour," the last Roman division of the night, so we assume that Jesus was finally brought to Pilate toward 6:00 A.M.[44] Jesus' time before Pilate would last another six hours, being sentenced about 12:00 noon (see discussion below). When Pilate asks the Jewish leaders what the charge is against Jesus, they respond: "If he were not a malefactor, we would not have delivered him up unto thee" (John 18:30). Pilate, unwilling to make a judgment, responds: "Take ye him, and judge him according to your law. The Jews therefore said unto him, It is not lawful for us to put any man to death: that the saying of Jesus might be fulfilled, which he spake, signifying what death he should die" (John 18:31–32; cf. John 12:32f). What John makes very clear is that the Jews want Jesus executed; and since they cannot do it themselves, they want to do so via Pilate. Otto Betz's research supports John's report: "The Jews did not have the *ius gladii* under the Roman administration; it was reserved for the prefect."[45]

Pilate moves again from the outside to inside the judgment hall itself: "Then Pilate entered into the judgment hall again, and called Jesus, and said unto him, Art thou the King of the Jews?" (John 18:33). Jesus' kingship is one of the main focuses of all the Passion narratives.

Jesus responds with a counterquestion: "Sayest thou this thing of thyself, or did others tell it thee of me?" (John 18:34). This forced Pilate to distinguish between two interpretations of kingship (Jewish and Roman).

"Pilate answered, Am I a Jew? [This probably does not reveal contempt for Jews as some argue.] Thine own nation and the chief priests have delivered thee unto me: what hast thou done? Jesus answered, My kingdom is not of this world: if my kingdom were of this world, then would my servants fight, that I should not be delivered to the Jews: but now is my kingdom not from hence. Pilate therefore

said unto him, Art thou a king then? Jesus answered, Thou sayest that
I am a king. To this end was I born, and for this cause came I into the
world, that I should bear witness unto the truth. Every one that is of
the truth heareth my voice" (John 18:35–37). In response to Jesus'
statement, Pilate asks the questions, "What is truth?" (John 18:38).

Nowhere is the dramatic aspect of the narrative more poignant
than here, which in one sense forces the reader to confront the obvious—Pilate is on trial, not Jesus. No one, the reader is led to conclude, can avoid Jesus' challenge to hear the truth when standing
before him. John carefully prepared this visual image through his
artful telling of the story of a man caught between good and evil,
light and darkness, truth and falsehood as Pilate physically moves
between Jesus in the judgment hall and the Jewish leaders outside
(see John 18:28–40). In a desperate and utterly fruitless attempt to
avoid hearing the truth, Pilate cynically responds: "What is truth?"
and then leaves the judgment hall. John records: "And when he had
said this, he went out again unto the Jews, and saith unto them, I
find in him no fault at all" (John 18:38).

In another attempt to hide from the truth, Pilate offers: "But ye
have a custom, that I should release unto you one at the passover:
will ye therefore that I release unto you the King of the Jews? Then
cried they all again, saying, Not this man, but Barabbas. Now Barabbas was a robber" (John 18:39–40). Some may have hoped for
Barabbas' release independent of the action against Jesus. Here we
see John's focus since he does not even take the time to tell us that
Barabbas was released.

Ironically, Pilate next makes Jesus sit so he can proclaim Jesus
king: "When Pilate therefore heard that saying, he brought Jesus
forth, and sat down in the judgment seat in a place that is called the
Pavement, but in the Hebrew, Gabbatha" (John 19:13).[46] "Sit
down" may mean that Pilate "sat him down."[47] In all likelihood, the
logical place for this dramatic scene "would have been at its eastern
gate opening on a square where the prefect would have had a *bema*
or *stella curulis*, 'judgment seat.'"[48] For John, Christ is the legitimate
judge of men; in condemning him, the Jewish leaders are judging
themselves.

As in Luke's narrative, John records that Pilate insists on three occasions that Jesus was innocent: "I find in him no fault at all" (John 18:38); "I find no fault in him" (John 19:4); and "I find no fault in him" (John 19:6). John continues: "Then Pilate therefore took Jesus, and scourged him" (John 19:1). The purpose seems to be to avoid executing Jesus. Pilate, however, seriously miscalculated the crowd. The story details the actions: "And the soldiers platted a crown of thorns, and put it on his head, and they put on him a purple robe, and said, Hail, King of the Jews! and they smote him with their hands" (John 19:2–3). The New International Version of the New Testament captures this best by adding the words "again and again" to the end of verse 3.

While Pilate attempted, through this scourging and mocking, to elicit sympathy for the prisoner, it only heightened the cry for blood. His ploy failed. As in Mark and Luke, the crowd in John's account demanded that Jesus be executed; nevertheless, we learn what really moved Pilate to hand Jesus over to his soldiers to die a cruel death on the cross: a political threat. John notes: "But the Jews cried out, saying, If thou let this man go, thou art not Caesar's friend: whosoever maketh himself a king speaketh against Caesar" (John 19:12). Two insights should be noted here. First, the mob obtains the release of someone guilty of the very crime of which they accuse Jesus. Second, Pilate eventually condemns Jesus because his kingdom is of this world, the Jews reject Jesus because his kingdom is not of this world.

Passover (John 19:14)

John records the place of these events explicitly, even noting the time: "it was the preparation of the passover, and about the sixth hour" (John 19:14). Passover eve, he says—or, since *paraskeue* (preparation) acquired in Jewish Greek the special sense of "sabbath eve," that is, Friday, the phrase could be rendered, "It was Friday of Passover Week at about 12 o'clock noon."[49]

John sees a deeper meaning in Pilate's words, just as he had seen a prophecy in Caiaphas's words (see John 11:49–51). The Roman governor exclaims, "Behold your King!" (John 19:14). Pilate implies that Jesus is the true king of the true Israel, of all the people of God who obey the voice of God. Spoken at midday on Passover Eve, we can infer that Jesus is the true Paschal Lamb about to be sacrificed at the appropriate hour of the appropriate day for the life of his people.

Apparently for John, the Jewish trial is a mockery of a prophet and the Roman trial a mockery of a king. Judas, a disciple, hands Jesus over to the Jewish leaders, the chief priests hand Jesus over to a Roman leader, and Pilate hands Jesus over to the soldiers to be crucified. While no one is completely responsible, each person or group hands Jesus over to another individual or group. Therefore, all collectively are responsible.

The Place of Execution (John 19:16–27)

"Then delivered he him therefore unto them to be crucified. And they took Jesus, and led him away. And he bearing his cross went forth into a place called the place of a skull, which is called in the Hebrew Golgotha" (John 19:16–17).

John identifies the general vicinity of the execution as "a place" (*kraniou topon*), not a specific spot on the ground. Likely, Golgotha was a large area where there was a place of execution and a garden, two different spots not necessarily close to one another. We learn from Hebrews: "Jesus also, that he might sanctify the people with his blood, suffered without the gate" (Hebrews 13:12). This reference could refer to the suffering in the garden located at the Mount of Olives, but context seems to indicate the suffering at the place of execution. John adds: "And Pilate wrote a title, and put it on the cross. And the writing was, JESUS OF NAZARETH THE KING OF THE JEWS. This title then read many of the Jews: for the place where Jesus was crucified was nigh to the city" (John 19:19–20). From the above we learn that Jesus was executed near the city, outside a gate, and close enough to a road so those passing by could read the title attached to the cross.

As already noted, some people believe the name comes from the topology of the place, namely that it was a hill with a rough resemblance to a human skull, like the one found near the Garden tomb.

The Joseph Smith Translation suggests an alternative view (see pages 59-60, 107).

Apart from the two most popular locations which are identified as the site of Jesus' execution, there is a possible third site. One scholar identifies a recently discovered gate as the Gennath Gate (Gardens Gate). This gate was apparently located in the western wall of the first-century city.[50] Two roads, one leading westward to Lydda and Joppa and a second one leading northward to Samaria may have joined at the gate. If this is a correct reconstruction, then it was a major entry point for Jews coming from the coast, Egypt, and Cyrenaica, and it was an appropriate site for executions designed to be seen by as many people as possible. At this site, those passing by were forced to look down into the area of Golgotha, an oval-shaped disused quarry, at the execution of Jesus and the two other men. Typical of Roman execution sites, a common burial pit was located nearby to dispose of the victims' remains. For those interested in this proposed site, it is located a little southwest of where David Street meets Habad Street, but north of St. Mark Street in the Old City.

Alternatively, the general location of the Garden Tomb also fits the description John provides. It was undoubtedly beyond the north city wall at the time. The small hill where a Muslim cemetery is now located meets the requirements of high visibility for executions, though the text never mentions a hill. Additionally there is an old tradition associating the area with the stoning of Stephen (see Acts 7:54–60). Finally, the location was very near a busy intersection, north of the main gate from which two roads branched out toward Damascus, Galilee, Phoenicia, and Samaria, again meeting the high visibility requirement for a Roman execution.[51]

Wherever the site of the execution was located, it would have been a gruesome sight and a miserable shock to possibly as much as one hundred and eighty thousand Passover pilgrims who were streaming into the city.

John continues his story of death: "Then the soldiers, when they had crucified Jesus, took his garments, and made four parts, to every soldier a part; and also his coat: now the coat was without seam, woven from the top throughout. They said therefore among themselves, Let us not rend it, but cast lots for it, whose it shall be" (John 19:23–24).

Only John explains that the execution squad was a quaternion. In Roman practice, those members of the executionary detail had a right to the victim's possessions. What items were taken from Jesus is not detailed (sandals, head covering, outer robe, and girdle?) though John specifically notes Jesus' *chitōn* (tunic or KJV coat). Normally, most tunics, a long garment worn next to the skin, were made of two rectangular or square sheets of the same width, sewn together to form a long piece. A slit was left in the seam for the head. The sides were also sewn together except at the top, where a hole was left for the arms.

John indicates that Jesus' tunic was seamless, a more expensive type and probably a rare personal item.[52] It was made in one piece on the loom, and a hole for the head was cut and hemmed afterwards making it appear like a modern poncho. In all likelihood, this precious garment was given to Jesus by a wealthy person he knew.

John then provides another intimate view of Jesus' last actions: "Now there stood by the cross of Jesus his mother [Mary], and his mother's sister [Salome], Mary the wife of Cleophas, and Mary Magdalene. When Jesus therefore saw his mother, and the disciple standing by, whom he loved [John], he saith unto his mother, Woman, behold thy son! Then saith he to the disciple, Behold thy mother! And from that hour [the hour of Jesus' return to the Father, not that very moment] that disciple took her unto his own home" (John 19:25–27).[53]

In all likelihood, now that her firstborn son's death approached, Mary had no one in her immediate family to rely on. Her other children apparently rejected their older brother's mission and possibly rejected her for following him (see John 7:1–5). Joseph, who had not been mentioned since Jesus' trip to the temple when he was twelve years of age, presumably was dead. At this moment, Jesus asks the disciple whom he loved (presumably John himself) to take care of his mother, probably John's aunt.[54]

Jesus' Thirst (John 19:28–30)

An often misunderstood passage follows: "After this, Jesus knowing that all things were now accomplished [all was finished], that the scripture might be fulfilled, saith, *I thirst*. Now there was set a vessel full of vinegar: and they filled a spunge with vinegar, and put it upon hyssop, and put it to his mouth. When Jesus therefore had received the vinegar, he said, It is finished: and he bowed his head, and gave up the ghost" (John 19:28–30; emphasis added). The allusion to Psalms seems possible: "And in my thirst they gave me vinegar to drink" (Psalm 69:21).

At this moment Jesus knew that the Passion was almost over. He is not a victim who is involuntarily caught in a situation he cannot handle anymore, as so often happens in ordinary human experience; rather, he knew everything in advance and has been in charge all along (see John 18:4)—this seems to be John's point. As noted above, the Passion narrative begins with "Now before the feast of the passover, when Jesus knew that his hour was come that he should depart out of this world unto the Father" (John 13:1), indicating that he understood that his suffering and death was the means by which he would go back to his Father.

While Mark and Matthew inform their readers that before Jesus died he uttered a loud cry, without telling us the contents, Luke indicates that he said: "Father, into thy hands I commend my spirit" (Luke 23:46). John adds: "It is finished." Additionally, only John informs us that Jesus "bowed his head" just before "he handed over the spirit," the literal meaning of "gave up the ghost."

We recall Jesus' words at the beginning of the Gospel narrative: "For God so loved the world, that he gave his only begotten Son, that whosoever believeth in him should not perish, but have everlasting life. For God sent not his son into the world to condemn the world; but that the world through him might be saved" (John 3:16–17). Later, he wrote: "God is love" (1 John 4:8). John adds: "Herein is love, not that we loved God, but that he loved us, and sent his son to be the propitiation for our sins" (1 John 4:10). The fundamental element of the Passion narrative in John's Gospel is that this God of love uses the cross in his service to bring about his purposes.

Death and Burial (John 19:31–42)

John gives the reader a little cultural background as he describes the next scene: "The Jews therefore, because it was the preparation, that the bodies should not remain upon the cross on the sabbath day, (for that sabbath day was an high day,) besought Pilate that their legs might be broken, and that they might be taken away" (John 19:31).

John is clear that the provisions of Deuteronomy 21 were taken seriously—Jesus' body would not be left on the cross to defile the land. Additionally, John demonstrates how Jesus, instead of defiling the land, consecrated it by his blood and water (see John 19:34) and has fulfilled the prophecy found in Isaiah, "He was pierced for our transgressions" (Isaiah 53:5).[55]

Connected with this fulfillment theme, John informs us that the soldiers "brake the legs of the first, and of the other which was crucified with him. But when they came to Jesus, and saw that he was dead already, they brake not his legs: but one of the soldiers with a spear pierced [poked or stabbed at] his side, and and forthwith came there out blood and water" (John 19:32–34). Note that bones from the Passover sacrifice were not to be broken (see Exodus 12:46; Numbers 9:12). Here it seems that John links the death of Jesus with the Paschal lamb, that is, he says that Jesus is the real Passover sacrifice. The breaking of bones (*crurifragium*) "was done with a heavy mallet; usually only the legs were broken, but occasionally other bones as well. Originally a cruel capital punishment in itself, the *crurifragium*, despite its brutality, was a mercy when it accompanied the crucifixion, for it hastened death."[56] This event seems to fulfill several ancient prophecies: first, the unbroken bones of the paschal lamb in Exodus: "neither shall ye brake a bone thereof" (Exodus 12:46); second, "They shall leave none of it till morning, nor break any bone of it: according to all the ordinances of the passover they shall keep it" (Numbers 9:12); third, "He keepeth all his bones: not one of them is broken" (Psalm 34:20).

Many have speculated on the exact cause of death. The most prominent propositions include asphyxia, aspiration, cardiovascular collapse, fatal syncope, ruptured heart, and cardia arrhythmia.[57]

While John does not, nor do any of the Gospel writers, provide direct evidence on this issue, he is careful to provide Jesus' words: "No man taketh it [my life] from me, but I lay it down of myself. I have power to lay it down, and I have power to take it again" (John 10:18).

What is important for John at this point is to show that Jesus was the true paschal sacrifice, fulfilling scriptural injunctions: "And he that saw it bare record, and his record is true: and he knoweth that he saith true, that ye might believe. For these things were done, that the scripture should be fulfilled, A bone of him [Passover lamb] shall not be broken. And again another scripture saith, they shall look on him whom they pierced [Zechariah 12:10]" (John 19:35–37).

Away from the place of execution, in a quieter part of Golgotha, Joseph of Arimathea "being a disciple of Jesus, but secretly for fear of the Jews . . . [and] Nicodemus, which at the first came to Jesus by night, . . . laid they Jesus, . . . for the sepulchre was nigh at hand" (John 19:38–39, 42). Specifically, we are informed: "Now in the place where he was crucified there was a garden; and in the garden a new sepulchre, wherein was never man yet laid" (John 19:41). The Greek word *kēpos* means a place with vegetables, flowers, or trees.[58]

John provides more details regarding the burial and the tomb than any other author. Jewish burials at the time were generally carried out in two distinct phases. During the primary burial the body was taken to the tomb and laid in a niche (Hebrew *kokh*) seven feet long, cut perpendicular to the wall of an underground chamber, or on a bench hewn in the rock, along a wall, frequently with an arch over it, thus the Latin name *arcosolium* (also Greek *klinē*). No soil was used in the process, so as to ensure rapid decay of the flesh. During the secondary burial, when the flesh had fully decomposed, the bones were collected between twelve months and three years later in ossuaries made of stone or wood, the average size of which was 25 x 15 x 12.5 inches.

Hewn in the rock in a cliff or on a hillside, sometimes in abandoned quarries, the typical rock-cut tomb was accessible through a low square opening (see John 20:5) that was normally closed with a vertical flat stone shaped like a millstone, which could be rolled back in a grove in front of the tomb entry as described in John. The entrance hole opened to a chamber with *kokhim,* "niches," or *arcosolia,* "benches," in its walls. Several chambers could be connected together with tunnels and constitute underground necropolises of considerable size.

A group of Latter-day Saint commentators outlined what they believe scripture and Jewish custom provide for evidence of the tomb mentioned by the Gospel writers.[59] Of most interest is their argument, "Theological Rationale for Jesus' Burial Site," in which they provide an overview of the story of Abraham and Isaac and its correlation to the sacrifice of "the Passover Lamb . . . slain at Passover time on the north of the Altar of Moriah as an atonement for sin," that is, Jesus Christ.[60]

If they are right about the necessity of exact physical location, then the area of crucifixion and burial may be near or at the Garden Tomb, north of the present-day Damascus Gate.[61] However, as noted earlier, symbolic acts such as the ritual of the red heifer were important to provide "types and shadows" of the coming of Jesus, but the ultimate fulfillment was not tied to a specific location, only to a general relationship. The red heifer, it will be recalled, was slaughtered on the Mount of Olives. Jesus, however, died outside the city wall (the camp) but not on the Mount of Olives. It probably is taking the symbolism of the ritual to a false conclusion to demand such specificity to locale.

LDS biblical archeologist Jeffrey R. Chadwick suggests the Garden Tomb may have had two distinct sections: an ante-chamber which had a preparation bench, and a burial chamber with two benches for bodies and a narrow shelf for ossuaries.[62] He further argues that the preparation bench in the so-called "weep-room" may be the location where Jesus' body was placed awaiting final anointing.

Wherever the locations of the execution and burial of Jesus were located, the events of Jesus' passion and burial brought to a close one aspect of John's Gospel narrative as it reveals Jesus as the legitimate "king of the Jews" (John 19:19–21).

NOTES

1. A brief but well-written introduction to John and his Gospel is C. Wilfred Griggs's "The Testimony of John," in *Studies in Scripture, Volume Five: The Gospels*, Kent P. Jackson and Robert L. Millet, eds. (Salt Lake City, Utah: Deseret Book Company, 1986), 109–26.

2. While the other Gospels are not usually called the First, Second, and Third Gospels, we may assume the title "Fourth Gospel" highlights the distinctive nature of John's narrative; see John Dominic Crossan, *Who Killed Jesus? Exposing the Roots of Anti-Semitism in the Gospel Story of the Death of Jesus* (San Francisco: HarperCollins, 1995), 20.

3. M. S. Enslin, "John" in *The Interpreter's Dictionary of the Bible*, 4 vols. and Supplement (New York and Nashville: Abingdon Press, 1962–76), 2:930.

4. See Jeni Broberg Holzapfel and Richard Neitzel Holzapfel, *Sisters at the Well: Women and the Life and Teachings of Jesus* (Salt Lake City: Bookcraft, 1993), 30, 129–31.

5. Raymond E. Brown, *An Introduction to the New Testament* (New York: Doubleday, 1997), 333.

6. Ibid.

7. See C. H. Roberts, *An Unpublished Fragment of the Fourth Gospel* (Manchester: Manchester University Press, 1935).

8. See Allan Millard, *Discoveries from the Time of Jesus* (Bratavia, Illinois: Lion Publishing Corporation, 1990), 165.

9. For example, how the issue regarding Jesus' royal status comes to Pilate's attention is not explained by John (see John 18:33–39).

10. P. G. W. Glare, *Oxford Latin Dictionary* (Oxford: The Clarendon Press, 1982), 1973.

11. John J. Rosseau and Rami Arav, *Jesus and His World: Archaeological and Cultural Dictionary* (Minneapolis: Fortress Press, 1995), 152.

12. In October 1997 Jerusalem was hit with a sudden rainstorm; within a short time water flowed quickly down into the valley below the BYU Jerusalem Center for Near Eastern Studies on Mount Scopus. Later the local news reported the death of several small children caught in the raging water flowing through the Kidron.

13. Summary based on Jerome Murphy-O'Connor, *The Holy Land: Oxford Archaeological Guides* (New York: Oxford University, 1998), 116–28.

14. Among the names inscribed on the ossuaries are Martha, Mary, Simeon, John, Joseph, and Salome; see Bellarmino Bagatti and J.T. Milik, *Gli Scavi del 'Dominus Flevit,' Gerusalemme* (Gerusalemme: Tipografia dei P.P. Franciscanum, 1958).

15. Murphy-O'Connor, *The Holy Land*, 128.

16. See Dennis Rasmussen, "Three Gardens," *New Era* 2 (April 1972): 14–15.

17. See Bruce R. McConkie, "The Purifying Power of Gethsemane," *Ensign* 15 (May 1985):9–11.

18. Jerome Murphy-O'Connor, "What Really Happened at Gethsemane?" *Bible Review* 14 (April 1998):39.

19. Raymond E. Brown, *The Anchor Bible: The Gospel According to John* (Garden City: New York: Doubleday, 1970), 2:815.

20. Ibid.

21. Edward Schillebeeckx, *Jesus: An Experiment in Christology* (New York: Crossroad Publishing Company, 1981), 313.

22. One can only imagine the scene: a large trained military and police unit armed with weapons and authority. They march from the western hill down through the deep Kidron and then with lights and an informer approached a darkened garden on the slope of the Mount of Olives in the middle of the night. Suddenly from out of the darkness Jesus confronts the toughened police and army personnel, demanding to know whom they are looking for, physically showing evidence of the anguish of the Atonement just performed (blood-stained clothing, at the least). For a group in such a clandestine operation it may have been surprising that the object of their search confronts them instead of forcing them to search for him. John reports their hesitancy in arresting him at this critical moment.

23. For a discussion of the use of *egō eimi* in John, see Gerhard Kittel's *Theological Dictionary of the New Testament* (Grand Rapids, Michigan: William B. Eerdmans Publishing Co., 1964), 2:352–54.

24. Bruce Chilton, "Annas," *Anchor Bible Dictionary*, 6 vols. (New York: Doubleday, 1992), 1:257–58.

25. Raymond F. Collins, "John," *Anchor Bible Dictionary*, 6 vols. (New York: Doubleday, 1992), 3:887.

26. Josephus, *Jewish War* 2.17.5; see H. St. J. Thackeray, trans., *Josephus II: The Jewish War, Books I-III* (Cambridge, Massachusetts: Harvard University Press, 1926), 489.

27. For example, see Alan Millard, *Discoveries from the Time of Jesus* (Batavia, Illinois: Lion Publishing Corporation, 1990), 12–18.

28. Martin Goodman, *The Ruling Class of Judaea: The Origins of the Jewish Revolt Against Rome* A.D. 66–70 (New York: Cambridge University Press, 1987), especially 29–108.

29. Representing the two views are Murphy-O'Connor, *The Holy Land*, 107, and Rainer Riesner, "Jesus, the Primitive Community, and the Essene Quarter of Jerusalem," *Jesus and the Dead Sea Scrolls*, James H. Charlesworth, ed. (New York: Doubleday, 1992), 204; see also David B. Galbraith, D. Kelly Ogden, and Andrew C. Skinner, *Jerusalem: The Eternal City* (Salt Lake City: Deseret Book Company, 1996), 174–75.

30. See Murphy-O'Connor, *The Holy Land*, 107.

31. See Ernst Haenchen, *John 2: A Commentary on the Gospel of John Chapters 7–21* (Philadelphia: Fortress Press, 1984), 167.

32. In 1971, based on the Madaba Map and other ancient sources, Broshi excavated the Armenian site and found a short segment of a Herodian wall and remains of houses from the time of Herod located here.

33. Otto Betz, "Jesus and the Temple Scroll," in *Jesus and the Dead Sea Scrolls*, James H. Charlesworth, ed. (New York: Doubleday, 1992), 84–87.

34. For other issues, see Richard Neitzel Holzapfel, "The 'Hidden Messiah,'" in *A Witness of Jesus Christ: The 1989 Sperry Symposium on the Old Testament*, Richard D. Draper, ed. (Salt Lake City: Deseret Book Company, 1989), 80–95.

35. Ellis Rivkin, "What Crucified Jesus?" *Jesus' Jewishness: Exploring the Place of Jesus within Early Judaism*, James H. Charlesworth, ed. (New York: Crossroad Publishing Company, 1991), 242.

36. Ibid., 242–43.

37. Richard A. Horsely and Neil Asher Silberman, *The Message and the Kingdom: How Jesus and Paul Ignited a Revolution and Transformed the Ancient World* (New York: Grosset/Putnam, 1997), 79.

38. See Murphy-O'Connor, *The Holy Land*, 74–76.

39. Horsely and Silberman, *The Message and the Kingdom*, 78.

40. Bruce Chilton, "Caiaphas," *Anchor Bible Dictionary*, 6 vols. (New York: Doubleday, 1992), 1:806.

41. See Richard Neitzel Holzapfel and David Rolph Seely, *My Father's House: Temple Worship and Symbolism in the New Testament* (Salt Lake City: Bookcraft, 1994), 102–5.

42. See R. E. Brown, *The Gospel According to John*, 2:828.

43. See Raymond E. Brown, *A Crucified Christ in Holy Week: Essays on the Four Gospel Passion Narrative* (Collegeville, Minnesota: The Liturgical Press, 1986), 10.

44. See R. E. Brown, *The Gospel According to John*, 2:844.

45. Betz, "Jesus and the Temple Scroll," 87–88.

46. A Roman pavement in the cellar of the Covenant of the Sisters of Zion was identified as the pavement (*lithostraton* in Greek or *Gabbatha* in Hebrew or Aramaic) where Pilate conducted his hearing. Spanning the street outside the Convent is an arch known today as *Ecce Homo* (Behold the man). Here, it is believed, was the spot where Pilate showed Jesus to the crowd (see John 19:5). Scholars today believe the pavement and arch were originally constructed by Hadrian in A.D. 135 in the new city of Aelia Capitolina.

47. Robert G. Bratcher, *Marginal Notes for the New Testament* (New York: United Bible Societies, 1980), 66. For a fuller discussion of this possible reading, see Barclay M. Newman and Eugene A. Nida, *A Translator's Handbook on the Gospel of John* (New York: United Bible Societies, 1980), 581, and Zerwick and Grosvenor, *A Grammatical Analysis*, 341.

48. John J. Rousseau and Rami Arav, *Jesus and His World: Archaeological and Cultural Dictionary* (Minneapolis: Fortress Press, 1995), 152.

49. Arndt and Gingrich argue that for the "Jewish usage it was Friday, on which day everything had to be prepared for the Sabbath, when no work was permitted"; Arndt and Gingrich, *A Greek-English Lexicon of the New Testament*, 637.

50. See Nahman Avigad, *Discovering Jerusalem: From the Canaanites to the Mamluks* (Sydney, Australia: Meditarch, 1993), 128–29.

51. Rousseau and Arav, *Jesus and His World*, 109.

52. For an alternative view see R. E. Brown, *The Gospel According to John*, 2:903.

53. See also Jeni Broberg Holzapfel and Richard Neitzel Holzapfel, *Sisters at the Well: Women and the Life and Teachings of Jesus* (Salt Lake City: Bookcraft, 1993), 129–32.

54. Ibid.

55. Betz, "Jesus and the Temple Scroll," 91.

56. R. E. Brown, *The Gospel According to John*, 2:934.

57. See W. Reid Litchfield, "The Search for the Physical Cause of Jesus Christ's Death," *BYU Studies* 37 (1997–98):93–109.

58. Arndt and Gingrich, eds., *A Greek-English Lexicon of the New Testament*, 431.

59. See Galbraith, Ogden, and Skinner, *Jerusalem*, 178–83.

60. Ibid., 182–83.

61. The argument that "a new sepulchre, wherein was never man yet laid" as possibly referring to a "newly remodeled tomb not yet used in the

newly cut form" advanced by them is not very satisfying and seems to be stretching the point beyond a reasonable interpretation. My rejection of this interpretation is based on the New Testament usage of the word *kainōs* (new) used in the text here. The Gospel authors used the word as meaning just what one generally understands it to mean: "pristine, never before used, not old." For example, see "new" wineskins in Matthew 9:17; Mark 2:22; Luke 5:38; or "new" piece of cloth in Mark 2:21; Luke 5:36. See also John's other usage: "a *new* commandment I give unto you" (John 13:34); cf. Arndt and Gingrich, eds., *A Greek-English Lexicon of the New Testament,* 394–95.

62. Personal conversations and correspondence with Jeffery R. Chadwick, July-August 1998.

The Raising Of Jesus

Part Two

$\mathcal{I}$NTRODUCTION

$\mathbf{P}$aul wrote the early Saints in Corinth a letter of counsel and reproof sometime between A.D. 50 and 59. Apparently some at Corinth believed that there was no bodily resurrection. Paul responded to this false teaching by drawing several conclusions: if the dead do not rise from the grave then—first, not even Jesus was raised from the dead; second, Paul's apostolic preaching of the resurrection was useless; third, the Saints' faith in the resurrection was also useless; fourth, the disciples' witness of the Resurrection was false before God; fifth, the Corinthians' faith was ultimately futile; sixth, each Saint was still in his or her sins and without the hope of redemption; seventh, the Saints already dead were lost forever; and eighth, the living Saints were of all men and women living in the Greco-Roman world most miserable (see 1 Corinthians 15:13–19).

Of the above list, the last argument is of most consequence for everyone who wishes to become a committed disciple of Jesus: "If in this life only we have hope in Christ, we are of all men most miserable" (1 Corinthians 15:19). Paul may mean that if our hope in Christ is based only on this life, then we should be most pitied among all the world's population for putting up with the heavy cost of discipleship. Yet Paul's categorical conclusion based on evidence presented in verses 3–8 is a straightforward testimony: "But now is Christ risen from the dead, and become the firstfruits of them that slept. For since by man came death, by man came also the resurrection of the dead. For as in Adam all die, even so in Christ shall all be made alive" (1 Corinthians 15:20–22).

Utilizing the same Greek verb form that expresses the certainty of Jesus' resurrection seven distinct times (see 1 Corinthians 15:4, 12–14, 16–17, 20), Paul emphasizes to the Corinthian congregation the central importance of the historical event on the first Easter morning—the raising of Jesus.

While the Gospels do not give us an account of the actual resurrection, what we will discover is that the four Gospels' "focus is rather on the experiences of those to whom the risen Jesus appeared."[1] On several occasions the verb *ōptanōmai* occurs in 1 Corinthians 15:5–8. And while some translate the word "he appeared," they may be missing the point because in this form the word is ambiguous: it might suggest a ghost or something. The form of the Greek verb used here has a rather different connotation; it means "he made himself visible," or as the King James Version provides, "he was seen."[2]

Over the years many attempts have been put forth to create an alternative explanation of the Resurrection. Richard Draper, a Latter-day Saint scholar, marshaled the internal evidence from the New Testament to demonstrate the reality of the physical resurrection in a well-crafted article published in 1991.[3]

Finally, such Resurrection narratives often imply and sometimes explicitly state "that it was the Jesus of the public ministry, crucified and buried, who appeared to his followers and who was proclaimed by his followers to others (see Acts 2:29–32). We may speak, then, of the *continuity* between Jesus of the ministry and the risen Jesus who appeared to some of his followers."[4]

NOTES

1. Frederick J. Cwiekowski, *The Beginnings of the Church* (New York: Paulist Press, 1988), 65.

2. William F. Arndt and F. Wilbur Gingrich, *A Greek-English Lexicon of the New Testament and Other Early Christian Literature* (Chicago: University of Chicago Press, 1957), 581–82.

3. See Richard D. Draper, "He Has Risen: The Resurrection Narratives As a Witness of a Corporeal Regeneration," in *The Lord of the Gospels: The 1990 Sperry Symposium on the New Testament*, Bruce A. Van Orden and Brent L. Top, eds. (Salt Lake City: Deseret Book Company, 1990), 39–55.

4. Cwiekowski, *The Beginnings of the Church*, 65.

$\mathscr{M}$ARK'S RESURRECTION NARRATIVE

F inding the empty tomb in Mark's Gospel (see Mark 16:1–8) is apparently part of a larger unit (see Mark 15:40–16:18).[1] Corresponding to the same elements in Paul's letter to the Corinthians (i.e., death, burial, and resurrection; see 1 Corinthians 15:3–4), Mark's story ties the larger unit together through a common set of participants: the women who watch Jesus die, see him buried, and then discover the empty tomb, thereby becoming witnesses to all three events.

Mark's story begins "when the sabbath was past" as several women (Mary Magdalene, Mary the mother of James, and Salome) "bought sweet spices, that they might come and anoint him. And very early in the morning the first day of the week, they came unto the sepulchre at the rising of the sun. And they said among themselves, Who shall roll us away the stone from the door of the sepulchre? And when they looked, they saw that the stone was rolled away: for it was very great. And entering into the sepulchre, they saw a young man sitting on the right side, clothed in a long white garment; and they were affrighted. And he saith unto them, Be not affrighted: Ye seek Jesus of Nazareth, which was crucified: he is risen; he is not here: behold the place where they laid him. But go your way, tell his disciples and Peter that he goeth before you into Galilee: there shall ye see him, as he said unto you. And they went out quickly, and fled from the sepulchre; for they trembled and were amazed: neither said they any thing to any man; for they were afraid" (Mark 16:1–8).

The Joseph Smith Translation clarifies somewhat the story as found in these important verses: "But when they looked, they saw that the stone was rolled away, (for it was very great,) and two angels sitting thereon, clothed in long white garments; and they were affrighted. But the angels said unto them, Be not affrighted; ye seek Jesus of Nazareth, who was crucified; he is risen; he is not here; behold the place where they laid him; and go your way, tell his disciples and Peter, that he goeth before you into Galilee; there shall ye see him, as he said unto you. *And they, entering into the sepulcher, saw the place where they laid Jesus.* And they went quickly, and fled from the sepulcher; for they trembled and were amazed: neither said they any thing to any man; for they were afraid" (JST, Mark 16:4–8; emphasis added).

Interestingly, Mark does not narrate the appearance of Jesus to the disciples in Galilee alluded to in verse 7; Matthew and John will tell the story, however.

Our current version of Mark ends with a long description of what happened following the appearance of the angel to the women at the empty tomb: "Now when Jesus was risen early the first day of the week, he appeared first to Mary Magdalene, out of whom he had cast seven devils. And she went and told them that had been with him, as they mourned and wept. And they, when they had heard that he was alive, and had been seen of her, believed not. After that he appeared in another form unto two of them, as they walked, and went into the country. And they went and told it unto the residue: neither believed they them. Afterward he appeared unto the eleven as they sat at meat, and upbraided them with their unbelief and hardness of heart, because they believed not them which had seen him after he was risen. And he said unto them, Go ye into all the world, and preach the gospel to every creature. He that believeth and is baptized shall be saved; but he that believeth not shall be damned. And these signs shall follow them that believe; In my name shall they cast out devils; they shall speak with new tongues; they shall take up serpents; and if they drink any deadly thing, it shall not hurt them: they shall lay hands on the sick, and they shall recover. So then after the Lord had spoken unto them, he was received up into heaven, and sat on the right hand of God. And they went forth, and preaching every where, the Lord working with them, and confirming the word with signs following. Amen." (Mark 16:9–20).

The most reliable early manuscripts of Mark's Gospel do not contain Mark 16:9–20. Generally, New Testament scholars doubt whether these verses were part of the original Mark narrative.[2] For the Latter-day Saints such a conclusion provides no difficulties. Joseph Smith taught that we "believe the Bible to be the word of God as far as it is translated correctly" (Articles of Faith 1:8).[3]

As noted, the verses are absent from important early manuscripts, and they display certain peculiarities of style and vocabulary unlike the rest of Mark's narrative. Many scholars speculate that Mark's Gospel ended at 16:8 or that the original ending has been lost. They surmise that some later editor added these verses so Mark's Gospel ended similar to the other Gospels.

In any event, the true climax to Mark's Gospel story is the powerful phrase: "He is risen!"

NOTES

1. George W. E. Nickelsburg, "Resurrection (Early Judaism and Christianity)," *Anchor Bible Dictionary*, 6 vols. (New York: Doubleday, 1992), 5:689.

2. This is true of conservative New Testament scholars.

3. That Joseph Smith intended more than just "translation" from either Hebrew to English or Greek to English as constituting a problem in modern editions of the Bible is evident from his comments about the process of how the Bible came to be. Apparently, we might use the word "transmission" instead of "translation" to include Joseph Smith's broader comments about the Biblical text; see Robert J. Matthews, *A Plainer Translation: Joseph Smith's Translation of the Bible. A History and Commentary*, (Provo: Brigham Young University Press, 1985), 11-12.

MATTHEW'S RESURRECTION NARRATIVE

Matthew begins his narrative highlighting the raising of Jesus in a familiar mode: "In the end of the sabbath, as it began to dawn toward the first day of the week, came Mary Magdalene and the other Mary to see the sepulchre" (Matthew 28:1).[1] Then he adds one special detail that explains how the huge stone was rolled away for the women who came to visit the tomb: "And, behold, there was a great earthquake: for the angel of the Lord descended from heaven, and came and rolled back the stone from the door, and sat upon it. His countenance was like lightning, and his raiment white as snow: And for fear of him the keepers did shake, and became as dead men" (Matthew 28:2–4). Only Matthew tells of this "aftershock" to the physical calamities that accompanied Jesus' death (see Matthew 27:51).

Matthew indicates that the women joyfully ran from the empty tomb in order to tell the disciples the good news they heard and saw: "And the angel answered and said unto the women, Fear not ye: for I know that ye seek Jesus, which was crucified. He is not here: for he is risen, as he said. Come, see the place where the Lord lay. And go quickly, and tell his disciples that he is risen from the dead; and, behold, he goeth before you into Galilee; there shall ye see him: lo, I have told you. And they departed quickly from the sepulchre with fear and great joy; and did run to bring his disciples word" (Matthew 28:5–8).

The women discover that Jesus is already gone, but not far: "And as they went to tell his disciples, behold, Jesus met them, saying, All hail. And they came and held him by the feet, and worshipped him.

Then said Jesus unto them, Be not afraid: go tell my brethren that they go into Galilee, and there shall they see me" (Matthew 28:9–10).

As one observant commentator notes: "Although traditions about the empty tomb are ancient, they are not at the heart of the resurrection experience, for an empty tomb is simply a fact about the past that is compatible, as the Gospel of Matthew clearly shows, with a variety of explanations, including the theft of the body. More important, the absence of the body does not by itself empower a community. It is a new form of presence that need explanation, not an absence."[2]

Anti-Christian Propaganda (Matthew 27:62–66; 28:11–15)

Earlier, Matthew reports: "Now the next day, that followed the day of the preparation, the chief priests and Pharisees came together unto Pilate, saying, Sir, we remember that that deceiver said, while he was yet alive, After three days I will rise again. Command therefore that the sepulchre be made sure until the third day, lest his disciples come by night, and steal him away, and say unto the people, He is risen from the dead: so the last error shall be worse than the first. Pilate said unto them, Ye have a watch: go your way, make it as sure as ye can. So they went, and made the sepulchre sure, sealing the stone, and setting a watch" (Matthew 27:62–66).

Only Matthew records this aspect of the burial story. His Resurrection narrative clarifies why he did so: he intended to counteract claims by the Jews that the body of Jesus was taken by his disciples.[3] Matthew now tells the rest of the story: "Now when they were going, behold, some of the watch came into the city, and shewed unto the chief priests all the things that were done. And when they were assembled with the elders, and had taken counsel, they gave large money unto the soldiers, saying, Say ye, His disciples came by night, and stole him away while we slept. And if this come to the governor's ears, we will persuade him, and secure you. So they took the money, and did as they were taught: and this saying is commonly reported among the Jews until this day" (Matthew 28:11–15).

The Risen Christ in Galilee (Matthew 28:16–20)

The narrative's finale shifts from Jerusalem to Galilee. There the southern end of the fertile plain of Ginnosar is dominated by the twelve-hundred-foot sheer cliffs of Mount Arbel. From the highest point of the cliff one is exposed to a magnificent view of an eighteen-and-a-half-mile-long mountain chain with three towering peaks. Mount Hermon, snowcapped in March and April when Matthew's story occurs, is the highest peak in Israel. Additionally, one can see the northern end of the Sea of Galilee with the important sites visited by modern tourists, the Mount of Beatitudes, Capernaum, Tabgha, and Bethsaida.

As one's gaze begins a full 360° circle, eastward the plateau of the Golan comes into view. Its monotony is broken by the appearance of the truncated cones of extinct volcanos from time to time until one sees the Yarmuck Canyon which now divides the State of Israel from the Hashamite Kingdom of Jordan. Continuing the panoramic survey, one sees the southern end of the Sea of Galilee, then further southwest to the prominent, beautiful, round high hill, Mount Tabor. Finally, the Horns of Hittin, an extinct volcano, come into view as the circle is completed facing west.

This high overlook could easily be the site mentioned by Matthew in the closing verses of his Resurrection narrative: "Then the eleven disciples went away into Galilee, into a mountain where Jesus had appointed them. And when they saw him, they worshipped him: but some doubted. And Jesus came and spake unto them, saying, All power is given unto me in heaven and in earth" (Matthew 28:16–18). From this breathtaking location one can see the whole region effortlessly, and it may be in this setting that Jesus directs the eleven disciples: "Go ye therefore, and teach all nations, baptizing them in the name of the Father, and of the Son, and of the Holy Ghost: teaching them to observe all things whatsoever I have commanded you: and, lo, I am with you alway, even unto the end of the world. Amen" (Matthew 18:19–20).

Thus Matthew ends where he began his Gospel narrative, "Behold a virgin shall be with child, and shall bring forth a son, and they shall call his name Emmanuel, which being interpreted is, God with us" (Matthew 1:23; see also 18:20).

NOTES

1. See W. F. Albright and C. S. Mann, *The Anchor Bible: Matthew* (Garden City, New York: Doubleday, 1971), 357–64.

2. Luke Timothy Johnson, *The Real Jesus: The Misguided Quest for the Historical Jesus and the Truth of the Traditional Gospels* (San Francisco: HarperSanFrancisco, 1997), 135.

3. See M. Jack Suggs, Katharine Doob Sakenfeld, and James R. Mueller, eds., *The Oxford Study Bible* (New York: Oxford University Press, 1992), 1302–03.

$\mathcal{J}$OHN'S RESURRECTION NARRATIVE

J ohn's Resurrection narrative clearly differs from that of Matthew, Mark, and Luke.[1] The story of Mary Magdalene and the risen Christ as told by John is the most detailed about the women at Jesus' tomb. John divided the story into two separate scenes: Mary at the empty tomb, and Mary with the risen Christ (see John 20:1–10, 11–18). On the first day of the Jewish week, Mary arrived at Jesus' tomb only to find the stone rolled away from its opening. According to the Gospel of John, Mary Magdalene ran back within the city walls to tell Peter and the disciples that the Master's body was missing. She offered the only logical explanation: "They have taken away the Lord out of the sepulchre" (John 20:2).

Peter and the Beloved Disciple (John 20:3–10)

The pre-resurrection world could not make sense of an empty tomb. The only acceptable explanation would be grave robbing. Peter, the beloved disciple (John), and Mary returned to the site: "Peter therefore went forth, and that other disciple, and came to the sepulchre. So they ran both together: and the other disciple did outrun Peter, and came first to the sepulchre. And he stooping down, and looking in, saw the linen clothes lying; yet went he not in. Then cometh Simon Peter following him, and went into the sepulchre, and seeth the linen clothes lie, and the napkin, that was about his head, not lying with the linen clothes, but wrapped together in a place by itself. Then went in also that other disciple, which came first to the sepulchre, and he saw, and believed. For as yet they knew not the scripture, that he must rise again from the dead. Then the disciples went away again unto their own home" (John 20:3–10).

Apparently, "he saw, and believed" refers only to John himself. The other two, Peter and Mary, are "they" who "as yet . . . knew not the scripture" and have not, therefore, yet come to a full understanding of the implications of the empty tomb before them.

Mary and Jesus (John 20:11–18)

The first episode ends and the second begins with the departure of Peter and John: "But Mary stood without at the sepulchre weeping: and as she wept, she stooped down, and looked into the sepulchre, and seeth two angels in white sitting, the one at the head, and the other at the feet, where the body of Jesus had lain" (John 20:11–12). Apparently, puzzled and dazed at not finding Jesus' body, Mary bent down again to look inside the tomb. Mary then conversed with two white-robed messengers at the head and foot of the place where Jesus' body had been laid. They said to her, "Woman, why weepest thou? She saith unto them, Because they have taken away my Lord, and I know not where they have laid him" (John 20:13). Her words were more personal here than her first report to Peter and John, for she refers to the Christ as "*my* Lord," instead of "*the* Lord," and she said, "*I* know not where they have laid him," instead of "*we* know not where they have laid him" (John 20:2; emphasis added).

Mary then turned towards the garden, and she saw the resurrected Christ, not knowing it was him. The first recorded words of the risen Jesus are a series of questions that he asks Mary, "Woman, why weepest thou? whom seekest thou?" (John 20:15). At the beginning of his Gospel, John preserves Jesus' words to the disciples of John the Baptist as they approach him: "Then Jesus turned, and saw them following, and saith unto them, What seek ye?" (John 1:38). The question is an invitation that introduces one of the marks of discipleship in John—to look for Jesus. The repetition of that question, "What seek ye?" in the Resurrection narrative establishes continuity between the first disciples and Mary.

"She, supposing him to be the gardener, saith unto him, Sir, if thou have borne him hence, tell me where thou hast laid him, and I will take him away" (John 20:15). John employs this threefold repetition of Mary Magadalene's words to describe her ardent longing to find Jesus whom she loved so much.

The "gardener" then changed Mary's life, and the lives of those who hear the story, forever, when he called her by name: "Mary." She turned around again, but this time she saw Jesus, her Master. "She turned herself, and saith unto him, Rabboni; which is to say, Master. Jesus saith unto her, Touch me not; for I am not yet ascended to my Father: but go to my brethren, and say unto them, I ascend unto my Father, and your Father; and to my God, and your God" (John 20:16–17).

Mary did not recognize Jesus until he called her by name. Being called personally by Jesus is a special privilege in John's Gospel. In the parable of the good shepherd, Jesus said, "[The shepherd] calleth his own sheep by name" (John 10:3). The "sheep follow him: for they know his voice" (John 10:4). Jesus called Lazarus by name to summon him from the tomb at Bethany, and now his voice summoned Mary to a new reality—the tomb was empty, and life was restored (see John 11:43).

John highlights the encounter between Mary and the risen Lord by noting the exact word that Mary would use in Aramaic, *Rabboni*. "Lord Master" is the literal rendering of *rabbanoi*, rather than teacher or master in this case. Mary knew that this was the risen Lord, not just her teacher (see John 20:18).

Mary may have embraced Jesus after she recognized him, because he said to her, "Do not hold on to me" in the Greek, or "Hold me not" in the Joseph Smith Translation (JST, John 20:17), both of which potentially imply that she was already touching him when Jesus spoke to her. This is not a harsh rebuke; rather, it was the first post-resurrection teaching. Jesus' prohibition was followed by a positive exhortation, "but go to my brethren, and say unto them, I ascend unto my Father, and your Father; and to my God, and your God" (John 20:17).

Mary fulfilled messianic scripture when she heeded Jesus' words and went to the disciples with the announcement, "I have seen the Lord" (see John 20:18). In Psalms we find, "I will declare *thy name* unto *my brethren*, in the midst of the congregation will I praise thee" (Psalm 22:22; emphasis added). We must remember that the Greek word for Lord (*kyrios*) is the same word rendered in the Septuagint (Greek version of the Old Testament) for the tetragrammaton, *YHWH* (Yahweh or Jehovah), which is the proper name of the Lord.

Mary's witness was soon followed by others; nevertheless, in a sense she was the first disciple of the risen Jesus to declare his victory. Mary became an "apostle to the apostles." The term does not mean a member of the Twelve (the more significant title in the New Testament), but rather she is "one sent forth" to witness the good news of Christ's resurrection. Mary Magdalene was the first witness of the Resurrection in two important and significant ways. She was the first person to see the resurrected Messiah, and she was the first person to witness to others what she had seen. (See page 21, n. 14.)

The Upper Room (John 20:19–28)

John's Resurrection narrative next turns to events later in the day: "Then the same day at evening, being the first day of the week, when the doors were shut where the disciples were assembled for fear of the Jews, came Jesus and stood in the midst, and saith unto them, Peace be unto you. And when he had so said, he shewed unto them his hands and his side. Then were the disciples glad, when they saw the Lord. Then said Jesus to them again, Peace be unto you: as my Father hath sent me, even so send I you. And when he had said this, he breathed on them, and saith unto them, Receive ye the Holy Ghost: Whose soever sins ye remit, they are remitted unto them; and whose soever sins ye retain, they are retained" (John 20:19–23).

"And after eight days again his disciples were within, and Thomas with them: then came Jesus, the doors being shut, and stood in the midst, and said, Peace be unto you. Then saith he to Thomas, Reach hither thy finger, and behold my hands; and reach hither thy hand, and thrust it into my side: and be not faithless, but believing. And Thomas answered and said unto him, My Lord and my God" (John 20:26–28). Since 1883, when *Harper's Magazine* gave us the phrase "doubting Thomas," this disciple has not only been an example, but his name has had to suffer by allusion.

The Disciples in Galilee (John 21:1–8)

John continues his story of the Resurrection by sharing an experience in Galilee: "After these things Jesus shewed himself again to the disciples at the sea of Tiberias; and on this wise shewed he himself. There were together Simon Peter, and Thomas called Didymus, and Nathanael of Cana in Galilee, and the sons of Zebedee, and two other of his disciples. Simon Peter saith unto them, I go a fishing. They say unto him, We also go with thee. They went forth, and entered into a ship immediately; and that night they caught nothing" (John 21:1–3).

In this scene, divided into two separate sections, the geographical setting of the Resurrection narrative shifts from Jerusalem in Judea to the Sea of Tiberias in Galilee, where most of Jesus' ministry took place. The lake is the largest body of fresh water in Israel today and is known by several different names in ancient sources, including the Sea or Lake of Galilee, Lake of Gennesaret and Lake of Taricheae.

The probable site of this event may be present-day Tabgha (Arabic, from the Greek *Heptapēgon* meaning "the place of seven springs") some two miles west of Capernaum. Here, the *Tiapia Galilea*, improperly called "Saint Peter's fish" today, move closer to the shore in schools to seek warmer waters near the warm springs, where they are caught in large quantities with dragnets. It is well known that night fishing is generally better than fishing during the day, and the resulting catch could be sold fresh in the morning at a local market.

John continues his narrative early the next morning when "Jesus stood on the shore" (John 21:4). He specifically tells his readers: "but the disciples *knew not* that it was Jesus" (John 21:4; emphasis added). Then the Greek manuscripts indicate that in a colloquial way, Jesus says: "My boys [or my lads], you haven't caught anything yet, have you?"[2] John adds: "They answered him, No. And he said unto them, Cast the net on the right side of the ship, and ye shall find. They cast therefore, and now they were not able to draw it for the multitude of fishes. Therefore that disciple whom Jesus loved saith unto Peter, It is the Lord. Now when Simon Peter heard that it was the Lord, he girt his fisher's coat unto him, (for he was naked,) and did cast himself into the sea. And the other disciples came in a little ship; (for they were not far from land, but as it were two hundred cubits,) dragging the net with fishes" (John 21:5–8).

Bread and Fish (John 21:9–17)

"As soon then as they were come to land, they saw fire of coals there, and fish laid thereon, and bread. Jesus saith unto them, Bring of the fish which ye have now caught. Simon Peter went up, and drew the net to land full of great fishes, an hundred and fifty and three: and for all there were so many, yet was not the net broken. Jesus saith unto them, Come and dine. And none of the disciples durst ask him, Who art thou? knowing that it was the Lord. Jesus then cometh, and taketh bread, and giveth them, and fish likewise. This is now the third time that Jesus shewed himself to his disciples, after that he was risen from the dead" (John 21:9–14).

This first section of the scene (John 21:1–14) reminds us of a story recorded in Luke 5:4–11, which may have been known by John's audience.

The second section (John 21:15–23) focuses on Peter. As a result a modest Franciscan chapel was built at Tabgha in 1933 on the foundations of a late fourth-century church and was called the Church of the Primacy of Peter or St. Peter's Primacy. "So when they had dined, Jesus saith to Simon Peter, Simon, son of Jonas, lovest thou me more than these? He saith unto him, Yea, Lord; thou knowest that I love thee. He saith unto Him, Feed my lambs" (John 21:15). Here and only here in this verse do we have the addition, "lovest thou me more than these?"

We need to deal with three specific issues related to the above before moving on to a larger possible interpretation. First, what Jesus intended by *these* is discussed by numerous commentators. One view suggests the question should be recast as: "Peter, do you love me more than these other *disciples* do?"[3] recalling Peter's earlier boast at the Last Supper: "But Peter said unto him, Although *all* shall be offended, yet will not I" (Mark 14:29; emphasis added. See also Matthew 26:33; John 13:37). Some suggest "more than these" refers to the boats, nets, and fishes—the tools of his profession. However, some manuscripts omit this clause in the first question, and, at any rate, Peter's reply does not allude to the "more than these" and may confirm that the clause is not intended as some significant aspect of the story.

Second, Jesus asks Peter an additional two times basically the same question (see John 21:16–17). Shifting from fish to sheep, the symbolism may intend to place Peter in the dual role as missionary-apostle (fisher of men and women) and Church leader (pastoral shepherd of the flock of God). During this resurrection appearance, the third one according to John (see John 21:14), Jesus reminds Peter that in his calling to act as a shepherd (Jesus was portrayed as the sole Shepherd in John 10), he must love Jesus, the flock belonging to Jesus (my lambs and my sheep), and he must be willing to lay down his life for the flock, just as Jesus himself did.[4]

Renewing the Last Supper

Perhaps the dinner served here should remind us of the meal that Jesus served the disciples in the Upper Room where Jesus offered protection in return for their utmost loyalty. There is an important element of eating with Jesus, as noted earlier in our discussion of the Last Supper in Mark's Gospel (see pages 33-35). And while John does not mention the institution of the sacrament explicitly, he most likely assumes that the original readers know the story well, because as noted earlier he writes with the assumption that the Passion narrative is already known through other sources, including Mark, Matthew, and Luke.

Post-resurrection appearances in the other Gospels and in Acts also allude to eating with Jesus. The book of Acts begins by reviewing briefly the forty-day ministry: "In my former book, Theophilus, I wrote about all that Jesus began to do and to teach until the day he was taken up to heaven, after giving instructions through the Holy

spirit to the apostles he had chosen. After his suffering [KJV pas-
sion], he showed himself to these men and gave many convincing
proofs that he was alive. He appeared to them over a period of forty
days and spoke about the kingdom of God. On one occasion, while
he was eating with them he gave them this commandment: Do not
leave Jerusalem but wait for the gift my Father promised, which you
have heard me speak about" (NIV, Acts 1:1–4; emphasis added).

The King James Version states: "And being *assembled* together
with them" (KJV, Acts 1:4). The Greek text suggests both ideas:
"*share a meal with . . . meet, gather together.*"[5] The context of Acts 1
appears to be a meeting on Sunday evening, the day of the Resurrection. In another place Peter alludes to eating with Jesus during
this same period when proclaiming the "Good News" to Cornelius'
household in Caesarea: "Him God raised up the third day, and
shewed him openly; not to all the people, but unto witnesses chosen
before of God, even to us, who *did eat and drink with him* after he rose
from the dead" (Acts 10:40–41). This again confirms the importance of these post-resurrection meals. While some argue that the
main purpose for such activity was to provide convincing proof of
the Resurrection, there is another important context—covenantal
meals noted above in our discussion of Mark's account of the Last
Supper. Let us now examine the story detailed here by John at the
Sea of Galilee within a larger context.

It may be that Jesus' three questions reminded Peter of his triple
denial in Jerusalem on the night of the arrest: "He saith unto him
the third time, Simon, son of Jonas, lovest thou me? Peter was
grieved because he said unto him the third time, Lovest thou me?" (John
21:17; emphasis added).

Apparently, from a first-century perspective, Peter's earlier denial should be considered "both complete and publically recognized.
Repudiation of a patron, broker, or friend in public normally severed
the relationship irrevocably."[6] If such a framework is correct, then it
may be possible to deduce that this meal on the Sea of Galilee is a
renewal of the covenant instituted at the Last Supper in one more
dramatic way—it may demonstrate the far-reaching impact of Jesus
Christ's love and loyalty, which under conventional practice should

have "severed the relationship [between Peter and himself] irrevocably." Despite the triple denials and actions which broke the
covenantal relationship established between them, the risen Christ
offers Peter an opportunity to renew this covenant on the seashore
in Galilee. And remember that Peter is portrayed as the spokesman
of the Twelve before Jesus' death and continues to be the spokesman
for the collective, apostolic witness after the Resurrection (see Acts
1:15).

Apparently, the renewal aspect of the covenantal meal was alluded to at the Last Supper itself. The earliest written account of the
institution of the sacrament is preserved in a Pauline letter, dated
around A.D. 54–55, a decade before Mark wrote the first Gospel narrative. Paul addresses the Corinthian Saints: "For I received of the
Lord that which also I delivered unto you, That the Lord Jesus the
same night in which he was betrayed took bread: and when he had
given thanks, he brake it, and said, Take, eat: this is my body, which
is broken for you: this do in remembrance of me. After the same
manner also he took the cup, when he had supped, saying, This cup
is the new testament in my blood: *this do ye, as oft as ye drink it,* in
remembrance of me. For as often as ye eat this bread, and drink this
cup, ye do shew the Lord's death till he come" (1 Corinthians
11:23–26; emphasis added).

Implicit in Jesus' own word is the command to repeat the Lord's
Supper periodically (see JST, Mark 14:24-25), and Paul makes what
is implicit here explicit by saying: "For as often as ye eat this bread,
and drink this cup, ye do shew the Lord's death till he come." He
correctly interpreted Jesus' intent; that is, the meal was to be held
periodically until the Second Coming.

Whatever doubts, misgivings, and guilt may have been associated with their actions on the night of Jesus' arrest, Peter along with
the other disciples ended the forty-day ministry assured that the
risen Christ forgave them as he ate with them again, renewing the
promises made at the Last Supper.

John's Resurrection narrative ends with a discussion of Peter's
death, the fate of the beloved disciple, and the testimony of the author (see John 21:18–25).

NOTES

1. This section relies heavily upon Jeni Broberg Holzapfel and Richard Neitzel Holzapfel, *Sisters at the Well: Women and the Life and Teachings of Jesus* (Salt Lake City: Bookcraft, 1993), 148–50.

2. See Raymond E. Brown, *The Anchor Bible: The Gospel According to John (xiii-xxi)* (Garden City, New York: Doubleday, 1964), 1070.

3. See Brown, *The Anchor Bible,* 1103–04.

4. See Raymond E. Brown, *An Introduction to the New Testament* (New York: Doubleday, 1997), 361.

5. Max Zerwick and Mary Grosvenor, *A Grammatical Analysis of the Greek New Testament* (Rome: Biblical Institute Press, 1981), 349.

6. Bruce J. Malina and Richard L. Rohrbaugh, *Social Science Commentary on the Synoptic Gospels* (Minneapolis: Fortress Press, 1992), 405.

LUKE'S RESURRECTION NARRATIVE

L uke 24 and Acts 1 partly overlap but in doing so provide an important bridge between the story of Jesus and the story of his witnesses. Luke 24 is composed of four major scenes— the empty tomb, the journey to Emmaus, the appearance in Jerusalem, and the ascension of Jesus. All of these events are restricted to the vicinity of Jerusalem.

Women Present (Luke 24:1–11)

Luke's story of Jesus' death and resurrection follows a particular line.[1] It is important for Luke that women were present at Jesus' death and burial. These faithful disciples actually saw Jesus' dead body placed in the tomb and noted how it was laid (see Luke 23:55–56). They did so because they wanted to return and offer their final act of devotion to Jesus by anointing his body. However, when they returned, they found the tomb empty: "Now upon the first day of the week, very early in the morning, they came unto the sepulchre, bringing the spices which they had prepared, and certain others with them. And they found the stone rolled away" (Luke 24:1–2).

Arriving early in the morning was part of the mourning ritual that usually consisted of not eating (fasting), inability to sleep (keeping vigil), disregard about clothing (wearing sackcloth), and unconcern about appearance (showing unkempt hair and a dirty face, both indicated by ashes on the head).

Perplexed as they entered the tomb to find it empty, the angels chided them: "Why seek ye the living among the dead?" (Luke 24:5). Their perplexity seems to have lifted with the revealing words of the angels: "He is not here, but is risen: remember how he spake unto you when he was yet in Galilee, saying, The Son of man must be delivered into the hands of sinful men, and be crucified, and the third day rise again. And they remembered his words" (Luke 24:6–8).

In view of the empty tomb, the heavenly testimony of the two angels, and Jesus' previous prophecy of his resurrection, the women now have enough light to understand, seemingly for the first time, that Jesus had to suffer and die and that he rose from the dead in fulfillment of his own words. Previously, the disciples received Jesus' instructions on these points with a lack of understanding (see Luke 9:45; 18:34). Luke continues: "And [they] returned from the sepulchre, and told all these things unto the eleven, and to all the rest" (Luke 24:9). The "eleven" and "all the rest" remain incredulous (Luke 24:11).

On the Road to Emmaus (Luke 24:13–31)

Luke's description of two disciples going to Emmaus with shattered expectations is the next link in a chain of events on this day. As the two walked "to a village called Emmaus, which was from Jerusalem about threescore furlongs [about seven miles]," Jesus "drew near, and went with them" (Luke 24:15). While three modern sites are often identified as possible locations for this Gospel event, ancient Emmaus may be located on a rocky ridge, formerly occupied by the Arab village of Qoloniya near the Motsa Interchange on the modern Jerusalem-Tel Aviv Highway.[2]

Like the Passion narrative before, "perhaps the history of Christian art depicting the resurrection has had an unconscious effect on the way we read the stories."[3] Most visual representations of this event depict two men walking along the way. One of the individuals walking away from the Holy City is named and is clearly male, Cleopas, a shortened form of the Greek name *Kleopatros*, the masculine form of Cleopatra. Since the time of Origen (c. A.D. 185–253) the unnamed individual has been identified as Peter or, in the tenth century, as Nathanael. Much later in the nineteenth and twentieth centuries, the unnamed disciple is often identified with a man named Emmaus and with Luke, the author of the Gospel narrative.

It is possible that the unnamed traveler is a woman, not to be confused with "Mary, the wife of Cleophas"(see John 19:25). The context of the story may suggest that a couple is returning home to Emmaus that day, for when they arrived they invited the risen Lord to have dinner with them in their home. The two travelers heard the women's report, including their account of the angels.

They had also heard that some of the disciples had verified that the tomb was indeed empty. Yet the two were now leaving Jerusalem and the assembled disciples. They were dejected and despondent, as the first part of their dialogue with Jesus indicates: "And he said unto them, What manner of communication are these that ye have one to another, as ye walk, and are sad?" (Luke 24:17).

Their recognition of the risen Lord is an essential aspect of the story. The two travelers at first failed to recognize the risen Christ. They expressed their lack of understanding of Jesus' identity and mission and their loss of hope because of Jesus' suffering and death, despite the women's report of "a vision of angels, which said that he was alive" (Luke 24:23). Their failure to recognize him was probably caused by their lack of insights into God's purpose as attested to in scripture and now realized in Jesus' suffering, death, and resurrection.

When questioned by Jesus they respond: "Art thou only a stranger in Jerusalem, and hast not known the things which are come to pass there in these days?" (Luke 24:18). Jesus attempts to lead them with a question and asks: "And he said unto them, What things?" (Luke 24:19). They begin to reveal the reversal they experienced at his death: "And they said unto him, Concerning Jesus of Nazareth, which was a prophet mighty in deed and word before God and all the people: and how the chief priests and our rulers delivered him to be condemned to death, and have crucified him. But we trusted that it had been he which should have redeemed Israel" (Luke 24:19–21).

The two, like many Judeans, Galileans, and Pereans of nonelite standing, were for various reasons hungry for a living symbol of their willingness to endure a bleak present in the face of a forthcoming re-versal in the political economy in their favor. Such a reversal in the political economy is what the term *redemption* means in Leviticus 25, and Luke records that this was what the two disciples expected of Jesus: "we trusted that it had been he which should have re-deemed Israel" (Luke 24:21).

The couple's lack of insight into Jesus' mission is emphasized in that the title "Christ" was missing from their summary description of Jesus' identity, activities, and mission. Equally absent was any refer-ence to Jesus' prophecy of his death and resurrection. This was underscored by Jesus' response: "O fools, and slow of heart to believe all that the prophets have spoken: Ought not Christ to have *suffered* these things, and to enter into his glory?" (Luke 24:25; emphasis added). Typical of Luke is the use of *suffer* for the whole Passion nar-rative (Luke 22:15; 24:26, 46; Acts 3:18; 17:3; 26:23).

What restrained these disciples from believing was their poor understanding of the scriptural witness to the Passion and Resurrec-tion events. Their study of the Hebrew scriptures should have pre-pared them. Jesus then opened the scriptures to them: "And begin-ning at Moses [Torah] and all the prophets [Prophets], he expounded unto them in all the scriptures the things concerning himself. And they drew nigh unto the village, whither they went: and he made as though he would have gone further. But they constrained him, say-ing, Abide with us: for it is toward evening, and the day is far spent. And he went in to tarry with them" (Luke 24:27–29).

That they invited the stranger to stay with them is nothing out of the ordinary. The first-century Mediterranean person, like those living in Judea-Palestine, "valued the free circulation of persons be-tween its communities. People traveled, for example, on pilgrimage, to seek out healing, to collect and distribute money, to attend meet-ings at central locations, to bring information, news or instruction to others, and the like. Such a society required a law of hospitality: Do as you would be done by; receive the strangers so that you will be well received."[4]

At some point after entering the home, the two are no longer the hosts: "And it came to pass, as he sat at meat with them, he took bread, and blessed it, and brake, and gave to them. And their eyes were opened, and they knew him; and he vanished out of their sight" (Luke 24:30–31). According to the *Oxford Study Bible*, "The scene obviously suggests a eucharistic [sacramental] setting."[5]

In each of the first three scenes, there is reference to earlier parts of the story, especially to Jesus' recent passion and his prophecies of death and resurrection (see Luke 24:6–7, 18–27, 44–46). In this way Luke links each scene with the other, thus presenting a continuous, developing discussion of Jesus' death and resurrection. In the end, the chapter provides an important commentary on the significance of Jesus' passion and resurrection. Ultimately, the third scene acts as a preview of the major events to come, as the risen Christ commissions his disciples to go into the world (see Luke 24:47–49).

The commentary on Jesus' passion and resurrection repeats themes which have already been expressed in the passion prophecies recorded earlier, beginning in Luke 9:22 (see Luke 24:7, 25–26, 44, 46).

Connecting Luke and Acts (Acts 1:1–3)

Luke begins the second part (the book of Acts) of his twofold work with a greeting and a summary of his Gospel: "The former treatise have I made, O Theophilus, of all that Jesus began both to do and teach, until the day in which he was taken up, after that he through the Holy Ghost had given commandments unto the apostles whom he had chosen: to whom also he shewed himself alive after his passion by many infallible proofs, being seen of them forty days, and speaking of the things pertaining to the kingdom of God" (Acts 1:1–3). In the Greco-Roman world, much like today, the acceptable evidence for support arose from sensory experience—seeing, touching, or hearing. During the forty-day ministry Jesus was seen, felt, and heard.

That Jesus showed "himself alive after his passion by many infallible proofs" became the witness that Jesus' cruel execution was the saving event *par excellence*. And while condemned in Jewish and Roman courts, the crucified Jesus was vindicated by the Father, who raised him from the dead. For the early disciples the raising of Jesus was the Father's means of reversing the verdict of the human court (the trial and crucifixion); furthermore, it provided the key to understanding the humiliation, scandal, and apparent tragedy of the Passion, and brought about a new redemptive act with universal import for everyone. Specifically, the raising of Jesus constituted the beginning of the process that eventually would have cosmic implications for humanity and the entire universe: "For God so loved the world that he gave his only begotten Son" (John 3:16).[6]

NOTES

1. This material is based on Jeni Broberg Holzapfel and Richard Neitzel Holzapfel, *Sisters at the Well: Women and the Life and Teachings of Jesus* (Salt Lake City: Bookcraft, 1993), 141–46.

2. The first, Emmaus-Nicopolis at Aijalon Park (near the present-day Latrun Interchange), was identified with the Gospel event by A.D. 330 and generally accepted during the entire Byzantine period (4th through 7th centuries); the second, Abu Ghosh (a village to the north of the Tel Aviv-Jerusalem highway some 9 miles from the Holy City) was identified by the crusaders and the tradition was firmly established by A.D. 1140; and the third, Qubeiba (located just under a mile from the Biddu crossroads), was identified sometime after the defeat of the Latin Kingdom at the Battle of the Horns of Hattin in 1187, at least from A.D. 1500 the site became associated with the event. Jerome Murphy-O'Connor posits correctly, I believe, that Luke had in mind the little town located on "the rocky ridge which forces the Jerusalem highway to make a right-angle turn below Motza"; see Jerome Murphy-O'Connor, *The Holy Land: Oxford Archaeological Guides* (New York: Oxford University Press, 1998), 319–21.

3. Stephen T. Davis, " 'Seeing' the Risen Jesus," in *The Resurrection*, Stephen Davis, Daniel Kendall, and Gerald O'Collins, eds. (New York: Oxford University Press, 1997), 126-47.

4. Bruce J. Malina, *The Social World of Jesus and the Gospels* (New York: Routledge, 1996), 233.

5. M. Jack Suggs, Katharine Doob Sakenfeld, and James R. Mueller, eds., *The Oxford Study Bible* (New York: Oxford University Press, 1992), 1364.

6. Found more than one hundred times in John's writings, the *world* is one of his favorite words and depending on context it means the universe, the earth, humanity, the majority of humanity, those opposed to the Lord, or the economic, political, religious or cultural systems opposed to the Lord's purposes. The *world* in John 3:16 means at least humanity, and possibly the universe.

THE EXALTATION OF JESUS CHRIST: ON THE RIGHT HAND OF GOD

It may be difficult for the modern reader to fully appreciate Paul's words to the early Saints at Corinth: "But we preach Christ crucified, unto the Jews a stumbling-block, and unto the Greeks foolishness" (1 Corinthians 1:23). In Galatians Paul relates the cross of Christ to Deuteronomy 21:22–23 (discussed briefly in the Passion narratives): "Christ hath redeemed us from the curse of the law, being made a curse for us: for it is written, Cursed is every one that hangeth on a tree" (Galatians 3:13). The passage from Deuteronomy is rendered in the King James Version (KJV): "And if a man have committed a sin worthy of death, and he be to be put to death, and thou hang him on a tree: his body shall not remain all night upon the tree, but thou shalt in any wise bury him that day; (for he that is hanged is accursed of God;) that thy land be not defiled, which the Lord thy God giveth thee for an inheritance" (Deuteronomy 21:22–23).

Otto Betz seems to be on the right course when he argues: "More than any other passage of scripture, Deuteronomy 21:22–23 may have convinced Paul that it was necessary to persecute the Christians. Belief in a crucified Messiah was a dangerous superstition; it was even blasphemy."[1]

One of the primary elements of the first apostolic preaching was the explanation of how a crucified man, and therefore one cursed of God, could actually be the Messiah. The book of Acts reveals this preaching, known as the *kerygma* (a Greek noun meaning "preaching" or "proclamation").[2] The *kerygma* was rooted in the life of Jesus, not just the resurrected Christ. It included what Jesus said (words) and did (deeds).

The heart of this message is found in Peter's sermon during Pentecost in Acts 2. Along with other speeches by Peter found in Acts, here we have the earliest account of what the collective apostolic witness group, for which Peter was the spokesman, believed about Jesus.[3] In Acts 2 Peter testifies, in light of the events described in the Resurrection narratives, that God not only made the crucified Jesus *Messiah*, but more important God made him *Lord*.

Peter's Answer (Acts 2:1–35)

Peter's answer to the question of why Jesus was allowed to die if he was God's anointed king came some fifty days following Jesus' last Passover among his disciples. The disciples gathered in the Upper Room in Jerusalem as Jesus had commanded (see Luke 24:49). Known as *Shavu'ot* (the Feast of Weeks), Pentecost marked the end of the grain harvest and the beginning of the bringing of the first fruit.[4] Additionally, it recalled the reception of the Torah (law of Moses) at Mount Sinai following the first Passover.

Luke introduces the story: "And when the day of Pentecost was fully come, they were all with one accord in one place. And suddenly there came a sound from heaven as of a rushing mighty wind, and it filled all the house where they were sitting. And there appeared unto them cloven tongues like as of fire, and it sat upon each of them. And they were all filled with the Holy Ghost, and began to speak with other tongues, as the Spirit gave them utterance" (Acts 2:1–4).

According to Luke, Jews from the Diaspora (dispersion, scattering) gathered in Jerusalem for this important pilgrimage feast from around the Greco-Roman world. "And there were dwelling [referring to visiting Jews and proselytes who were present for the festival] at Jerusalem Jews, devout men, out of every nation under heaven. Now when this was noised abroad, the multitude came together, and were confounded, because that every man heard them speak in his own language. And they were all amazed and marvelled, saying one to another, Behold, are not all these which speak Galilæans? And how hear we every man in our own tongue, wherein we were born?" (Acts 2:5–8).

Luke lists the various nations represented by the crowd and then continues: "And they were all amazed, and were in doubt, saying one to another, What meaneth this? Others mocking said, These men are full of new wine" (Acts 2:12–13).

At this point in the story line the first public preaching of the "Good News" occurs, interpreting for the first time the meaning of the events of the past fifty days (Jesus' suffering, death, resurrection, and exaltation). And while the Holy Ghost fell upon all the disciples gathered in the Upper Room, it is the Twelve who now present themselves to the Jews gathered at the feast as the leading witnesses. As has been the case in the past, Peter acts as the spokesman for the group (see Luke 9:20; Acts 1:15): "But Peter, standing up with the eleven, lifted up his voice, and said unto them, Ye men of Judæa, and all ye that dwell [are visiting] at Jerusalem, be this known unto you, and hearken to my words: for these are not drunken, as ye suppose, seeing it is but the third hour [from sunrise or about 9:00 A.M.] of the day" (Acts 2:14–15).

Peter tells the group that the Holy Ghost is the real speaker and that they, like the Old Testament prophets before, are only the mouthpieces of the Lord (see Acts 2:16–18). He indicates that they have witnessed the fulfillment of the prophecy of Joel (see Acts 2:16-21). Joel saw a day when the Lord would call Israel to repentance, which would be followed by forgiveness (a typical Old Testament pattern). This call to repentance and the mercy that follows is only a prelude to the coming of the kingdom of God, the day of the Lord which heralded a new day of reconciliation: "before that great and notable day of the Lord come: and it shall come to pass, that *whosoever shall call on the name of the Lord shall be saved*" (Acts 2:20–21; emphasis added). This starting point was something everyone present could agree upon, "*whosoever shall call on the name of the Lord shall be saved.*" The surprise comes when Peter reveals who the Lord is later in his discourse.

Now begins the proclamation in earnest: "Ye men of Israel, hear these words; Jesus of Nazareth, a man approved of God among you by miracles and wonders and signs, which God did by him in the midst of you, as ye yourselves also know: him, being delivered by the determinate counsel and foreknowledge of God, ye have taken, and by wicked hands have crucified and slain: Whom God hath raised up, having loosed the pains of death: because it was not possible that he should be holden of it" (Acts 2:22–24). Peter's contrast between the actions of the Jewish leaders in killing Jesus and that of the Father in exalting him is of immediate concern and becomes a primary way of explaining this historical event. Additionally, when Peter says "delivered by the determinate counsel and foreknowledge of God," he confirms that it was the Father's plan to give Jesus into the hands of wicked men.

Luke continues with the account of Peter's speech: "For David speaketh concerning him, I foresaw the Lord always before my face, for he is on my right hand, that I should not be moved: Therefore did my heart rejoice, and my tongue was glad; moreover also my flesh shall rest in hope; because thou wilt not leave my soul in hell, neither wilt thou suffer thine Holy One to see corruption. Thou hast made known to me the ways of life; thou shalt make me full of joy with thy countenance. Men and brethren, let me freely speak unto you of the patriarch David, that he is both dead and buried, and his sepulchre is with us unto this day. Therefore being a prophet, and knowing that God has sworn with an oath to him, that of the fruit of his loins, according to the flesh, he would raise up Christ to sit on his throne; he seeing this before spake of the resurrection of Christ, that his soul was not left in hell, neither his flesh did see corruption" (Acts 2:25–31).

In using the burial site of the famous King David as a point of reference (not just geographically but theologically), Peter is about to reveal who Jesus really is unto the crowd with this fundamental aspect of his argument: "This Jesus hath God raised up, whereof we all are witnesses. Therefore being by the right hand of God exalted, and having received of the Father the promise of the Holy Ghost, he hath shed forth this, which ye now see and hear. For David is not ascended into the heavens: but he saith himself, The Lord said unto my Lord, Sit thou on my right hand, until I make thy foes thy footstool" (Acts 2:32–35).

Lord and Christ (Acts 2:36)

The climax of the first public proclamation follows: "Therefore let all the house of Israel know assuredly, that God hath made that same Jesus, whom ye have crucified, both Lord and Christ" (Acts 2:36). This refers back to "*whosoever shall call on the name of the Lord shall be saved.*" What Peter has in mind is: "Whosoever shall call on the name of *Jesus* shall be saved." This should remind us of Jesus' own words recorded in Luke's earlier writing, the Gospel of Luke: "Then opened he their understanding, that they might understand the scriptures, And said unto them, Thus it is written, and thus it behoved Christ to suffer, and to rise from the dead the third day: And that repentance and remission of sins should be preached *in his name* among all nations, beginning at Jerusalem. And ye are witnesses of these things" (Luke 24:45–48; emphasis added).

What is entailed here is a three-step process: first, wicked men raise up Jesus on the cross; second, God overrides their condemnation by raising up Jesus through the Resurrection; and finally, God made him both *Christ* and *Lord* by raising up Jesus to the *right hand*. The irony of the situation is apparent—wicked men helped Jesus in his movement back to God.

Joseph A. Fitzmyer correctly deduces that the "title [Lord] is given to Jesus with various nuances by many NT writers."[5] In many cases it simply means "sir." While it may be impossible to determine what the author meant for every reference of Jesus as Lord during his early ministry, Peter's proclamation makes the necessary connections for us to understand what was intended when he identified Jesus as both *Messiah* (Christ) and *kyrios* (Lord). From at least this point forward, the *kyrios* title was part of the apostolic preaching, or what we have called the Resurrection Faith.

Following his explanation to the Jewish pilgrims in Jerusalem, Peter asked them to begin the process which would make them beneficiaries of Jesus' atoning death: "Repent, and be baptized every one of you in the *name of Jesus Christ* for the remission of sins, and ye shall receive the gift of the Holy Ghost" (Acts 2:38). Only through Jesus' suffering and death could they be saved: "And with many other words did he testify and exhort, saying, Save yourselves from this untoward [crooked] generation" (Acts 2:40; emphasis added).

Peter's Discourse in Acts 3

The second Petrine discourse is found in Acts 3. Following the healing of the man at the entrance to gate Beautiful at the temple, Peter declares: "Ye men of Israel, why marvel ye at this? or why look ye so earnestly on us, as though by our own power or holiness we had made this man to walk? The God of Abraham, and of Isaac, and of Jacob, the God of our fathers, hath glorified his Son Jesus; whom ye delivered up, and denied him in the presence of Pilate, when he was determined to let him go. But ye denied the Holy One and the Just, and desired a murderer to be granted unto you; And killed the Prince of Life, whom God hath raised up from the dead; whereof we are witnesses" (Acts 3:12–15).

Here it should be noted that "Holy One" and "Righteous One" or "Just One" may not be titles, or at least at one level they may be "the expression of an ethico-religious verdict on the life of Jesus."[6] These two phrases apparently became titles, but in the first instance they may describe something about Jesus. Again, Peter contrasts the two courts, human and heavenly. Jesus' vindication comes from God "who raised [him] from the dead."

Peter's Preaching in Acts 4

What Luke preserves for us in the following chapter (Acts 4) is how the early Saints interpreted Jesus' mission in light of prophetic writings through two distinct but related events. The first is Peter's preaching before the Jewish leadership, and the second is a combined utterance among the Saints, led by Peter and John.

Luke records the first sermon: "Then Peter, filled with the Holy Ghost, said unto them, Ye rulers of the people, and elders of Israel. If we this day be examined of the good deed done to the impotent man, by what means he is made whole; Be it known unto you all, and to all the people of Israel, that by the name of Jesus Christ of Nazareth, whom ye crucified, whom God raised from the dead, even by him doth this man stand before you whole" (Acts 4:8–10).

Like the Passion narratives themselves, Peter found in the Psalms the way to interpret Jesus' suffering and death: "This is the stone which was set at nought of you builders, which is become the head of the corner" (Acts 4:11). The allusion is to Psalm 118:22. Peter concludes: "Neither is there salvation in any other: for there is none other name under heaven given among men, whereby we must be saved" (Acts 4:12). This reminds us of his statement in Acts 2 regarding being saved by calling upon the *name* of the Lord (see Acts 2:21).

Following a release from being held by the Jewish leadership, Peter and John returned to one of the gathering places of the Saints in Jerusalem: "And being let go, they went to their own company, and reported all that the chief priests and elders had said unto them. And when they heard that, they lifted up their voice to God with one accord, and said, Lord, thou art God, which hast made heaven, and earth, and the sea, and all that in them is: Who by the mouth of thy servant David hast said, Why did the heathen rage, and the people imagine vain things? The kings of the earth stood up, and the rulers were gathered together against the Lord, and against his Christ" (Acts 4:23–26).

This citation comes from Psalm 2, one of the enthronement psalms (royal coronation psalms). In this particular psalm, the Lord promises to sustain the newly appointed monarch. And though nations and kings may conspire against him, God calls him *anointed*, *king*, and *son*, promising him final victory over his enemies: "Why do the heathen rage, and the people imagine a vain thing? The kings of the earth set themselves, and the rulers take counsel together, against the Lord, and against his anointed, saying, Let us break their bands asunder, and cast away their cords from us. He that sitteth in the heavens shall laugh: the Lord shall have them in derision. Then shall he speak unto them in his wrath, and vex them in his sore displeasure. Yet have I set my king upon my holy hill of Zion. I will declare the decree: the Lord hath said unto me, Thou art my Son; this day have I begotten thee. Ask of me, and I shall give thee the heathen for thine inheritance, and the uttermost parts of the earth for thy possession. Thou shalt break them with a rod of iron; thou shalt dash them in pieces like a potter's vessel. Be wise now therefore, O ye kings: be instructed, ye judges of the earth. Serve the Lord with fear, and rejoice with trembling. Kiss the Son, lest he be angry, and ye perish from the way, when his wrath is kindled but a little. Blessed are all they that put their trust in him" (Psalm 2:1–12).

This particular psalm, as noted above, is not just about opposition to God's anointed one, but about the ultimate vindication of the servant identified by three distinct and significant titles: Anointed One (*Messiah* from Hebrew and *Christ* from the Greek), King on Mount Zion; and the Son of God. All three titles are discussed during the hearings Jesus was subjected to shortly before his crucifixion.

In a significant way, Psalm 2 helped these Saints understand God's plan. Specifically, the Saints interpreted those in opposition to Jesus as "Herod, and Pontius Pilate, with the Gentiles, and the people of Israel" (Acts 4:27). All of them conspired against Jesus, just as Psalm 2 prophesied.

Peter and Cornelius (Acts 10)

In one of the most celebrated chapters in the book of Acts, Peter arrives in the Roman capital of Judea to find a receptive audience among the household of a Roman officer, Cornelius. Luke records Peter's announcement of the "Good News" among the Gentiles for the first time: "Then Peter opened his mouth, and said, Of a truth I perceive that God is no respecter of persons: But in every nation he that feareth him, and worketh righteousness, is accepted with him. The word which God sent unto the children of Israel, preaching peace by Jesus Christ: (he is Lord of all:) That word, I say, ye know, which was published throughout all Judea, and began from Galilee after the baptism which John preached; How God *anointed* Jesus of Nazareth with the Holy Ghost and with power: who went about doing good, and healing all that were oppressed of the devil; for God was with him. And we are witnesses of all things which he did both in the land of the Jews, and in Jerusalem; *whom they slew and hanged on a tree:* Him God *raised up* the third day, and shewed him openly; Not to all the people, but unto witnesses chosen before of God, even to us, who did eat and drink with him after he rose from the dead. And he commanded us to preach unto the people, and to testify that it is he which was ordained of God to be the Judge of quick and dead. To him give all the prophets witness, that *through his name* whosoever believeth in him shall receive remission of sins" (Acts 10:34–43; emphasis added).

The main elements of the Resurrection Faith are present: first, the comparison between the human and heavenly courts; second, Jesus as Christ and Lord; and finally, the importance of salvation through the name of Jesus.

The Expression of a Collective Witness

As an example of how closely Peter's initial speeches are an expression of the "collective, apostolic witness," we conclude with Paul's discourse at Antioch in Pisidia.[7]

The divine plan of salvation is connected with the death of Jesus. "For they that dwell at Jerusalem and their rulers, because they knew him not, nor yet the voices of the prophets which are read every sabbath day, they have fulfilled them in condemning him. And though they found no cause of death in him, yet desired they Pilate that he should be slain. And when they had fulfilled all that was written of him, they took him down from the tree, and laid him in a sepulchre. But God raised him from the dead: And he was seen many days [40 days ministry] of them which came up with him from Galilee to Jerusalem, who are his witnesses unto the people" (Acts 13:27–31).

What at first seems a simple story—Jesus is arrested, sentenced, and executed as a result of a conspiracy to kill him—really turns out to be exactly the opposite. He is not arrested in the ordinary sense of the word, but he gives himself over to his captors. While his enemies mock, scourge, and crucify him, Jesus turns out not to be the victim, but the King of Israel. The suffering and death became the first steps back to glory, where he was from the beginning (see John 1:1–6).

In the end, without a belief in the resurrection and exaltation of Christ, his mortal ministry, suffering, and death give occasion for sorrowful abandonment and despair rather than grounds for a lively hope (see 1 Corinthians 15:19).

NOTES

1. Otto Betz, "Jesus and the Temple Scroll," in *Jesus and the Dead Sea Scrolls*, James H. Charlesworth, ed. (New York: Doubleday, 1992), 89.

2. The noun comes from the verb *keryss*, "announce, make known by a herald . . . proclaim aloud . . . speak of, mention publicly . . . spread the story widely"; William F. Arndt and F. Wilbur Gingrich, *A Greek-English Lexicon of the New Testament and Other Early Christian Literature* (Chicago: The University of Chicago Press, 1957), 431.

3. See Hans F. Bayer, "The Preaching of Peter in Acts," in *Witness to the Gospel: The Theology of Acts* (Grand Rapids: Wm. B. Eerdmans Publishing Co., 1998), 257–74.

4. Many times the scriptures distinguish the resurrection of Jesus from his exaltation, in other cases the resurrection appears to be identical with the exaltation (see Acts 2:2–33).

5. Joseph A. Fitzmyer, *The Semitic Background of the New Testament* (Grand Rapids, Michigan: William B. Eerdmans Publishing Company, 1997), 115.

6. Edward Schillebeeckx, *Jesus: an Experiment in Christology* (New York: Crossroad, 1981), 289.

7. Bayer, "The Preaching of Peter," 269.

*E*PILOGUE:
A Lively Hope in Jesus Christ

T errence Prendergast assiduously reviews the use of the word *hope* in the four Gospels and correctly concludes: "Even if the noun 'hope' (Gk *elpis*) is not found at all in the Gospels and the verb 'to hope' (Gk *elpizein*) is found only five times in the Gospels—with the OT sense of 'to trust' (Matt 12:21; John 5:45) or with a purely secular and nonreligious sense (Luke 6:34; 23:8; 24:21)—the idea of hope as confidence in God 'whose goodness and mercy are to be relied on and whose promises cannot fail' . . . is everywhere presupposed in the New Testament."[1]

Highlights from Paul

A few passages highlight the teachings of the one who preached "Christ crucified" to his fellow Jews and to the Gentiles. First, from Paul's great letter to the early Saints in Rome: "And hope maketh not ashamed; because the love of God is shed abroad in our hearts by the Holy Ghost which is given unto us" (Romans 5:5). At another time he wrote to the Saints in Ephesus: "That at that time ye were without Christ, being aliens from the commonwealth of Israel, and strangers from the covenants of promise, having no hope, and without God in the world" (Ephesians 2:12). For the small group of believers in Colossea, Paul writes: "If ye continue in the faith grounded and settled, and be not moved away from the hope of the gospel, which ye have heard" (Colossians 1:23). To a new group of

203

Saints in Greece he wrote: "Now our Lord Jesus Christ himself, and God, even our Father, which hath loved us, and hath given us everlasting consolation and good hope through grace" (2 Thessalonians 2:16). To his fellow worker Titus he testified: "In hope of eternal life, which God, that cannot lie, promised before the world began" (Titus 1:2).

Peter's Letter of Hope

Often called the "letter of hope," Peter's epistle is apparently addressed to a group of Saints subjected to persecution. This letter expresses the basis of our continued hope upon the promises of the Lord and is one of the most profound summaries of the apostolic proclamation from the first century.[2]

> PETER, an apostle of Jesus Christ, to the strangers scattered throughout Pontus, Galatia, Cappadocia, Asia, and Bithynia,
> Elect according to the foreknowledge of God the Father, through sanctification of the Spirit, unto obedience and sprinkling of the blood of Jesus Christ: Grace unto you, and peace, be multiplied.
> Blessed be the God and Father of our Lord Jesus Christ, which according to his abundant mercy hath begotten us again unto *a lively hope* by the resurrection of Jesus Christ from the dead,
> To an inheritance incorruptible, and undefiled, and that fadeth not away, reserved in heaven for you, Who are kept by the power of God through faith unto salvation ready to be revealed in the last time. Wherein ye greatly rejoice, though now for a season, if need be, ye are in heaviness through manifold temptations:
> That the trial of your faith, being much more precious than of gold that perisheth, though it be tried with fire, might be found unto praise and honour and glory at the appearing of Jesus Christ:
> Whom having not seen, ye love; in whom, though now ye see him not, yet believing, ye rejoice with joy unspeakable and full of glory:
> Receiving the end of your faith, even the salvation of your souls. Of which salvation the prophets have enquired and searched diligently, who prophesied of the grace that should come unto you:

Searching what, or what manner of time the Spirit of Christ which was in them did signify, when it testified beforehand the sufferings of Christ, and the glory that should follow.

Unto whom it was revealed, that not unto themselves, but unto us they did minister the things, which are now reported unto you by them that have preached the gospel unto you with the Holy Ghost sent down from heaven; which things the angels desire to look into.

Wherefore gird up the loins of your mind, be sober, and hope to the end for the grace that is to be brought unto you at the revelation of Jesus Christ;

As obedient children, not fashioning yourselves according to the former lusts in your ignorance: But as he which hath called you is holy, so be ye holy in all manner of conversation;

Because it is written, Be ye holy; for I am holy.

And if ye call on the Father, who without respect of persons judgeth according to every man's work, pass the time of your sojourning here in fear:

Forasmuch as ye know that ye were not redeemed with corruptible things, as silver and gold, from your vain conversation received by tradition from your fathers; But with the precious blood of Christ, as of a lamb without blemish and without spot:

Who verily was foreordained before the foundation of the world, but was manifest in these last times for you,

Who by him do believe in God, that raised him up from the dead, and gave him glory; that your faith and hope might be in God.

Seeing ye have purified your souls in obeying the truth through the Spirit unto unfeigned love of the brethren, see that ye love one another with a pure heart fervently:

Being born again, not of corruptible seed, but of incorruptible, by the word of God, which liveth and abideth for ever.

For all flesh is as grass, and all the glory of man as the flower of grass. The grass withereth, and the flower thereof falleth away:

But the word of the Lord endureth for ever. And this is the word which by the gospel is preached unto you (1 Peter 1:1–25; emphasis added).

While no single term is adequate for expressing the reality of God's promises, *hope* brings to mind a broad range of images associated with these promises. For Peter and the other disciples of Jesus, the hope found in the "Good News" is a living hope rather than a futile one because it is connected to and grounded in the suffering, death, resurrection, and exaltation of Jesus Christ. These four transcendent events are inseparable.

And while we can find examples of human goodness and achievement in the story of civilizations, we can no longer hope for any *final* good from our human history. In the end, all hope is founded in the crucified and risen Christ, who is coming again to create a "new heaven and a new earth" (Revelation 21:1). For while his passion and subsequent triumph have been told and proclaimed by his faithful disciples, the story is not yet over.

NOTES

1. Terrence Prendergast, "Hope," *Anchor Bible Dictionary*, 6 vols., (New York: Doubleday, 1992), 3:282–85.

2. W. Harrelson, "Hope," in *Interpreter's Bible Dictionary*, 4 vols. and Supplement (Nashville: Abingdon Press, 1962–76), 2:643.

$\mathcal{I}$NDEX